Portugal's
Political Development

Westview Special Studies

The concept of Westview Special Studies is a response to the continuing crisis in academic and informational publishing. Library budgets for books have been severely curtailed. Ever larger portions of general library budgets are being diverted from the purchase of books and used for data banks, computers, micromedia, and other methods of information retrieval. Interlibrary loan structures further reduce the edition sizes needed to satisfy the needs of the scholarly community. Economic pressures on the university presses and the few private scholarly publishing companies have severely limited the capacity of the industry to properly serve the academic and research communities. As a result, many manuscripts dealing with important subjects, often representing the highest level of scholarship, are no longer economically viable publishing projects-- or, if accepted for publication, are typically subject to lead times ranging from one to three years.

Westview Special Studies are our practical solution to the problem. We accept a manuscript in camera-ready form, typed according to our specifications, and move it immediately into the production process. As always, the selection criteria include the importance of the subject, the work's contribution to scholarship, and its insight, originality of thought, and excellence of exposition. The responsibility for editing and proofreading lies with the author or sponsoring institution. We prepare chapter headings and display pages, file for copyright, and obtain Library of Congress Cataloging in Publication Data. A detailed manual contains simple instructions for preparing the final typescript, and our editorial staff is always available to answer questions.

The end result is a book printed on acid-free paper and bound in sturdy library-quality soft covers. We manufacture these books ourselves using equipment that does not require a lengthy make-ready process and that allows us to publish first editions of 300 to 1000 copies and to reprint even smaller quantities as needed. Thus, we can produce Special Studies quickly and can keep even very specialized books in print as long as there is a demand for them.

About the Book and Author

Portugal's early developmental experience created a highly centralized administrative state that continues to have a powerful influence on the nature and style of the country's government and politics. Emphasizing this theme, Dr. Opello shows that, contrary to the conclusions of scholars who have analyzed Portugal from Latin American or Third World perspectives, Portuguese political development is more comparable to the pattern of development of West European countries, especially France. He compares Portugal's political experience with that of other West European countries and concludes by speculating about the future of Portugal's fledgling democracy.

Walter C. Opello, Jr., is associate professor of political science at the University of Mississippi. His articles on Portuguese politics and government and on Portuguese-speaking Africa have appeared in several books and journals.

Portugal's Political Development
A Comparative Approach

Walter C. Opello, Jr.

Westview Press / Boulder and London

Westview Special Studies in West European Politics and Society

All rights reserved. No part of this publication may be reproduced or transmitted in any form or by any means, electronic or mechanical, including photocopy, recording, or any information storage and retrieval system, without permission in writing from the publisher.

Copyright © 1985 by Westview Press, Inc.

Published in 1985 in the United States of America by Westview Press, Inc., 5500 Central Avenue, Boulder, Colorado 80301; Frederick A. Praeger, Publisher

Library of Congress Catalog Card Number: 84-62208
ISBN: 0-8133-7020-5

Printed and bound in the United States of America

10 9 8 7 6 5 4 3 2 1

Para os meus pais

Contents

List of Tables and Figures xi

1 INTRODUCTION: WHY PORTUGAL? 1

   Analyzing the Portuguese Case 3
   The Plan of the Book 7

2 HISTORICAL BACKGROUND: CRISES AND SEQUENCES
  IN THE EVOLUTION OF THE PORTUGUESE
  NATIONSTATE 13

   Identity: From Feudal Province to
     Independent Kingdom 15
   Legitimacy: From Absolutist Monarchy to
     Democratic Republic 24
   Penetration: From Feudalism to the
     Administrative State 28
   Participation: From Legal to Popular Control
     of Government 34
   Distribution: From Infrastructure Development
     to Distributional Policies 40
   Conclusions: The Asymmetrical Polity 41

3 THE NEW STATE: THE INSTAURATION AND COLLAPSE
  OF AUTHORITARIANISM 49

   Authoritarian Regimes 49
   The Emergence and Instauration of the New
     State 52
   Failure to Institutionalize Corporatism . . . 56
   Conclusions 60

4 APRIL 25, 1974: THE <u>GOLPE</u> AND PERIOD OF
  EXCEPTION 65

   The Armed Forces Movement 66
   The Period of Exception 69
   The Containment of Spontaneous Action 75
   Conclusions 79

ix

5	THE PARTY SYSTEM: THE POLITICAL ARCHAEOLOGY OF PORTUGUESE PARTIES	83
	Origins of the Party System	84
	The Emergence of Modern Political Parties	90
	Political Parties after April 25, 1974	94
	Conclusions: Electoral Systems and Party Systems	108
6	ELECTIONS: SOCIO-ECONOMIC ECOLOGIES AND VOTING BEHAVIOR	117
	Societal Cleavages and Voting Behavior before 1974	118
	Social Cleavages and Voting after 1974	121
	Electoral Dynamics since 1974	128
	Conclusions: Parties as Determinants of Electoral Behavior	138
7	THE 1976 CONSTITUTION: CYCLES IN PORTUGUESE CONSTITUTION MAKING	143
	Cycles in Portuguese Constitutional History	143
	The 1976 Constitution	147
	The Politics of Constitutional Revision	151
	Constitutional Revisions	155
	Conclusions	156
8	THE POLICY PROCESS: MAKING THE ADMINISTRATIVE STATE RESPONSIVE TO DEMOCRACY	161
	Assessing the Administrative Elite	163
	Social Origins	165
	Political Attitudes	169
	Conclusions	171
9	LOCAL GOVERNMENT: POLITICAL CULTURE AND STRUCTURE	175
	Local Political Structure: Continuity and Change	176
	Local Political Culture	182
	Conclusions	190
10	CONCLUSION: WHITHER PORTUGAL?	197
	ACRONYMS	207
	BIBLIOGRAPHY	213
	INDEX	223

Tables and Figures

TABLES

6.1 Turnout for National Assembly elections, 1934-1973 121

6.2 Vote for CDS, PSD, PS, and PCP by labor sector, 1976 126

6.3 Nonvoters and party vote as a proportion of the elegible electorate 128

6.4 The correlation between the proportion of eligibles supporting the same party in 1975 and 1980 130

6.5 The correlation between partisan change between 1980 and 1975 and the support level of each party in 1975 131

6.6 Correlations between the degree of partisan change for all parties, 1975-1980 . 133

6.7 Regression estimates of "change" proportions from 1975 to 1980 134

8.1 Backgrounds and careers of a sample of Portuguese directors-general 166

8.2 Frequencies for background characteristics by when appointed to post of director-general 168

8.3 Mean scores for the tolerance for politics, programmatic commitment, elitism, and tolerance for conflict indices by when appointed to post of director-general . . . 169

TABLES

8.4	Mean scores on tolerance for politics and elitism indices for Portugal, Britain, Italy, Germany, and Sweden	170
9.1	Revenues of Porto de Mós, by source, 1977	180
9.2	Citizen level of political awareness	183
9.3	Citizen level of political knowledge	184
9.4	Citizen expectation of fair treatment	185
9.5	Citizen level of evaluation of local political system	185
9.6	Citizen evaluation of local assemblies	186
9.7	Level of salience of input structures	187
9.8	Citizen political role perception	188
9.9	Citizen level of competence as political actors	188
9.10	Qualities of local elected officials	189
9.11	Citizen attitudes toward bribes	190

FIGURES

2.1	Periods of conflict for the five crises in Portugal	42
5.1	The evolution of the Portuguese party system	110
6.1	Distribution of the vote for the winning parties in the 1915 election, by concelho	120
6.2	Distribution of the vote for the democratic opposition (CDE + CEUD) in the 1969 election, by concelho	122
6.3	Distribution of the vote for the four major parties in 1975, by concelho	123

1
Introduction: Why Portugal?

Political scientists who study West European politics have traditionally focused their attention on the major powers--Great Britain, France, West Germany, and Italy--and neglected the smaller countries of the region. Lately, however, some scholars have begun to turn their attention toward West Europe's smaller democracies.[1] Of these, Portugal has been perhaps the most neglected. The reasons for this neglect are several. First, of course, and perhaps foremost, Portugal was not a democracy until relatively recently when a military golpe de estado on April 25, 1974 put an end to one of the world's longest running authoritarian regimes. Second, although Portugal during the fifteenth and sixteenth centuries was a world power and spearheaded European expansion and discovery, the center of economic and political power in Europe has long since shifted northward leaving Portugal, situated on the southwestern most edge of the continent, far from the mainstream of events. Today, Portugal, Spain, Greece and southern Italy form the underdeveloped periphery of the continent and share a host of common economic, political and social problems.[2] Third, until the collapse of authoritarianism in 1974, Portugal tended to be oriented economically and politically toward Africa where she had three colonies--Angola, Mozambique, and Guinea (Bissau) --and toward her former colony, Brazil. The African colonies, which were the subject of grandiose dreams of Portuguese policymakers during the authoritarian period, acted as a political and economic counterweight to Portugal's small size and meager natural resources and magnified her international importance and prestige. Finally, Portugal has been neglected because few political scientists possess competency in the Portuguese language. Those who do are usually concerned with Brazil or Portuguese-speaking Africa (Portugal's former colonies). Moreover, political scientists with an interest in Iberian politics are invariably drawn toward Portugal's neighbor, Spain.

It should be pointed out that this neglect of Portugal extends to the Portuguese academic community as well.[3] Except from a historical perspective, Portuguese society and politics have not been studied to any significant degree by its own academy. There are several reasons for this state of affairs: first, the lack of political freedom during the authoritarian period meant that there was no academic freedom of inquiry as well. As social science research often raises difficult questions for authoritarian regimes, such research projects had to receive government approval. Few gained such approval, and those that did frequently had to disguise the real nature of the project.[4] Second, the social sciences generally and political science particularly are in their infancy as recognized, legitimate academic disciplines in Portugal. Social science has not been encouraged because of the humanistic and legalistic orientation which predominates in Portuguese classical universities and the belief by much of the Portuguese-trained professoriat that the social sciences do not deal with moral, legal, and philosophical questions of sufficient significance to warrant their time and attention.[5]

Therefore, little is known of Portuguese society and politics from a social science point of view and Portugal has not been included to any significant degree in the comparative political research tradition on West Europe. It is vitally important that Portugal now be included in this tradition. First, as political scientists we are concerned with making broad generalizations about politics. Portugal is a political system and now has a very active democratic political life. Like other political systems the experience of Portugal may serve to suggest new hypotheses and invalidate or support existing ones. Despite the arguments of some political scientists--namely, the corporatists, of which more below--the various approaches that have been used to study West European politics can be as fruitfully applied to Portugal as anywhere. The Portuguese political tradition, although no doubt different in important ways from that of the major powers, is as much West European as is that of France, West Germany or Italy. The inclusion of Portugal within the tradition of comparative scholarship adds one more case to the universe of pluralist democracies and can aid our understanding of the West European political experience generally.

Second, it is important to add Portugal to the body of comparative studies on Western Europe because it is highly relevant to a host of specialized theoretical problems of comparative politics, especially those having to do with the breakdown of authoritarianism and the instauration of democracy. How is it that a country with practically no democratic tradition almost overnight turned away from authoritarianism and established a pluralist democracy? The inclusion of Portugal in the tradition of comparative scholarship can shed additional light on this question as well as more "mundane" ones concerning nationstate formation, political party and party system development, electoral behavior, national-local linkages, political culture, and so on.

Third, and more practically, it can be argued that comparative scholarship, by virtue of the fact that it increases understanding of difficult and complex problems, can contribute, as it has in other countries, to the maintenance and betterment of democratic government itself.[6] Such scholarship can help defeat the tendency of many Portuguese of all social classes to see their country's limited experience with democratic forms in a very negative light and to believe that this experience is the result of Portugal's lack of political sophistication or the cultural "immaturity" of its people. Comparative scholarship can show that Portuguese political history and development fits patterns found elsewhere, especially more advanced countries in Western Europe. In time such scholarship could make its way into Portuguese schools and contribute to the political socialization process itself.

For these reasons, this book is being written. Taken as a whole, it is a country study in the classic tradition because it covers topics normally found in such books: constitutions, parties, voting behavior, local government, and the like. It is different from many such works, however, because it seeks to shed additional theoretical light on several of what might be called the "perennial" problems of comparative politics using data from the Portuguese case: e.g., the relationship between party systems and electoral system, voting behavior and socio-economic cleavages, political culture and structure, and the like. The overall thrust will be to begin to fill the knowledge gap that exists about the organization and workings of one of Western Europe's newest democracies as well as to shed new light, where possible, on old theoretical issues.[7]

ANALYZING THE PORTUGUESE CASE

Although marginal to comparative political research on Western Europe, Portugal has received fairly extensive treatment in the context of scholarship on Latin America. In the late 1960s and early 1970s, before April 25, 1974 when the old regime appeared to be as firmly entrenched as ever, analyses of the Portuguese political system sought to understand this case by placing it within the context of the Latin American experience. The general thrust of these analyses was that Portugal, like countries in Latin America, could not be comprehended within the general framework of political development because its political processes and institutions were fundamentally different from those in the rest of the less developed world. It was also argued that Portugal, because of its authoritarian regime and underdevelopment, could not be comprehended through the perspective of "advanced industrial society"; that is, from the West European perspective.[8]

The central organizing concept of these analyses was "corporatism." It was argued that corporatism was a unique and distinctive feature of Iberian political systems which had been transferred to Latin America during the colonial epoch. Portugal, like Spain and the countries of Latin America, was viewed as uniquely elitist, authoritarian, bureaucratic, and patrimonial, qualities which set these political systems apart from all others.[9]

Within this body of scholarship two modes of analysis emerged. One mode, which has been dubbed "culturalist,"[10] stressed attitudinal variables, individual orientations, and a comprehensive view of Portuguese society, politics, and history.[11] This mode of analysis assumed that the superstructure of political and social institutions found in Portugal during the authoritarian period depended upon the content of the Portuguese political culture in which they were embedded.[12] The culturalists argued that corporatist values and attitudes form an immutable, procrustean bed in which the superstructure of Portuguese social and political institutions have been, ever since medieval times, securely anchored. Culturalists dismissed structural changes, such as those which followed April 25, 1974, as being superficial and not fundamentally affecting the supposed "stronger and more deeply-engrained corporative tradition characteristic of all Portuguese regimes regardless of their self-imposed labels."[13]

The second mode of corporative analysis has been called "structuralist."[14] This mode viewed corporatism primarily in institutional and structural terms and as a specific elite response to the various problems associated with modernization. For structuralists, Portugal's authoritarian regime was considered to be a unique twentieth-century reaction to socioeconomic change such that Portugal seemed to be "treading water" or "swimming against the tide," isolated, idiosyncratic, and backward, having taken its own particular route to development and citizen participation.[15]

The golpe de estado of April 25, 1974, came like a bombshell to the corporatists, none of whom had the slightest notion that Portugal's "corporatist" regime was in a state of imminent collapse. The reason for this shortsightedness, as has been argued by one of the corporatist theorists himself, is that the "conceptual spectacles" through which Portugal was being observed were in need of "regrinding" and were better at "producing snapshots than motion pictures."[16] The corporatist framework of both varieties distorted reality by exaggerating those aspects of the political system each believed to be the most important. The culturalist mode placed too much emphasis on culture as a determinant of political and social institutions. Moreover, the culturalist position was conceptually and methodologically weak. No precise definition of corporatism was offered with sufficient precision to distinguish it from other forms of authoritarian rule and subject political culture. The tendency was to define corporatism in non-unique terms and infer from the presence of a few governmental institutions, that later proved to be hollow and insignificant, and elite interviews the existence of an extensive corporatist state and culture. On the other hand, the structuralist mode of corporatist analysis tended to overemphasize the ideology and master plans of the elite and paid insufficient attention to the actual implementation of the corporatist apparatus and to the structures and policy process by which the old regime was governed. Structuralists tended to infer from ideology the presence of a well-entrenched, extensive and functioning corporatist system of "interest intermediation"[17] when the reality of the political system was quite different, about which more in Chapter 3.

Although the Portuguese case may have distinctive features, it is the underlying assumption of this book that corporatism per se is not one of them. No matter how exotic corporatists claim Portugal to be, what is the case for Portugal may be substantially the same as elsewhere in Western Europe. Of course, the only satisfactory way of knowing if Portugal is unique, or has distinctive attributes, is to compare it to other cases. This can be accomplished basically in two ways: first, one of the several general functional models of the political system which comprehend the process of development could be adopted as an organizing frame of reference.[18] This approach is not to be followed here, however, because the high level of abstraction of such frameworks makes them exceedingly difficult to apply to concrete cases. Second, comparisons could be made by examining Portugal's formal institutions and comparing them with similar ones in other cases. Such a purely institutional approach is also rejected because it cannot automatically be assumed that institutions bearing the same name in different cases perform the same function in each. Such an approach would also result in an analysis which would disregard important historical, social, economic, and cultural factors which affect the operation of the institutions under examination.

Therefore, to avoid the shortcomings that would result if pure behavioral or institutional approaches were chosen, an attempt will be made to walk the tightrope between the excessive abstraction of behavioral analysis and the excessive concreteness of institutionalism. The approach, in general, views behavior and organization as complementary, as establishing mutual limits for one another. Thus, an attempt will be made to understand the Portuguese case in terms of the interactions between the political organization of the regime and its behavioral and cultural aspects. Such an approach will avoid the assumption of uniqueness and determinism found in the corporatist approach and the opposite tendency of institutional analysis to assume that nothing else matters.[19]

Although this study seeks to steer a course between the Scylla of pure behavioralism and the Charybdis of pure institutionalism, it contains a certain bias toward the latter as well as toward history. This is because of the author's conviction that the Portuguese case cannot be fully understood without a certain amount of detail about the organizational aspects of the system and its historical development. This is necessary especially in this case because so little is generally known even of the basics. The bias toward institutionalism and historical analysis also stems from the author's belief that institutions in general and the rules that guide the decisionmaking process within them establish a system of positive and negative sanctions, incentives and disincentives which exercise a very powerful effect on the attitudes and behaviors of individuals.[20] It is the main thesis of this book that much of Portugal's political history and development can be understood as a struggle to create new political institutions to deal with social and economic problems in the face of excessive institutionalization of older structures which prevent the routinization of new modes of behavior and institutions. The presence of such "confining conditions" has served, more often than not, to contain, frustrate, and otherwise prevent "breakthroughs" to new political forms.[21]

In this study the Portuguese political experience is approached by juxtaposing it with that of other political systems especially those of Western Europe. This is done in two ways. First, where appropriate, comparisons are made in terms of the various bodies of middle-range theory that are available on the key attributes of West European political systems such as nation-state development, electoral behavior and the like. Second, in those areas where there is little theoretical literature, such as constitution making, comparisons are made in terms of the patterns of development found elsewhere in Western Europe. The Portuguese political experience will be, in either case, put in historical perspective. In other words, the present democratic regime will not be viewed as a single snapshot but, rather, as part of a long-running motion picture of which it is only the latest reel. Thus, Portugal will be used as a kind of laboratory for testing and, perhaps, even refining the theoretical insights found in the various extant bodies of theory and developmental patterns identified.

In a general sense this book seeks to shed light on two questions, one theoretical, the other practical. First, how do well-entrenched institutions and legal rules shape political attitudes and behavior? An answer to this question is being sought because of the author's conviction that behavioral analysis, which was, of course, a reaction to pure institutionalism, has gone too far and has tended to neglect the importance of institutions and other formal arrangements as systematic variables affecting attitudes and behavior.[22]

Second, what are the factors which contribute to or detract from the survivability of Portugal's new democratic regime? Speculation on this question is important because of Portugal's previous unsuccessful experiments with democracy. Is Portugal's present democratic regime to go the way of its own First Republic (1910-1926), the Weimar Republic, and the French Third and Fourth Republics? Or does the regime change which took place on April 25, 1974 represent a significant breakthrough from the confining conditions of the past? Although predictions about the lifespan of a newly established regime are fraught with danger, it is this author's belief that it can be done with a reasonable degree of confidence if the case in question is analyzed carefully and without the bias of a unique framework which purports to explain but actually distorts reality.

THE PLAN OF THE BOOK

The book's plan is as follows: Chapter 2 seeks to comprehend the broad sweep of Portuguese history up to the beginning of the New State (<u>Estado Novo</u>) established by António de Oliveira Salazar between 1928 and 1932. This is done in terms of the crises and sequences model developed by the Social Science Research Council (SSRC). The model is used to analyze the developmental experience of Portugal as a nationstate. It suggests that the particular pattern in which Portugal developed has had a profound impact on contemporary politics. The chapter "tests" several hypotheses derived from the model about the relationship between the sequence and timing of the various developmental crises identified by the SSRC and the extent to which nationstate development will be either smooth or stressful and lead to either democratic or authoritarian forms.

Chapters 3 and 4 deal with the regime change which took place on April 25, 1974. Chapter 3 examines the first phase of this change: the collapse of the New

State. This chapter seeks to understand why the New State, which appeared to be monolithic, disintegrated almost overnight without significant resistance. This is done by examining the emergence, instauration, and institutionalization of the New State in terms of the theory available on authoritarian regimes, especially their breakdown. Chapter 4 deals with the second phase of this change in regimes; that is, the golpe de estado and the subsequent period of exception under military rule which gave rise to the present democratic regime. This chapter offers an alternative explanation for the meaning of the events during the period of exception which is contrary to those who argue that Portugal was experiencing a profound revolution which was eventually contained by right-wing forces in the counter-revolutionary golpe attempted on November 25, 1975. The chapter argues that the actual dynamic of events was not revolutionary in the true sense of the word but, rather, the result of the activities of various rival elite factions, primarily military at this stage, frequently led by charismatic individuals using populist appeals, which were struggling to gain control of the "situation." Moreover, the chapter argues that the spontaneous mass-based activity that did appear was actually quite limited in scope and objective and eventually contained and frustrated by various "confining conditions."

Chapters 5 and 6 deal with Portugal's emergent political infrastructure of parties and elections and seek to shed light on the theoretical issues concerning the development of multi-party as opposed to two-party systems. Chapter 5 examines the evolution of Portugal's political parties in terms of "constitutional" and "political" explanations, specifically the electoral system. The second of these two chapters deals with social forces explanations. That is, the correlations between voting behavior and broad socio-economic cleavages. The chapter seeks to answer questions about the relationship between electoral outcomes and socio-economic characteristics in Portugal as well as about the formation of stable voter alignments in newly emergent democratic systems.

Chapter 7 discusses the 1976 constitution. This chapter seeks to show that Portuguese constitutional history, like that of France and other West European countries, can be analyzed in terms of cyclical patterns of legislative supremacy and executive dominance caused by changing constellations of political forces within the society around conflicting theories of constitutionalism. The chapter suggests that the 1976 constitution and the recent revisions that have been made to it can be understood in these terms. Moreover, Chapter 7 suggests that the rationale behind the 1976 constitution was not too different from that which was applied to the other constitutions written in Western Europe immediately after World War II. This discussion of the constitution appears at this stage of the book rather than earlier because the political struggle in Portugal is not conducted wholly within the constitutional framework, as is the case in more institutionalized West European democracies, but is, rather, manipulated by various elite factions for their own political ends. Thus, the recent revision of the constitution can be seen as a continuation of the political struggle among competing elites unleashed on April 25, 1974.

Chapters 8 and 9 are concerned with the policymaking process. Chapter 8 argues that the trends in the policy process in Western Europe generally from political to administrative policymaking has been to a certain extent revised in Portugal since April 25, 1974. That is, problems regarded as administrative and technical during the authoritarian period are now seen as political and Portugal's new governing elite has attempted to shift the policy process away from the administrative apparatus of the state. Chapter 8 focuses on the purges that were carried out in the wake of April 25, 1974 in order to replace high level administrative personnel with individuals whose backgrounds and attitudes are more compatible with and responsive to the new democratic policy formation process. Chapter 9 shifts the examination of the policy process to the local level. The purpose of the chapter is to determine the degree to which the changes in the policy formation process evident at the national level have ramified to the periphery of the political system. The analysis is carried out in terms of the theoretical debate within the political culture literature on the relative weight of structural vs. cultural factors as determinants of political behavior.

Chapter 10 concludes the book with a discussion of the contributions of the Portuguese case to theory and some speculations about the future of Portuguese democracy.

NOTES

1. See, for example, Earl H. Fry and Gregory A. Raymond, The Other Western Europe: A Political Analysis of the Smaller Democracies (Santa Barbara, Calif./Oxford, England: ABC-Clio, 1982).

2. See Stuart Holland, "Dependent Development: Portugal as Periphery," in Underdeveloped Europe: Studies in Center Periphery Relations, ed. Dudley Seers et al. (Atlantic Highlands, N. J.: Humanities Press, 1979), Chap. 8.

3. However, some anthropological research was carried out during the authoritarian period by a few foreign and Portuguese scholars. See, for example, Joyce Firstenberg Riegelhaupt, "Saloio Woman: An Analysis of Informal and Formal Political and

Economic Roles of Portuguese Peasant Women," *Anthropological Quarterly* 40 (July 1967): 109-26; "Festas and Padres: The Organization of Religious Action in a Portuguese Parish," *American Anthropologist* 75 (1973): 835-852; and José Cutileiro, *A Portuguese Rural Society* (Oxford: Clarendon Press, 1971).

4. The problem of government censorship was especially critical for scholars, foreign and Portuguese, doing research in the African colonies who did not support Portugal's colonial policy. In some cases researchers were detained, interrogated, and held incommunicado by the secret police, the infamous Internation Police for the Defense of the State (Polícia Internacional e Defensa do Estado: PIDE). See Ronald Chilcote, *Portuguese Africa* (Englewood Cliffs, N.J.: Prentice Hall, 1967), Preface; and John Marcum, *The Angolan Revolution*, Vol. I (Cambridge, Mass.: M.I.T. Press, 1969), Preface.

5. The nucleus for domestic social science research in Portugal has been a small, independent research group called the Gabinete de Investigações Sociais supported by grants from the Gulbenkian Foundation and the Ministry of Education. Recently, this group gained official status and was integrated into the structure of the University of Lisbon as the Instituto de Ciências Sociais (ICS).

6. This function of the discipline is suggested by David E. Apter, *Introduction to Political Analysis* (Cambridge, Mass.: Winthrop Publishers, 1977), pp. 14-17.

7. Such an approach is relatively unique in the West European research tradition where, when compared to the comparative studies that have been conducted in Asia, Africa, and Latin America, there has been only a sporadic effort at theory development. On this problem, see Stein Rokkan, "Dimensions of State Formation and Nation-Building: A Possible Paradigm for Research on Variations within Europe," in *The Formation of National States in Western Europe*, ed. Charles Tilly (Princeton, N. J.: Princeton University Press, 1975), pp. 562-600.

8. For an excellent statistical analysis of Portugal's position between the developed and less developed worlds see Carlos Roma Fernandes, *Portugal a Europa e o Terceiro Mundo* (Lisbon: Editorial Pórtico, 1980). See also, Howard J. Wiarda, *Does Europe Stop at the Pyrenees? Or Does Latin America Begin There? Iberia, Latin America, and the Second Enlargement of the European Community*. The Center for Hemispheric Studies, American Enterprise Institute, Occasional Papers Series No. 2.

9. Major theoretical statements of this school of thought can be found in Howard J. Wiarda, "Toward a Framework for the Study of Political Change in the Iberic-Latin Tradition: The Corporate Model," *World Politics* 25 (January 1973): 206-235; Howard J. Wiarda (ed.), *Politics and Social Change in Latin America: The Distinctive Tradition* (Amherst, Mass.: University of Massachusetts Press, 1974); and Frederick B. Pike and Thomas Stritch (eds.), *The New Corporatism* (South Bend, Ind.: University of Notre Dame Press, 1974).

10. Linn A. Hammergren, "Corporatism in Latin American Politics: A Reexamination of the 'Unique' Tradition," *Comparative Politics* 9 (July 1977): 443-461.

11. This is the position of Wiarda. See in particular his

Corporatism and Development: The Portuguese Experience (Amherst, Mass.: University of Massachusetts Press, 1977).

12. For a critique of this assumption see Carole Pateman, "Political Culture, Political Structure and Political Change," *British Journal of Political Science* 1 (July 1971): 291-305; and Brian Barry, *Sociologists, Economists and Democracy* (London: Macmillan, 1970), pp. 48-52.

13. Howard J. Wiarda, "Portuguese Corporatism Revisited," *Iberian Studies* 3 (1974): 79. See also Howard J. Wiarda, *Transcending Corporatism? The Portuguese Corporative System and the Revolution of 1974* (Columbia: Institute of International Studies, The University of South Carolina, 1976).

14. Hammergren, "Corporatism in Latin American Politics."

15. The leading spokesman for this position is Philippe C. Schmitter. See his *Corporatism and Public Policy in Authoritarian Portugal* (Beverly Hills, Calif./London: Sage Publications, 1975).

16. Philippe C. Schmitter, "Liberation by *Golpe*: Retrospective Thoughts on the Demise of Authoritarian Rule in Portugal," *Armed Forces and Society*, 2 (1974): 7. In fairness to Wiarda, it should be noted that he too has reevaluated the Portuguese experience in light of the *golpe* and has concluded that Portugal is less distinctive than he previously thought. See his *From Corporatism to Neo-Syndicalism: The State, Organized Labor, and the Changing Industrial Relations Systems of Southern Europe*, Monographs on Europe, Monograph #5 (Cambridge, Mass.: The Center for European Studies, Harvard University, 1981).

17. Moreover, such "interest intermediation" is said to be now the dominant form of elite-mass linkage in the industrialized democracies of northern Europe and to be on the increase in the United States. See the issue of *Comparative Political Studies* 10 (April 1977), edited by Schmitter, for a discussion of this point of view. Additional discussion can be found in Philippe C. Schmitter and Gerhard Lehmbruch (eds.), *Trends Toward Corporatist Intermediation* (Beverly Hills, Calif./ London: Sage Publications, 1979) and Lehmbruch and Schmitter (eds.), *Patterns in Corporatist Policy-making* (Beverly Hills, Calif./ London: Sage Publications, 1982). For a dissenting view see Frank L. Wilson, "Alternative Models of Interest Intermediation: The Case of France," *British Journal of Political Science* 12 (1982): 173-200, and Frank L. Wilson, "French Interest Group Politics: Pluralist or Neocorporatist?" *American Political Science Review* 77 (December 1983): 895-910.

18. Such as can be found in David E. Apter, *The Politics of Modernization* (Chicago: University of Chicago Press, 1965); Gabriel A. Almond and G. Bingham Powell, Jr., *Comparative Politics: A Developmental Approach* (Boston: Little, Brown, 1966); or Samuel P. Huntington, *Political Order in Changing Societies* (New Haven: Yale University Press, 1968), and David Easton, *A Systems Analysis of Political Life* (New York: John Wiley, 1965).

19. See Kenneth Jowitt, "An Organizational Approach to the Study of Political Culture in Marxist-Leninist Systems," *American Political Science Review* 58 (September 1974): 1171-1191.

20. This point is brilliantly made by Giuseppe Di Palma, *Surviving Without Governing: The Italian Parties in Parliament*

(Berkeley: University of California Press, 1977).

21. Otto Kirchheimer, "Confining Conditions and Revolutionary Breakthrough," American Political Science Review 59 (December 1965): 964-974.

22. For a discussion see Ronald Inglehart, "Changing Paradigms in Comparative Political Behavior," paper prepared for the 1982 Annual Meeting of the American Political Science Association, Denver, Colorado, September 2-5, 1982. See also Lee Sigelman and George H. Gadbois, Jr., "Contemporary Comparative Politics: An Inventory and Assessment," Comparative Political Studies 16 (October 1983): 275-305.

2
Historical Background: Crises and Sequences in the Evolution of the Portuguese Nationstate

The wide sweep of Portuguese history must be studied in order to identify the nature of the "confining conditions" from the past which contain and frustrate "breakthroughs" to and the institutionalization of new political forms. This chapter will not present a straight narrative of the history of Portugal but will, rather, organize that history in terms of a framework that has been presented as a means of understanding the general process by which nationstates have developed: that of the Social Science Research Council (SSRC).[1] Briefly put, the SSRC model seeks to comprehend the political transformation of nationstates in terms of five crises or areas of critical change that must be resolved as development proceeds. These crises are aspects of governmental decisionmaking which become serious problems and grow into significant "arenas of conflict." The five crises areas identified by the SSRC are the following:

1. The penetration problem is the problem of how much effective control the government has.
2. The participation problem is the problem of who takes part (who has some influence over) the making of governmental decisions.
3. The legitimacy problem refers to the basis on which and the degree to which the decisions of government are accepted by the populace of a society because of normative beliefs on the part of the populace as to the "rightness" of the ways in which decisions are made.
4. The distribution problem refers to the extent to which the decisions of government are used to distribute material benefits and other benefits of the society.
5. And the identity problem refers to the definition of the set of individuals whom it is believed appropriately fall within the decision-

making scope of the government, i.e., to the question of the appropriate members of the system.[2]

The five crises are not considered to be ever permanently resolved. They may be resolved at one point in time and reappear at a later time. They may appear as areas of conflict one at a time or several simultaneously. All are, therefore, potential areas of conflict at any point in the development of a nationstate. As such, they represent a set of continuous problems that are never solved in an absolute sense.

A crisis can be seen as a turning point in the solution of each problem area which requires new patterns of institutionalization. Thus, the most useful way of identifying the developmental sequence and resolution of the five crises for a particular nationstate is by examining these patterns of institutionalization; that is, by examining the sequence with which institutions have been created to deal with each problem area. Institutions, which are defined as "generally accepted regularized procedures for handling problems,"[3] persist, develop their own dynamic, and represent attempts to solve problems. The focus on institutions aids identification of the various crises in the development of the modern nationstate in Portugal. A crisis can be said to exist when a problem arises in any or all of the crisis areas which cannot be dealt with by already established, routine responses and requires some new, innovative institutional means of dealing with the problem. The degree of crisis will depend upon the degree of flexibility of routine responses. If the system has a high level of flexibility, it may be capable of responding with no change in institutional pattern. On the other hand, if a system's institutions are inflexible and incapable of adaptation, then the degree of crisis will be high until new innovations are accepted as routine.

It should be noted that the crises and sequences framework does not suggest an inevitable, constant evolution toward a final resolution of all five crises. Not all societies can generate a viable institutional response; some crises can become severe enough to lead to the collapse of the society itself. Crises may be extremely persistent, and, for various reasons, the society may reinstitutionalize very slowly thus plunging it into seemingly interminable periods of chaos, violence, civil strife, and even civil war.

Having said that, it should also be noted that it has been suggested by the formulators of the framework that the resolution of one particular crisis before another as well as the pace and timing of reinstitutionalization will have certain consequences for the resolution of subsequent crises. When considered in terms of the extent to which the resolution of one crisis facilitates the resolution of another the following sequential pattern is suggested as the optimum one: identity, which facilitates legitimacy, which in turn facilitates penetration, which then facilitates participation and distribution. In terms of the pace of resolution the optimum development is one of balanced institutionalization in all five crisis areas. With respect to timing, the spreading out of each crisis so that they are resolved one by one makes for smoother development.[4]

These theoretical considerations suggest several hypotheses concerning sequence and timing that can be "tested" with the Portuguese historical data. The first is that the resolution of the five crises will be smooth and less stressful if the first three crises--identity, legitimacy, and penetration--are resolved before the last two, participation and distribution. The second hypothesis is that the resolution of the five crises will be smooth and less stressful if development is of balanced institutionalization in all five crisis areas. The third hypothesis is that resolution of the five crises will be smooth and less stressful if the crises are prevented from accumulating and are resolved one at a time.

Each of the five crisis areas will be discussed in terms of the history of the development of the Portuguese nationstate up to the establishment of the New State, which will receive special treatment in Chapter 3. The order will be identity, legitimacy, penetration, participation and distribution.[5]

IDENTITY: FROM FEUDAL PROVINCE TO INDEPENDENT KINGDOM

The problem of defining the set of individuals whom it is believed appropriately fall within the decisional scope of the government was resolved relatively early in Portugal and has reached crisis proportions only once since. Portuguese historians claim that theirs was the first nationstate to emerge from medieval Europe. Although such claims are somewhat exaggerated, there is no doubt that a common Portuguese identity emerged in the late Middle Ages. The creation of this identification reached crisis proportions at two distinct turning points requiring new patterns of institutionalization. The first crisis occurred at the founding of the monarchy, commonly accepted to have taken place in 1143, and persisted until 1385 when complete independence from Castile was achieved. This crisis involved three successive phases of conflict. The first conflict was between the founder of the monarchy, Afonso Henriques and his barons on the one hand, and the Emperor of León on the other, and involved the question of Portugal's existence as an autonomous and independent kingdom. The second conflict was between Afonso

Henriques and his successors, on the one hand, and the Moslem peoples who occupied the southern half of Portugal. This conflict was an integral part of the Christian Reconquest (<u>Reconquista</u>) of the Iberian Peninsula which ended in Portugal in 1249. The third phase of conflict involved a crisis of succession which pitted Portugal against Castile from 1383 to 1385 over the Portuguese crown and the complete independence of the Portuguese state.

The second crisis of identity occurred almost 200 years after the first when Portugal was occupied by Spain from 1580 until 1640 and the crown was merged with that of Castile in the Spanish Union. This crisis involved two phases of conflict. The first phase was the crisis of succession in 1580 which divided Portugal into two camps: Hispanophiles, who wanted union with Spain, and commoners, who wanted to maintain Portuguese independence, distinct identity, and separate crown. The second phase of the crisis was the reassertion of Portuguese independence and the restoration of the crown in 1640 and the intermittent warfare with Spain until 1666 when Portugal's independence as a nationstate was finally recognized. These turning points, requiring new patterns of institutionalization, are now discussed in detail.

Successive generations of historians have attempted to explain the emergence of Portugal as an independent monarchy on the southwest corner of the Iberian peninsula. In the sixteenth century it was held that Ulysses had founded Lisbon or that a legendary figure named Lusus had established the kingdom of the Lusíads, forerunners of the Portuguese monarchs. In the seventeenth century it was argued that Afonso Henriques, Portugal's first king, was divine, having miraculously defeated the Moslems with God's help. Portugal's greatest historian, Alexandre Herculano, considered Portuguese identity to be the result of accidental and fortuitous political developments in the twelfth century. Twentieth-century historians have stressed the underlying cultural and linguistic distinctiveness of the region which can be traced back to the Middle Ages.[6]

Obviously, a number of factors explain the emergence of a separate Portuguese identity and its development into a significant arena of conflict with those around it. Long before there was a unified kingdom of Portugal there were Portuguese. The province of the Kingdom of León, which had been granted to Afonso Henrique's parents and from which the independent nationstate of Portugal would eventually emerge, had achieved a sense of regional identity by the late Middle Ages. This sense of identification was fostered by several factors. First, toward the end of the ninth century, the area south of the Minho and north of the Douro rivers, having been reconquered from the Moslems and sufficiently resettled by Christians, was detached from the Galician province of Asturia, or León, as it was to be called after the tenth century. This newly detached province was called Provincia Portucalense, taking its name from the port of Cale (where the present city of Porto is situated), which had been the principal transit point between the Roman provinces of Galicia in the north and Lusitania in the south. This new province was, like the others of Asturia, placed under the authority of a governor, a duke appointed by the crown.[7]

Second, throughout the ninth and tenth centuries the province of Portugal (the c was changed to g in the vernacular) was kept united under the same family which governed on a hereditary basis. Unity, self-reliance, and identification were encouraged by Viking attacks and repeated Moslem raids during the tenth and early eleventh centuries. Self-containment and particularism were also fostered by the province's relative isolation from the rest of the peninsula. Separated from León by mountains, the peoples of Portucalense occupied the basin of the Duoro River which oriented them toward the southwest and the Atlantic Ocean.[8]

A third factor which encouraged a separate identity for the new province was the development of a separate dialect of vernacular Latin which, because of the political and geographic separation of Portugal from León, gradually evolved into the modern Portuguese.

The development of this regionalism into a significant arena of conflict over its identity as a separate kingdom began in 1096 when Alfonso VI, the king of León Castile, Galicia, and Portugal bestowed upon a Bergundian knight named Henri, in return for his service against the Moslems, the entire territory south of the Minho to be governed as a fief. Count Henri was married to Teresa, the king's illegitimate daughter and personal favorite, and established his government and court in the town of Guimarães. Bound by the usual ties of vassality to his suzerain, the count was expected to be faithful and loyal to the king and give him advice when required. Until Alfonso's death in 1109, Henri attended royal councils, helped the king in his military campaign against the Moslems, and generally behaved as a feudal lord should. However, Alfonso's death in 1109 plunged the kingdom of León into civil war as Argonese, Castilian, and Galician nobles fought over the royal patrimony, which had been inherited by the king's wife, Urraca. Count Henri, who was also involved in this struggle, was careful not to commit too strongly to one faction or another and thereby maintained freedom of action. From 1109 he quit carrying out his feudal obligations but never rebelled openly. When he died in 1112 his wife inherited the government of the province and continued her husband's policy.[9]

When Alfonso VI's wife, Urraca, died in 1126,

Alfonso VII decided to assert his suzerainity over Teresa, his aunt, and her consort, a Galician nobleman named Fernando Peres. She refused to pay homage and was forced into submission after a six-week campaign in 1127. The Portuguese barons blamed Teresa for their declining fortunes which Henri's policy of independence had gained and aligned themselves with her son and heir, Afonso Henriques, who had been about seven years old when his father died. Now a young man of twenty-four, Afonso, supported by the barons, rebelled against his mother's rule. On July 24, 1128, Teresa's army attacked Afonso and his liegemen at São Mamede near Guimarães. Teresa's forces were defeated and she and Peres were forced to flee to Galicia. Afonso Henriques thus gained control of the province of Portugal.[10]

In 1130 Afonso Henriques occupied a portion of southern Galicia, which had been earlier annexed by his mother. Alfonso VII, who was bent on acquiring fame as a warrior, recaptured the territory and stationed his troops there. In 1135 Alfonso VII, secure in his control over León and Castile, called himself "Emperor" and convoked a great assembly so that the princes of northern Spain could pay him homage. Afonso Henriques, encouraged by his barons to resist domination by León, refused to attend and even marched on Galicia to regain the territory north of the Minho lost to Alfonso five years earlier. The emperor met this challenge by ordering Galician barons to make war on Afonso. However, negotiations between Afonso Henriques and Alfonso VII prevented open conflict. After an earlier attempt in 1137 broke down, a permanent peace between Portugal and León was negotiated in 1143. By the terms of the treaty, Afonso Henriques was recognized as King of Portugal but was required to give military aid to the emperor and pay him homage.[11]

At the time of Afonso Henrique's recognition as king about one-half of the Iberian peninsula was under Moslem control. It was also at this time that a period of peaceful coexistence between Moslems and Christians was broken by a renewed military challenge from the Almohads, north African Berbers who swept into the Iberian Peninsula, Al-Andalus, as it was called by the Moslems. Like other Christian kings on the peninsula, Afonso Henriques reacted by launching a campaign against the Moslem south. In 1135 he built a castle at present day Leiria to act as base of operations. And in 1139, Afonso Henriques achieved his most famous victory against the Moslems in a daring raid across the Tejo River deep into their territory.[12] Some ten years later, in 1147, he took advantage of a series of religious rebellions among the Moslems and, with the help of passing crusaders sailing for Palestine, captured Lisbon. Continued Moslem internal dissent aided the Portuguese and gradually they advanced across the Tejo

River into the heartland of Al-Andulus, the Alentejo. Beja fell in 1162, and in 1165 a local freebooter and adventurer named Geraldo Geraldes, considered by some to be the Portuguese cid, attacked Evora and captured several towns in what is now Spain's Estremadura province. In 1166 Geraldo attacked Serpa and in 1168 Badajoz, still Moslem but under Leonese protection. The last attack, unauthorized by the king, provoked the intervention of Ferdinand II of Leon. As the Leónese forces were approaching Badajoz to oust the Portuguese, Afonso Henriques who had subsequently arrived to take charge of the situation, accidentally broke his right leg and was captured. After two months captivity, he was ransomed in return for a promise to abandon all territorial claims in Galicia and Castile. Unable to ride, Afonso's military career came to an end. At his death in 1185 the Portuguese had extended their front lines well into the Alentejo, where they would remain for the next fifty years.[13]

Sancho I (1185-1211), Afonso Henriques' son and heir, continued the reconquest of the peninsula but devoted most of his energy to the institutional development of the new Portuguese monarchy. He carried out a vigorous program of repopulation and the founding of new towns. Portugal's third king, Afonso II (1211-1233), however, was not much interested in military matters but continued to clarify the overarching authority of the crown in the already conquered areas. Sancho II (1223-1246), the heir of Afonso II, was the least successful of Portugal's early kings. Dominated by a clique of powerful barons, his reign was marked by considerable internecine fighting and he was eventually deposed. His younger brother, Afonso III (1246-1279), was placed on the throne. It was during the reigns of these last three kings that, owing to the collapse of the Almohad empire, the Portuguese, again aided from time to time by passing fleets of crusaders and the military orders of Santiago, Templers, Calatrava, and Hospitlers, were able to conquer the entire Alentejo and the eastern part of the Algarve. The reconquest of Portuguese Iberia was completed early in the reign of Afonso III, when an isolated enclave of Moslems in the extreme south of the Algarve was overrun in 1249. This last campaign brought the Portuguese to the sea and established the approximate boundaries that Portugal has had ever since.[14]

Although the military phase of the reconquest had given Portugal its territorial limits, the problem of national identity still remained. The immediate problem facing the monarchy was the forging of a unified society from two different entities: Christian north and Moslem south. This process of amalgamation took about 100 years and began when Afonso III ascended the throne. Several factors encouraged the molding of a single national Portuguese identity.

The first factor was the vast emigration of the Moslem population from the southern part of Portugal into the unconquered areas of Spain and to Africa and the simultaneous immigration of large numbers of Christians from the north. It is estimated that towns in the south lost between one-third and one-half of their populations. The Moslems who remained, usually individuals from the lower classes, were kept separate from the Christian population, lost all property rights, and were heavily taxed. As the social and economic importance of those who stayed was not significant, they were unable to exercise much influence over their Christian overlords. Emigration continued, and gradually over the next several centuries the Moslems who had remained behind were completely assimilated into Christian society.[15]

A second factor in the development of a common Portuguese national identity was the introduction of a unified market system which created an economic infrastructure linking northern and southern economic zones as well as urban and rural areas. Until the introduction of official markets, a feudal subsistence, barter system was the general mode of economic exchange. The introduction of a system of markets stimulated not only the conversion of surpluses into coin but also the manufacture and selling of various goods. Thus, economic exchanges between towns and the surrounding countryside stimulated the development of a national currency system.[16]

A third factor in the amalgamation of north and south was the adoption of the Portuguese vernacular as the national language. During the reign of King Dinis (1279-1325) it was decided that all official documents were to be written in Portuguese instead of Latin, which had been the practice until then. This decision not only helped to create a sense of national identification but also stimulated the improvement and perfection of the national language.[17]

A fourth factor was the growth of what might be called an "official culture." This culture was spawned by the founding of schools in various cathedrals and in 1288 a university. The most important agent for the dissemination of this culture was, however, the activity of learned tutors in manor houses and the presence of educated priests and friars at the king's court. This culture was further disseminated among the population at large by troubadores, who created an original and unique form of Portuguese literature and poetry.[18]

A fifth factor in the amalgamation process was the role that the Catholic Church played in defining and sustaining a sense of Portuguese identity. The revival of the church on the peninsula involved the restoration of the bishoprics as they were thought to exist before the Moslem conquest. The struggle for an independent Portuguese kingdom was intimately connected to the problem of the restoration of ecclesiastical administration during this period. The restoration of the bishopric of Braga in 1070 and the collaboration between its bishops, especially John Peculiar, with Afonso Henriques, gradually led to a coincidence of Portuguese spiritual ties to the political ambitions of her early kings. Although the struggle to elevate Braga to a metropolitanate was resisted by the Spanish bishoprics of Toledo, Santiago, and Lugo, the bishop was able to maintain de facto religious supremacy over Portugal. At the end of the reconquest, Portugal thus had its own church hierarchy organized into nine bishoprics all united under the archbishop of Braga. Homogeneity of religious practice throughout the national territory was fostered by the fact that the Portuguese Church was thoroughly orthodox owing to Portugal's isolation which insulated it from various medieval religious and cultural movements.[19]

The final factor which contributed to an overarching sense of national identification was the rise of Lisbon as Portugal's capital. Afonso III, who apparently liked Lisbon's climate, moved his court there in the thirteenth century. Because the south belonged to the king's patrimony and that of the military orders, he spent considerable time in the region. Despite the fact that Portugal's medieval monarchs, like kings everywhere in Europe at that time, constantly wandered from place to place within their patrimony carrying with them their court and administrative officials, Lisbon gradually became the center of Portuguese political, economic, social, and cultural life. This enhanced the position of the south and helped transfer its political and cultural values throughout the national territory.[20]

Although a sense of identification with the territorial limits of Portugal had been fairly well established by the time of the great plague of 1348, enabling the Portuguese to weather its destruction better than otherwise would have been the case, the first crisis of identity was not, however, finally resolved until forty years later. The third and final phase of conflict concerning the question of identity involved a domestic civil conflict and international war with Castile.

During the reign of Afonso IV (1325-1357), various disputes and fighting occurred with Castile to whom some ties of vassality still existed. After the relatively peaceful interlude of the reign of Afonso IV's son and heir, Pedro (1357-1367), the conflict with Castile resurfaced with the death of his grandson, Fernando (1367-1383). Fernando, who left no heir, was the last king of the Burgundian dynasty. His only daughter, Beatriz, was married to Juan I of Castile, providing that their offspring would inherit the Portuguese throne. When Fernando died, the government fell to his queen,

Eleanor Teles, who was seen as a foreign interloper and was thus extremely unpopular. The queen's main rival was Fernando's bastard son, João, master of the Order of Avis, the Portuguese section of the Knights of Calatrava. A revolt by João and his supporters drove Teles from Portugal which resulted in an invasion by Castile. From 1383 to 1384 the fighting waxed and waned, neither army able to inflict a decisive victory over the other. Finally, in the summer of 1385, the conflict reached its climax when Portuguese troops, under the command of João's brilliant military leader, Nun'Alvares Pereira, inflicted a crushing defeat on the Castilians on the plain of Aljubarrota. Random hostilities continued until peace was made in 1411.[21] The establishment of a new dynasty, the House of Avis, and the end of hostilities marked the end of the third phase of conflict and resolved Portugal's crisis of identity.

The second crisis of identity began in 1578 when the young and impetuous King Sebastião lost his life in Morocco leading a foolhardy military expedition against the Moslems at Alcácer-Quivir. He left no heir, which plunged Portugal into a period of confusion and intrigue over the succession. This involved a split between Portugal's hispanophile elite who saw themselves as a part of a broader Spanish community and the commoners who wanted to maintain Portuguese independence. Castilianization had reached a high point during the sixteenth century when every educated Portuguese was either bilingual or could at least read Castilian. The Spanish monarch sought the incorporation of the Portuguese throne in order to realize a long-held desire to unify the peninsula under one crown.[22]

Initially, Henry, the last surviving son of King Manuel I, was proclaimed king. This did not solve the problem of succession, however, because Henry was an infirmed and aged cardinal and was unable to gain a dispensation from the pope to marry. The King of Spain, Philip II, who was the grandson of Manuel I, had the strongest claim to the throne and began bribing the hispanophile members of the Portuguese nobility to gain their support for his claim. In January 1580 the Portuguese Court (<u>Cortes</u>) met to decide the succession but the commoners resisted the selection of a Spanish king. In order to cut through this opposition, Philip II promised to take Portuguese into his household, to defend Portugal and her overseas possession, and to ransom prisoners still held in Morocco.[23]

Active opposition to Philip's machinations came from António, the prior of Crato and an illegitimate son of Luís, one of King Manuel's brothers. Although he was disliked by the nobility he had the support of the commoners. When Henry died in January 1580, António was proclaimed king by the populace and marched on Lisbon with an improvised   Eight days later, a well-organized Spanish force invaded Portugal and attacked Évora, Arraiolas, Montmôr, and Setúbal. A few days following, the Spanish routed António's rag-tag army at Alcántara, on the outskirts of Lisbon. The pretender fled northward but could not stop the Spanish advance. After a period incognito, he left for France in 1581. Portugal's crown had thus been annexed by force.

In 1581 Philip II of Spain was declared Philip I of Portugal. In the following year he issued a proclamation of unity of the two crowns. This document provided that the governance of Portugal would take place through a six-member Council of Portugal, that the Portuguese Cortes would meet only on Portuguese soil; that all civil, military, and ecclesiastical officers would remain in Portuguese hands; and that the language, judicial system, coinage, and military would remain autonomous.[24]

In 1582, Philip's admirals subdued the island of Terceira in the Azores, which had remained loyal to António. In 1586, preparations were begun for the conquest of England. The combined Portuguese-Spanish Armada, which was supposed to accomplish this task, was, of course, defeated in 1588. In response, Queen Elizabeth sent Sir Francis Drake with a small army to capture Lisbon and install António on the Portuguese throne. Drake's expedition failed because of the strength of Spanish defenses and the inexperience of António's troops.[25] After this defeat no further immediate attempts were made to dislodge the Spanish from Portugal and António died in Paris in 1595, thus ending the House of Avis and closing the first phase of conflict in Portugal's second identity crisis.

During Philip II's reign, the terms of the union of the two crowns were generally upheld. However, with his death in 1598 and the accession to the Spanish throne of his son, Philip III, less respect began to be paid to the provision which guaranteed Portuguese autonomy. Philip III did not visit Portugal until 1619, very near the end of his reign, and began appointing Spaniards to the Council of Portugal as well as to important lower posts. When Philip III died, the crown was inherited by his son Philip IV, who, having little interest in government, turned over the administration of Portugal to the Count-Duke of Olivares. The Count-Duke began to alienate Portuguese of all classes when, in order to reassert the waning power of the Spanish monarchy, he levied excessive taxes and troop requisitions on Portugal to support military adventures against Spain's enemies, which now included France.[26]

The French, for their part, offered to support a Portuguese pretender with men and ships. The most likely candidate was Duarte, Duke of Bragança, the son of João's niece, and an extremely powerful and wealthy landowner. In 1640 the Catalonians rebelled against

Philip IV and, thus encouraged, a group of nobles persuaded Duarte to take the Portuguese throne for himself. On December 1, 1640, his supporters overran and occupied the royal palace in Lisbon. Five days later the Duke was crowned King João IV, restoring the Portuguese monarchy and founding a new dynasty, the House of Bragança. Unable to intervene militarily because they were occupied with the Catalonian rebellion, the Spanish were unable to send troops to prevent the restoration. Later attempts were also unsuccessful. Intermittent attempts to reincorporate Portugal into the Spanish Union continued until 1666 when a permanent peace was arranged and Portuguese independence was finally recognized, thus ending the second phase of conflict of the second identity crisis, and resolving Portugal's identity crisis more or less permanently.

LEGITIMACY: FROM ABSOLUTIST MONARCHY
TO DEMOCRATIC REPUBLIC

The problem of determining the basis on which the regime is accepted by the population because of normative beliefs about its right and duty to rule reached crisis proportions twice in Portuguese history. The first crisis of legitimacy occurred at the founding of the monarchy and involved two phases of conflict. The first phase pitted Afonso Henriques against Alfonso VII over the claim by the former to be King of Portugal. The second phase of conflict was between Afonso Henriques and the pope and involved recognition by the Holy See of the former's claim of monarchy. The second crisis of regime legitimacy arose in the nineteenth century as liberal ideology began to spread throughout Portugal. The crisis also can be divided into two phases of conflict. The first, which began in the 1820s and persisted until 1842, involved a struggle between Portuguese Jacobins and absolutists over the nature of the monarchy and the question of participation in the governmental process. The second phase of conflict, which began in the later part of the nineteenth century with the rise of republican ideology, persisted until the establishment of the military dictatorship in 1926 and pitted republicans and monarchists against one another over the future of the crown and the complete secularization of political authority. This second crisis has been much more intense, violent, and lengthy (running over 100 years) because it involved fundamental principles of regime legitimacy whereas the first was resolved relatively quickly.

The relatively quick resolution of Portugal's first crisis of legitimacy was facilitated by the fact that the conflict between Afonso Henriques and Alfonso VII was not over fundamental principles of the sources of political authority, which had been well established by the time of Afonso's claim to be the Portuguese sovereign. All early Christian kings on the peninsula legitimized themselves by tracing their ancestry to the monarchs of the Visigothic empire. Their suzerainity over territory reconquered from the Moslems was legitimized by reference to their hereditary ties to Visigothic kings and the idea that they were simply reestablishing the Visigothic empire as it existed before the arrival of Islam. The myth of the peninsula unified under an overarching kingdom nourished the dreams and ambitions of certain kings to become the emperor of all Spain. As one of the theoretic heirs to the old Gothic rulers, the Kings of León, who harbored such ambitions, began in the tenth century to use the title of emperor. Thus, for Afonso Henriques, the problem was one of gaining recognition for his claim to be a king, not establishing the principles of monarchy.

In Afonso Henriques' view, his claim was legitimate because he was the grandson of an emperor (Alfonso VI) and because he had been successful in reconquering territory from the Moslems. Afonso's position was buttressed when, in 1135, Alfonso VII proclaimed himself emperor and by the fact that Afonso Henriques' domain was larger than either Aragon and Navarre, the two other Christian kingdoms on the peninsula in addition to León. From the point of view of Alfonso, however, the claim was illegitimate because Afonso Henriques' father had been a mere count and his province was not an independent state, officially being a feudal parcel subordinate to king and pope. Considered this way, Afonso Henriques was little more than a rebel who had taken up arms against his mother, the legitimate ruler, as well as his king.[27] This phase of the legitimacy conflict came to a close, of course, when, in 1143, permanent peace was arranged and Afonso Henriques was acknowledged by Alfonso VII as the king of Portugal.

The second phase of the first legitimacy crisis involved the acceptance of the de facto kingdom of Portugal by the Holy See. When he was recognized by Alfonso VII as king in 1143, Afonso Henriques declared himself a liegeman of St. Peter and the pope, promising to pay tribute in return for official recognition. This recognition was not immediately forthcoming, however, because papal policy of the day was to encourage unification of the peninsula under one crown in order to be better able to defeat the Moslems. Afonso Henriques' claim ran counter to this policy, and it was not until thirty-six years later that the Holy See recognized the Portuguese kingdom. This recognition came primarily because of Afonso Henriques' vigorous prosecution of the reconquest which had won him vast territories in the south, far outdistancing the other kings of the peninsula. On May 23, 1179, a papal bull issued by Pope Alexander III granted to Afonso Henriques possession of all his conquests and recognized the rights of his successor to the throne of Portugal. Thus, the kingdom was granted full papal recognition and protection and the right to all lands conquered over which neighboring kings could not prove rights.[28]

The legitimacy of the crown and monarchical principle of governance were not seriously questioned in Portugal until the 1800s when liberalism began to undermine them. Although liberal ideology was known in Portugal in the late 1700s by way of the French and American revolutions, it was not until the turn of the eighteenth century that it became a force to be dealt with. Freemasonry played an active role in spreading liberalism in Portugal. In 1801 Portugal had five masonic lodges in Lisbon and the first Portuguese grandmaster was elected in 1804. The French invasion encouraged the spread of liberalism, and by 1812 the number of masonic lodges had grown to thirteen. Several years later, in 1818, freemasons established the Sinédrio, a secret society which was a major motive force in the liberal revolution of 1820. Liberalism was also spread by Portuguese exiles living in London and Paris where they had observed and been impressed by the functioning of the French and English systems. Newspapers and pamphlets published by these exiles were smuggled into Portugal and widely read. After the Napoleonic wars, the exiles themselves returned home and began to work for the establishment of a liberal regime.[29]

Portugal was ripe for a new set of legitimizing principles and institutions. The king, João VII, had been absent from the country since 1808 when the Portuguese court was moved to Rio de Janeiro to escape Napoleon's armies; the Regency, which stayed behind to govern the country in the king's absence, was almost bankrupt from the constant drain on the treasury in order to maintain the crown overseas; and the people were exhausted and war-weary after three French invasions. Liberalism was thus an attractive ideology at least among certain segments of the population, principally the urban middle classes in coastal towns, because it held out a new mode of political organization which would allow new elites to realize their desires to participate in the governmental process as well as resolve Portugal's pressing economic and social problems. Liberalism was also attractive because liberals posed themselves not as revolutionaries who wanted a clean break with the past, but, rather, as restorers of traditional individual rights supposedly suppressed by absolutism. Therefore, liberals were content with a constitutional monarch and the church would remain united with the state.[30]

The first phase of overt conflict within this

second crisis of legitimacy appeared in the early days of 1820 when a liberal insurrection broke out in Spain and gradually spread until Ferdinand VII was obliged to accept the Spanish Constitution of 1812 (Cadiz). These events, as well as the departure for Brazil of William Beresford, the commander of a combined British and Portuguese army which had been organized to defeat the French, encouraged Portuguese liberals and spread their influence in the army. In August 1820 military units in Porto revolted and the revolution soon spread to other regions of the country. A provisional government was organized and elections held for a constituent cortes. The constitution which emerged established a hereditary, constitutional monarchy in which the government would embody liberalism's tripartite division of power among legislative, judicial, and executive branches of government.

The constitution was short lived, however, lasting less than two years, and Portugal was plunged into a protracted civil war between Jacobins and absolutists, which waxed and waned in varying degrees of intensity until 1842 when a constitution, called the Constitutional Charter (Carta Constitucional), which compromised liberal and absolutist principles, was established. The Charter remained in force until 1910 when the constitutional monarchy was overthrown by republicans.[31]

Although the liberal era is frequently distinguished from the republican period (1910-present) it can be more appropriately understood not as a distinct new crisis of legitimacy, but, rather, as the second phase of the crisis which began with the advent of liberalism one-hundred years earlier. The roots of republican ideology can be traced back to the beginning of the nineteenth century but it was only by the second half of the century that republicanism began to command a large following. As the ideals of liberalism and its institutions began to solidify displacing absolutist principles of monarchy, republican ideology began to spread throughout Portugal, especially in the cities among the bourgeoisie. This movement was encouraged by the triumph of republicanism in France (1870), Spain (1873-74), and Italy as well as the instability of liberal governments and their humiliating foreign policy defeat at the hands of the British over Portugal's African territories (i.e., the Ultimatum of 1890). In 1899 three republicans were elected to parliament from Porto and, in 1906, four from Lisbon. Supported by the activities of the secret societies (Masons and the Carbonária), the republicans succeeded in overthrowing the moribund constitutional monarchy on October 5, 1910.

Adhering to the ideals of logical-positivism, the republicans viewed the monarchy, Catholic Church, and nobility as irrational and indefensible institutions that sapped the strength of the nation and were determined to replace them with republican ones. In May 1911 the republican provisional government held elections for a constitutent assembly which produced a new constitution which enshrined republican ideals. An elected bicameral legislature and presidency were created. Titles of nobility were abolished and the civil service was opened on the basis of merit. Workers were given the right to strike and tenancy laws modified. The government was thoroughly secularized by disestablishing the church; abolishing religious instruction in schools; forbidding the military from taking part in religious observances; excluding saint's days from the list of national holidays; and not recognizing religious oaths as binding.[32]

Although the republicans had come to power, Portugal's second legitimacy crisis was not yet resolved. Political life during the First Republic (1910-1926) was extremely unstable and violent. Maneuvering and military challenges mounted by monarchists resulted in violent attempts at counter-revolution in 1911, 1912, and 1919. Gradually, it became clear that the only institution capable of bringing to an end the political and economic chaos of the time was the military, which, after three previous attempts, succeeded in establishing a military dictatorship on May 28, 1926.

However, the soldiers carefully avoided actions that might be interpreted as meaning that a restoration of the monarchy was at hand. A majority of the officers were themselves republicans who needed the support of the population which they knew did not favor a restoration. Realizing that the tide was against them, the monarchists decided to wait for a more propitious time to push their cause. With the death of ex-king Manuel in 1932 all serious chances of a restoration also died, and most monarchists accepted the republic.[33] Thus, the second phase of conflict came to a close effectively ending Portugal's second crisis of legitimacy.

PENETRATION: FROM FEUDALISM TO
THE ADMINISTRATIVE STATE

The problem of effective control of the central government reached crisis proportions twice in Portuguese history. The first crisis of penetration, which began very early on during the reign of Portugal's third monarch, Afonso II (1211-1223), and persisted until the time of King Dinis (1279-1325), involved conflict between the crown and church over the control of the royal patrimony. The second penetration crisis occurred during the reigns of João II (1481-1495) and Manuel I (1495-1521) and involved conflict between the crown, on the one hand, and the nobility and military orders, on the other. Like the crises already discussed these two crises of penetration can be broken down into identifiable phases of conflict, in this case, each roughly corresponding to the reign of three particular monarchs.

Before the reconquest Portugal was subdivided into territories (terras), each of which was a political unit of feudal suzerainty and governed by a local nobleman confirmed by the king. Religious administration was carried out by the church which was divided into dioceses roughly corresponding to each terra. Central administration, especially the administration of justice, was the prerogative of the king. In the southern part of the country, however, after the reconquest, a second type of administrative system appeared. Because most of the reconquest was carried out by the religious military orders the crown granted almost all of the land in the Alentejo to them as well as to the monastic orders as payment and as protection against future invasions by the Moslems. The towns, and a certain amount of land surrounding them, were retained in the king's patrimony. Although each town had its own governing council the king was always represented by an official called the alcaide, appointed by the crown, and empowered to interfere in local matters on behalf of the king, as necessary.[34]

Outside the towns the king's tutelary power and authority were greatly curtailed in the north by the prevailing feudal system over which the crown retained only the ultimate word in matters of high justice but little else and in the south by the military and monastic orders which were either self-governing or integrated into the church hierarchy. The principal source of revenue for the crown was taxes collected from the signorial lands as well as tithes derived from lands owned directly by the king. As the latter were an extremely important source of income, the maintenance and enlargement of the royal patrimony became the source of conflict between the crown, on the one hand, and, initially, the church, and, later the nobility and the military orders, on the other.

The first phase of this early penetration crisis began in 1211 when Afonso II ascended the throne and discovered that his father had given away to the church large amounts of the royal patrimony. In 1216, after a lengthy legal battle with Rome over various provisions of his father's will, the Holy See recognized the king's right to maintain the royal patrimony in tact. Therefore, from 1216 to 1221 the crown asserted this general right by requiring those entities that had received donations from previous monarchs to apply for a letter of confirmation from the king currently on the throne. Thus, the crown gained the right to revise grants and donations to the church, nobility, and other corporate bodies.[35]

This practice gave rise to the appointment of royal commissions authorized to investigate land ownership, especially in the north where much of the feudal land tenure predated the creation of a unified Portugal. These inquiries (<u>inquerições</u>), as they were called, gathered evidence (oral history) from the oldest most experienced men in each <u>terra</u>, without consulting local nobles or church officials. They revealed a large number of illegal extensions of land boundaries and attempts to defraud the crown of income, the first inquiries finding that the church was the biggest expropriator of the royal patrimony. The archbishop of Braga, angered by the activities of the commissions and their findings, excommunicated the king in 1219. Afonso II responded by seizing church property and forcing the archbishop to flee Portugal for Rome. In 1220, the pope confirmed the king's excommunication and relieved him of his oath of fealty to the Holy See. The conflict between church and crown over disputed land ended temporarily when the excommunicated king died in 1223 and his chancellor arranged an ecclesiastical burial in exchange for the return of property confiscated from the church and a promise that future inquiries would respect canon law. Thus, the first phase of conflict involving the establishment of central government control ended with a defeat for the crown,[36] which proved, however, to be only temporary.

It was not long, however, before conflict over the problem of control of the royal patrimony resurfaced. In 1258, during the reign of Afonso III (1246-1279), the <u>inquerições</u> were revived and commissioners began taking depositions from the oldest members of the parishes so that lands taken from the crown could be restored. Once again the church was found to be the biggest violator. In response, seven of Portugal's nine bishops revolted against the crown and, in 1267, the archbishop and four bishops went to Rome where they accused Afonso of illegally confiscating church property and of bad government. Afonso placated the Holy See by launching a new campaign against the Moslems which influenced the pope to raise his interdict order. The crown then appointed a new archbishop and bishops in the four abandoned bishoprics and retained the confiscated church property in the royal patrimony. The pope responded by excommunicating Afonso who did not however pledge obedience until shortly before his death in 1277.

Portugal's first penetration crisis involving conflict between church and crown was finally resolved during the reign of King Dinis (1279-1325). In 1284, Dinis launched new <u>inquerições</u> and in the following year he promulgated laws forbidding the church and the military and monastic orders to purchase land and requiring the sale of land purchased since the beginning of his reign. For this action against the church, Dinis, like his father and great-grandfather before him, was excommunicated. This time, however, the king refused to pledge obedience to the pope and established once and for all the authority of the crown against that of the church to regulate and control the royal patrimony.37

The problem of effective control from the center was not again to reach crisis proportions for two-hundred years. In the meantime, the crown asserted its undisputed control over the administration of justice and order in the municipalities. After the middle of the thirteenth century, the <u>alcaides</u> were assisted by new officials appointed by the king to ensure that justice was fairly administered and order enforced. These new officials were the "bailiffs" (<u>meirinhos-mores</u>) who travelled from locale to locale overseeing justice and the justices (<u>corregedores</u>) who kept the peace. In addition, outside judges (<u>juízes de fora</u>) were sent to those places where fair trials were not possible from local magistrates. By the time Afonso IV (1325-1357) ascended the throne even local magistrates had to be confirmed by the crown, which could order the election of new judges and lay assessors (<u>vereadores</u>) when deemed necessary.38

During the reign of Afonso V (1438-1481), however, much of the effective central control over the royal patrimony built up by previous kings had been eclipsed and precipitated Portugal's second penetration crisis. Owing to the lax rule of Afonso V, the nobility had accrued enormous wealth and power by overstepping their rights and privileges; usurping large parcels of land from the king's patrimony; involving themselves in municipal affairs; and administering their own justice. When João II (1481-1495) ascended the throne he found the royal patrimony so reduced and the king's authority so diminished that he is reported to have remarked that he was little more than "king of the roads of Portugal." One of Portugal's ablest monarchs, João resolved to regain effective control over the nobility and the national territory.39

The bulk of the king's patrimony had been usurped by about fifteen noble families of which the Braganças, Menenses, Coutinhos, and the Melos were the most important. The most powerful of these was the Duke of Bragança and Guimarães who was also Marquis of Vila Viçosa, and Count of Barcelos, Ourém, Arraiolas, and Neiva. The duke controlled more than fifty towns and castles and commanded a private army of 15,000 troops and cavalry.40 João's first step in reasserting the power and authority of the crown was to require the nobility to take a rigid oath of allegiance and show evidence of title to their possessions. The Duke of Bragança and the other prominent nobles refused, saying the oath was incompatible with the dignity of their position and that they were legally entitled to all of their possessions. A search by the king's agents of the duke's papers revealed correspondence with Ferdinand and Isabella concerning a marriage between a Bragança and one of the Castilian king's illegitimate children. João used this correspondence as a pretext to try the Duke of Bragança for treason. In June 1484, he was found guilty, sentenced to death, and beheaded in Évora. The nobility, who saw that João intended to assert complete authority, conspired to assassinate him and make one of their own, the Duke of Viseu, king. As there were a large number of conspirators, the king learned of the conspiracy and took appropriate precautions. Knowing the precise day and place of the attempt on his life, João surprised the conspirators with an armed force. The king himself stabbed to death the leader of the conspiracy and imprisoned the rest, three of whom were later beheaded.[41] This brief but bloody confrontation was a complete victory for the crown and established permanently the political and juridical subordination of the nobility in Portugal.

During the reign of João II's successor, Manuel I (1495-1521), the final steps were taken to establish the effective control of the crown over the national territory. Manuel completed the process of turning the separate military landed aristocracy into a dependent court nobility which relied on royal appointments and annual allowances from the crown. He also completed the process of nationalizing and secularizing the military religious orders which had begun under João II, who himself had already united the masterships of Avis and Santiago in 1481. Manuel took over the Templars, now called the Order of Christ, and, in 1550, the pope sanctioned their integration into the king's patrimony. At the same time, the power and influence of the monastic orders, except for the largest and most prestigious, such as the Cistercians at Alcobaça, were declining, and much of their holdings were sold. By the middle of the sixteenth century, the royal patrimony encompassed about one-half the national territory.

Effective control was further achieved by centralizing and systematizing public finance, administration, law enforcement, and justice. Beginning in 1472 the town charters (<u>forais</u>) granted by the crown were revised, at first in response to excessive illegal taxation and later as a royal attempt to standardize the various types of local revenue. A code, known as the Manuelean Ordinances (<u>Ordenações Manuelinas</u>), was published in 1512 and was intended to reorganize the payment of land taxes and the collection of revenue. In addition, codes regulating the national treasury (<u>Regimentos e Ordenações da Fazenda</u>) and local finance (<u>Regimento dos Contadores das Comarcas</u>) were promulgated in 1516 and 1514, respectively. In 1473 the budget first appeared as a carefully organized document.

It was during this period that Portugal was divided into six provinces (comarcas) for administrative purposes. These administrative units, although based on traditional regions of the country, replaced the feudal division of terras and alcaidárias. Within each, the crown was represented by an official (corregador) who administered the district and ensured the king's justice and peace. In order to efficiently collect taxes, the national territory was also divided into financial districts called alms-shires (almoxarifados) each under the authority of an alms-sheriff (almoxarife), who was responsible for collecting the crown's revenue. The effectiveness of the king's justice was also enhanced during this period by increasing the number of outside judges and the powers of the king's officials. By 1538 even local magistrates became employees of the crown, being paid from the national treasury instead of by the local population, a practice which had resulted in much corruption. Finally, it was also at this time that the national government began to be differentiated from the crown. Because of increasing complexity a true cabinet appeared comprising six secretaries or ministers: the Great Chancellor (chancelor-mor), responsible for the royal chancellary; the private scribe (escrivão da puridade), the king's private secretary; the public secretary (secretário d'el Rei), who accompanied the king whenever he travelled; two attorney's-general (corregadores de corte), one for criminal and the other for civil matters and an administrator of justice (meirinhos-mor). The king was also assisted by a Council of State (Conselho de Estado) composed of twenty-seven members of the nobility and clergy.[42]

Thus, by the end of Manuel I's reign, the monarchy had so thoroughly established the power and authority of the crown and its government over the national territory that it was never to be seriously challenged again. Portugal's second penetration crisis thus resolved, increasing amounts of power and authority gradually accrued to the crown and central government over the next two centuries. During these centuries the government became increasingly complex and bureaucratized. Government became more and more the prerogative of the king and his cabinet. In 1736, the titles of the king's secretaries were changed to correspond to their functions: Secretary of State for the Interior, Foreign Affairs, War, Navy, Oversea, etc. The Secretary of State for the Interior acted as the Prime Minister. During the eighteenth century the number of comarcas in each province gradually increased from twenty-seven to forty-four indicating a growth in the penetration of national territory by the central government. Centralization and state power probably reached their apogee during the prime ministership of the Marques de Pombal (1750-1777) when all remaining residues of feudalism were abolished and general law was established for the entire national territory. Pombal also reformed the police forces making them more efficient and established the concept of a state police with the power to arrest those who opposed the government. The growing complexity and centralization of government began to require specialized training, which the nobility could no longer provide. Thus, administrators began to be recruited on the basis of expertise and merit. By the time of Pombal, then, Portugal had become a highly centralized administrative state.[43]

PARTICIPATION: FROM LEGAL TO POPULAR CONTROL OF GOVERNMENT

The problem of who should take part in or influence governmental decisionmaking has reached crisis proportions once in Portugal's history. Questions of who should participate as well as which institutions should have the greatest amount of influence in policymaking became a significant arena of conflict in the early 1800s and persisted until relatively recently. This conflict roughly parallels that of the second legitimacy crisis but persists about fifty years longer, until 1974. Portugal's participation crisis can be divided into two phases of conflict. The first, which corresponds to the struggle between Portuguese Jacobins and absolutists in the civil war in the early nineteenth century, was concerned with bringing the absolute monarchy under the legal control of a written constitution. The second phase, which began in the late nineteenth century, was essentially concerned with bringing government under popular control.[44] This phase did not end until April 25, 1974, when universal suffrage was established and mass based political parties appeared for the first time in Portuguese history.

The first phase of the participation crisis was produced by Portugal's transitions from a predominantly rural, agricultural society into a predominantly urban, nascent industrial state. As economic modernization and industrialization progressed, especially after 1800, land gradually became a less important source of wealth and power. Increasingly the tenets of monarchical power were challenged, first, by the adherents of liberalism and, later, by supporters of republicanism, principally the new urban upper and middle classes. As the power of the crown began to wane, that of new middle class oligarchies began to rise thus producing demands for a greater voice in government. This transformation was prolonged and intensified by Portugal's slow and uneven rate of economic development which resulted in violent conflict between traditionalists and modernizers over the legal control of the state and question of which groups should be allowed to participate in governmental decisionmaking.

At the founding of the monarchy decisions affecting the entire realm were, of course, the king's prerogative. He was assisted by royal advisers, the head of the army, the head of the royal household, and the chancellor, being the most important, as well as members of the royal family. When matters required, the circle of advisers was increased to include bishops, the abbots of the largest monasteries, the most respected of the nobility, and the masters of the military religious orders. It was from such gatherings that the principle of consultation with the cortes or parliament, was established.

Initially, the cortes, which was composed of the three estates of the realm, clergy, nobility, and commoners, met infrequently. However, after the resolution of Portugal's first identity crisis in 1385, and the resultant strengthening of the direct ties between the crown and populace, the cortes was summoned with much greater frequency. For example, during the reigns of João I (1383-1433), Duarte (1433-1438), and Afonso V (1438-1481), a period of a little less than 100 years the cortes was called on average every two years.[45] During the reign of João II (1481-1495), however, as the ability of the crown to extract revenue through its own instrumentalities grew, the responsibility of the cortes to provide monies and advice declined. Thus, from 1481 until 1502 the elapsed time between meetings increased from every two years to every three. Between 1502 until 1544, the cortes was called only three times for an average of once every fourteen years. During the last half of the sixteenth century, the cortes continued to decay as an important consultative body, its role increasingly becoming symbolic. Between 1562 and 1579, the cortes met three times, but only to discuss the problem of royal succession. During the sixty years in which the crown of Portugal was united with that of Castile in the Spanish Union the cortes was summoned only three times, in 1581, 1583, and 1619. Although the cortes met a little more frequently after the restoration, five times between 1641 and 1668, this resurgence did not last. When it attempted in 1674 to expand its purview into matters of royal policy, the cortes was disbanded by Pedro II. Although it was summoned in 1679 to discuss the marriage of Pedro's daughter, the cortes was not called again until 1697, its last meeting.[46]

With the disappearance of the cortes the problem of participation lay dormant until the early 1800s when liberalism began to spread in Portugal. As constitutionalism is a key element in liberal doctrine, the struggle to bring Portugal's absolute monarchy under the control of a written constitution began. As already mentioned in the above discussion of the legitimacy crisis, the Jacobin victory in the civil war resulted in the writing of Portugal's first constitution in 1822. This document proclaimed Portugal to be a hereditary, constitutional monarchy, and divided power among three branches of government. The executive power was granted to the king and his ministers. The legislative went to a unicameral parliament, and the judicial to the courts. The right to vote was granted to all literate males.

However, this unicameral cortes had a precarious existence and did not long endure. From the outset the liberal regime had antagonized the nobility and clergy by failing to give them representation and was seen as having humiliated the monarchy by stripping the king of royal prerogatives. Moreover, the Jacobins even succeeded in antagonizing some of their original supporters, particularly merchants, because they were unable to formulate a coherent policy to improve Portugal's economy, devastated by the Peninsular Wars.[47]

At the same time the whole complexion of European international politics was changing. In 1823, the Holy Alliance was preparing to intervene diplomatically and militarily in Spain, whose turbulence was considered a threat to European peace. In Portugal, thus encouraged, leading absolutists who were still a force to contend with, established a headquarters in Vila Real in the province of Trás-os-montes. When the French entered Spain in April 1823 and restored Ferdinand, impetus was given to an absolutist uprising (known as the Vila Francada) which took place at the end of May in Vila Franca de Xira, near Lisbon. The rebels were joined by João VI's youngest son, Miguel, who had fallen under the influence of young nobles who saw their power threatened by Jacobinism and its institutions. The constitution of 1822 was suspended and absolutism restored, but with the promise that a new constitution would be promulgated more in keeping with traditional Portuguese institutions. In June 1823 João dissolved the cortes and appointed a committee to prepare a new constitution. The promised document was never to materialize, however, and many liberals went into exile in France and England. Portugal was governed by João's moderate absolutism until his death in March, 1826.[48]

João's death created a problem of royal succession. The rightful heir to the throne was his eldest son, Pedro, who was then emperor of Brazil. Neither the Portuguese nor the Brazilians wanted a unified monarchy. Consequently, Pedro abdicated the Portuguese crown in favor of his daughter, Maria da Glória, a child of seven, on the condition that, when of age, she marry his brother Miguel. In April 1826, as part of the settlement of the succession question, Pedro granted a new constitution to Portugal, known as the Constitutional Charter (Carta Constitucional).[49]

This document attempted to reconcile monarchists

and Jacobins by allowing them both to participate in the decisionmaking process. The cortes was divided into two houses: the upper house, the House of Peers (Câmara de Pares), was composed of life and hereditary peers and clergy appointed by the king without numerical limit. The lower house, the House of Deputies (Câmara de Deputados), was composed of 111 deputies elected for four year terms by indirect suffrage from local assemblies which were themselves selected by a franchise restricted by tax-paying and property-owning requirements.

The compromise embodied in the charter between the historical cortes of appointed delegates and the unicameral parliament of 1822, however, did not satisfy the absolutists. In February 1828, Miguel, who had been exiled for his role in a failed absolutist uprising of 1824 (the Abrilada), returned to Portugal to take the oath of allegiance to the charter. Immediately upon his arrival, he was proclaimed king by his supporters. Although it initially appeared that Miguel would abide by the charter, pressure for a return to absolutism mounted. A month after his return, Miguel dissolved the House of Deputies and, in May, summoned the traditional cortes of the three estates of the realm to legitimate his accession to absolute power. At the same time the charter was nullified.[50]

Miguel's accession to absolutism sparked a military uprising by the Jacobins in Porto and other regions of Portugal. This led to six years of repression against Portuguese liberals. Many thousands fled, and among those who remained many thousands were detained by Miguel's police. This oppression eventually plunged Portugal into a violent civil war.[51]

The war was essentially a struggle for power among three main elite factions, each with its own ideology and notions about representative institutions and popular participation. The absolutists, who derived their power from the aristocracy and the peasantry, especially in the north, wanted no written constitution and the traditional appointed cortes of the three estates of the realm. The moderates, who derived their power from the upper bourgeoisie in the cities and towns, wanted the charter and a parliament of two houses, one indirectly elected and the other appointed by the crown. The radicals, who derived their power from the newly emergent urban bourgeoisie and merchants in the major cities, wanted a return to the constitution of 1822 and the directly elected unicameral parliament.[52]

In July 1833, allied moderate and radical Jacobin troops under the command of Pedro IV, who had a romantic belief in liberal principles and who had abdicated the Brazilian throne, established a beachhead in Porto. Later that month, Pedro's naval commander succeeded in defeating Miguel's fleet and a second landing was made at Faro in the Algarve. The Jacobin army marched northward and captured Lisbon on July 24. A stalemate of nine months ensued, with the absolutists controlling the rural areas, where they were supported by the aristocracy and the peasantry, and the Jacobins occupying Portugal's two major cities, Lisbon and Porto, where they commanded a sizeable following among the lower and middle classes. The stalemate was finally broken when liberal forces supported by the Quadruple Alliance defeated the absolutists in May 1834. Miguel was banished from Portugal, never to return, and Pedro restored the charter.[53]

A new cortes met in August 1834. Although there were no political parties as such, the delegates were deeply divided between moderates, who supported Pedro and the charter, and radicals called Vintistas, who wanted a return to the Constitution of 1822. In September 1836 the radicals rebelled and reestablished the constitution of 1822. At the same time, the Septemberists, as the radicals were now called, convoked a constituent assembly which was given the task of revising the 1822 document to make it more compatible with changed social and economic circumstances. This resulted in a violent reaction from the moderates, who saw their power threatened and considered the charter the symbol of the Jacobin victory in the civil war. As a compromise, the constituent assembly was remanded to make alterations in both the constitution of 1822 and the charter with the aim of establishing a constitutional monarchy similar to those elsewhere in Europe. In April 1838 Portugal's third constitution was promulgated.[54]

The constitution of 1838 attempted a compromise between the charter and the constitution of 1822. It abolished the moderative power and returned to liberalism's classical tripartite division of power into legislative, executive, and judicial branches of government. The 1838 document reaffirmed, as in 1822, that sovereignty rested with the nation. It abolished the House of Peers and substituted a House of Senators (Câmara de Senadores) and it established the direct election of the House of Deputies, although under a restrictive franchise. The king's role was enhanced and the senate was restricted to notables.[55]

After four years of inept radical government and a marked decline in Jacobin sentiment, the charter was restored in 1842, after a bloodless golpe by the moderates. This second restoration did not, however, immediately bring stability to Portugal's political life. There were still two distinct concepts of who ought to participate in the decisionmaking process. The moderates advocated a House of Peers nominated for life and a House of Deputies elected indirectly. The radicals, on the other hand, wanted direct election of both

houses. It was finally recognized by the moderates that
the charter had to be modified to allow more participation by the population in the governmental process.
Therefore, beginning in 1852, amendments to the charter
called Additional Acts (<u>Actos Adicionais</u>) gradually
introduced a number of democratic reforms. The first
of these amendments introduced the direct election of
the House of Deputies but maintained income qualifications for voting and for holding office. The second,
in 1885, eliminated hereditary parity, limited the number of life peers to 100, created fifty elected peers,
and restricted the king's moderative power. The third,
in 1896, mitigated the reforms of the 1885 amendment
somewhat by restoring life peerages.[56]

Despite continued differences between the moderates, now called Regenerators (<u>Regeneradores</u>), and the
radicals, now called alternatively Historicals (<u>His-
tóricos</u>) and Progressives (<u>Progressistas</u>), these amendments, as well as the agreed upon practice of governments governing as long as they were able and then turning power over to their rivals, lent some measure of
stability to Portuguese government from 1871 onward.
This system, known as Rotativism (<u>Rotativismo</u>), survived
until the first decade of the twentieth century.[57]

Although it is possible to say that since the
beginning of the nineteenth century there have been
some advocates of a republican form of government in
Portugal, they did not command much of a following until
the later half of the century. As the ideals of absolutism began to fade with the death of Miguel in 1866
and as liberalism and its institutions were solidified,
republicanism began to spread throughout Portugal, especially in the cities and towns. In 1899 three republicans were elected to the House of Deputies from Porto,
and in 1906, four were elected from Lisbon. As has
already been mentioned, republicans succeeded in overthrowing Portugal's moribund monarchy on October 5,
1910.[58]

Republicans were determined to secularize the state
and design a constitutional system which would adequately represent Portugal's nascent industrial and
merchant middle class, who were by the turn of the century a significant factor in the nation's social and
economic life and from whom they derived the bulk of
their support. The Constitution of 1911 granted legislative power to the Congress of the Republic (<u>Congresso
da República</u>), composed of two houses. The upper house,
called the Senate (<u>Senado</u>) was comprised of senators
directly elected for six-year terms from the administrative districts of the country as well as from overseas
territories. The lower house, the House of Deputies
(<u>Câmara de Deputados</u>), was made up of directly elected
deputies who served three year terms.[59]

However, political life during the First Republic

was characterized by extreme parliamentary, presidential, and governmental instability. In its sixteen years, there were seven congressional elections, and eight for president; and forty-five governments rose and fell. The primary reason for the poor performance and eventual collapse of the First Republic, as will be discussed in greater detail in Chapter 5, was its failure to institutionalize new means of dealing with popular participation; that is, its failure to institutionalize a coherent party system capable of mobilizing and controlling participation. The collapse of the monarchy, the decimation of the nobility through the appointment of life peers for political purposes, and the disestablishment of the church had by this time severed nearly all of the traditional institutions which linked the populace to the national government. The political infrastructure of political parties and the congress did not adequately fill this void.[60]

As was mentioned above, the army intervened in May 1926 in an attempt to bring some semblance of order to the economic and political chaos of the day. Unable itself to govern effectively, the military gradually relinquished power to a civilian regime created by António de Oliveira Salazar. The manner in which Salazar sought to solve the participation crisis and the reasons for his failure will be the subject of the next chapter.

DISTRIBUTION: FROM INFRASTRUCTURE
DEVELOPMENT TO DISTRIBUTIONAL POLICIES

The problem of distribution has not been an arena of serious conflict until relatively recently in Portuguese history. Until the beginning of the twentieth century, Portugal's population, for the most part, was made up of self-sufficient peasants who no doubt resented and at times resisted state taxation and feudal obligations which made their survival more difficult but never demanded basic changes in the distribution of the material benefits of Portuguese society. Except for church lands, which were taken out of mortmain in 1834 and sold to individual peasants, the policy of the Portuguese crown and its governments had been to encourage the development of agriculture and the industrial infrastructure. Possibly the only exception to this generalization would be the Sesmarias decree of 1375 which was promulgated to ensure that all arable land was put into cultivation. According to the decree, a response to the devastation of Portuguese agricultural production wrought by the plague of 1348, land in the hands of the nobility and church not being cultivated was to be confiscated and resold on reasonable terms to landless peasants.[61]

However, after 1900, the distribution of material and non-material benefits became a significant arena of conflict in Portugal. As industrialization began to increase the productive capacity of the Portuguese economy and create an urban working class, distributional type demands began to appear. The first phase of significant conflict over distribution occurred during the first quarter of this century. During these years Portugal experienced a large number of strikes and demonstrations by workers demanding more reasonable working hours, better working conditions, and higher salaries. Although the governments of the day frequently gave in to such demands, government policy did not change from its basic orientation toward infrastructure development. Indeed, during the Salazar period, distributional demands were suppressed and infrastructure development was emphasized above all else.

The second phase of conflict over the distribution of Portugal's material benefits is intimately associated with the collapse of the old regime on April 25, 1974 and has persisted until the present. Since then distributional demands have reached unprecedented heights and government policy has become concerned with such issues. Political conflict in Portugal since 1974 has been for the most part structured by the participation and distribution crises, especially the latter.

CONCLUSIONS: THE ASYMMETRICAL POLITY

Figure 2.1 demonstrates graphically the sequences and timing of the periods of conflict for the five crises as they have occurred in Portuguese history. The figure shows that the crises have appeared and have been resolved roughly in the following sequence: legitimacy, identity, penetration, participation, and distribution. This pattern is complicated somewhat, however, by the fact that there has been considerable overlap of various crises and because the legitimacy and identity crises, resolved early on, resurfaced at a later time simultaneously with other crises, specifically participation and distribution.

Figure 2.1 shows that there appear to be two broad periods in Portuguese history as far as the five crises are concerned. The first period begins at the founding of the nationstate and runs roughly to the sixteenth century. Three problem areas--identity, legitimacy, and penetration--were significant areas of conflict during this early period. If it is considered that participation was resolved without having become a significant arena of conflict (the medieval <u>cortes</u> seems to have evolved without too much tension from the royal court) and distribution was never a significant issue, then the five crises seem to have been solved early on for

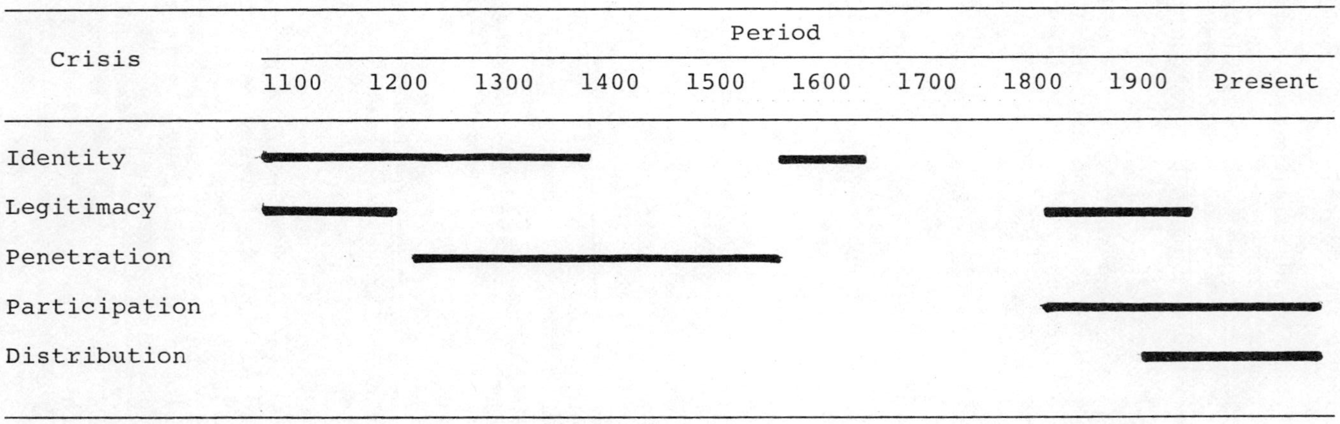

Crisis	1100	1200	1300	1400	1500	1600	1700	1800	1900	Present
Identity										
Legitimacy										
Penetration										
Participation										
Distribution										

Figure 2.1 Periods of conflict for the five crises in Portugal

Portugal in the form of a centralized absolutist monarchy of the late medieval period.

The second broad period began about 1800 with the arrival of liberalism and the subsequent resurfacing of the legitimacy crisis and the surfacing first of participation and distribution problems as arenas of conflict. This period marks the beginnings of the modern Portuguese state. Thus, in the first period, conflict was most likely to be caused by questions of legitimacy, identification, and penetration, while in the modern period conflict and tension are oriented about questions of participation, distribution, and, to a lesser extent, legitimacy.

Figure 2.1 also shows that the resolution of Portugal's five crises has been quite slow and, as was shown in the historical discussion of each, fraught with difficulties. This suggests that, except in the case of the first legitimacy crisis, the processes of institutionalization and reinstitutionalization have been difficult and stressful. It required 245 years for a Portuguese identity as a unified monarchy to be institutionalized sufficiently to withstand the second identity crisis which occurred between 1580 and 1640 when Portugal was part of the Spanish Union. A period of 310 years was required to institutionalize the central control by the crown and its administrative apparatus. Portugal's second legitimacy crisis occupied slightly more than 100 years and involved a civil war, which suggests great difficulty getting new legitimizing principles institutionalized. The fact that the crisis of participation began about 150 years ago and was only recently resolved also suggests great difficulty getting representative participatory structures and processes based on new legitimizing principles established and institutionalized. Finally, the conflict surrounding distribution, which surfaced about eighty years ago and continues today, indicates considerable difficulties getting accepted the notion that government ought to be involved in distributional policymaking as a normal activity.

How does the Portuguese sequence compare with those of other West European nationstates? Grew[62] found two basic patterns in European nationstate development. One was represented by those cases (Great Britain, Scandinavia, and Belgium) where the legitimacy and participation crises were resolved early and the second, those cases (Germany, Poland, and Russia) where penetration was resolved first. The cases which exemplify both of these types suggest that democratic participatory forms are more likely to result if the participation crisis is resolved early rather than later, after other crises, such as penetration have been dealt with. Grew also found a third pattern somewhere between type one and two, exemplified by France and Italy, in which the identity crisis was resolved early but closely tied to participation as in the Italian case and penetration as in the case of France. Although the precise sequence and timing of the appearance and resolution of the crises are unique to Portugal, the overall pattern is closest to Grew's intermediary type, especially that of France.

What light does Portugal's pattern of development shed on the theoretical questions raised at the beginning of the chapter? One hypothesis was that the successful resolution of one crisis will guarantee the successful resolution of later ones and that the early resolution of the first three crises--identity, legitimacy, and penetration--will facilitate the resolution of the last two crises--participation and distribution. The Portuguese case is particularly good for testing this proposition because it comes very close to replicating this ideal sequence. It does not appear, however, from the Portuguese experience that the early resolution of the first three crises facilitates the resolution of the last two. Indeed, the high levels of conflict and stress connected with the participation and distribution crises suggest exactly the opposite; that is, a much greater difficulty institutionalizing responses to these later crises than would have been the case. Established polities seem to meet new challenges with the institutions that have already been built up. Thus, the participation crisis has been a long, drawn out and often violent affair because the problem of institutionalizing new structures and processes of popular involvement have been resisted tooth and nail by those elites who wished to maintain the institutions of the absolute monarchy and/or centralized state. The Portuguese case, as well as those analyzed in Grew, shows that political systems tend to respond to new crises with the institutional patterns which have been already established. Thus, it is important whether a nationstate's sequence begins with the identity and participation crises or identity and penetration crises. Thus, the ideal sequence posited by the theorists of the crisis framework does not necessarily lead to a smooth transition and an easier resolution of participation and distribution crises. Just the opposite appears to be the case, that is, the early resolution of the penetration crisis, in particular, makes the resolution of participation and distribution considerably more difficult and stressful.

The second hypothesis was that balanced, simultaneous institutionalization in all five crisis areas will encourage a smooth and less stressful resolution of conflict. The Portuguese data tend to support this hypothesis, or at least its opposite: that development will be stressful if institutionalization is unbalanced. The Portuguese data show not a smooth, balanced institutionalization in all five areas more or less simultaneously but, rather, a series of fits and starts with certain areas rushing ahead and others lagging behind. Thus, legitimacy preceded identity which preceded penetration, while all three of these were resolved far in advance of participation and distribution. This asymmetrical development has made the resolution of the participation and distribution crises more difficult because of the great institutional weight, as it were, of the early forms and processes which inhibit the creation of and act as a constraint upon new ones relevant to later crises. Nowhere is this more true than between penetration and participation. The fact that the penetration crisis was so thoroughly resolved by the sixteenth century has clearly inhibited the resolution of the participation crisis because the absolutist state overpowered the traditional cortes so that it was unable to evolve in a balanced fashion into a modern parliament. Thus, there was no tradition of participation or structure on which liberals and republicans could build modern representational institutions. Indeed, the fact that the penetration crisis was resolved early and very well has created a fundamental tension in Portuguese politics which persists today between a highly centralized administrative apparatus and weak and fragile participatory institutions; that is, a fundamental tension between the power and authority of the administrative infrastructure when compared to that of the political infrastructure.

The third hypothesis was that the accumulation of crises will result in their stressful resolution. The Portuguese pattern certainly tends to support this hypothesis. There is little doubt that participatory and distributional demands were held in abeyance and, therefore, accumulated as the system responded with institutionalized, routine responses inappropriate to the distributional and participatory needs that were growing among the population. This has resulted in several forceful attempts, principally by the military, as in 1916, 1926, and 1974, to break through the confining conditions created by the early and complete resolution of the penetration crisis by offering to the population greater levels of participation in the decisionmaking process and a larger share in the country's material rewards.

In conclusion, the frame of reference employed here to analyze Portuguese history helps explain much about Portugal's development as a nationstate. It shows that while the specifics of Portugal's particular sequence and pattern of crisis resolution are unique, the general pattern has been reproduced elsewhere in Western Europe, particularly in France and Italy. The crisis framework also suggests reasons why Portuguese political history has been at times so violent and unstable. Moreover, the framework gives a clear understanding of the reasons why democracy has come late to Portugal, why it has been so very difficult to create, and what obstacles need to be surpassed in order to institutionalize democratic participatory structures and democratic decision-making routines and behavior.

NOTES

1. For the definitive statement of this framework see Leonard Binder et al., *Crises and Sequences in Political Development* (Princeton, N. J.: Princeton University Press, 1971). For a critical review of its utility as a theory-building device see Robert T. Holt and John E. Turner, "Crises and Sequences in Collective Theory Development," *American Political Science Review* 69 (September 1975): 979-994.
2. Sidney Verba, "Sequences and Development," in *Crises and Sequences*, ed. Binder et al., p. 299.
3. Ibid., p. 301.
4. Ibid., pp. 310-314.
5. This framework has been applied to Portugal but only in a very tentative way with little or no historical detail. See Stanley G. Payne, "Spain and Portugal," in *Crises of Political Development in Europe and the United States*, ed. Raymond Grew (Princeton, N.J.: Princeton University Press, 1978), pp. 197-218.
6. See H. V. Livermore, *A New History of Portugal* (Cambridge: Cambridge University Press, 1969), pp. 9-10; and Stanley G. Payne, *A History of Spain and Portugal*, Vol. 1 (Madison, Wis.: University of Wisconsin Press, 1973), p. 113.
7. Livermore, *A New History of Portugal*, pp. 10-11; Payne, *A History of Spain and Portugal*, Vol. 1, pp. 114-115.
8. Payne, *A History of Spain and Portugal*, Vol. 1, p. 115.
9. A. H. de Oliveira Marques, *History of Portugal*, Vol. 1: *From Lusitania to Empire* (New York: Columbia University Press, 1972), pp. 34-38.
10. Livermore, *A New History of Portugal*, pp. 47-49.
11. Ibid., pp. 50-51.
12. According to Livermore, *A New History of Portugal*, p. 52, there is considerable doubt as to the location of this legendary victory. The town where the battle is reported to have taken place, Ourique, was too deep inside Moslem territory. Livermore suggests that the most probable place was Chão de Ourique, near Santarém.
13. Ibid., pp. 63-64.
14. Payne, *A History of Spain and Portugal*, Vol. 1, p. 119.
15. Marques, *History of Portugal*, Vol. 1, p. 79.
16. Ibid., p. 94.
17. Charles E. Nowell, *A History of Portugal* (New York: D. Van Nostrand, Inc., 1952), p. 12.
18. Marques, *History of Portugal*, Vol. 1, pp. 103-104.

19. Payne, A History of Spain and Portugal, Vol. 1, pp. 123-124.
20. Marques, History of Portugal, Vol. 1, p. 78.
21. Payne, A History of Spain and Portugal, Vol. 1, pp. 127-129.
22. Ibid., p. 243.
23. Livermore, A New History of Portugal, p. 161.
24. Ibid., p. 164.
25. Ibid., p. 165.
26. Ibid., pp. 166-167.
27. Marques, History of Portugal, Vol. 1, p. 41.
28. Livermore, A New History of Portugal, pp. 65-66.
29. Marques, History of Portugal, Vol. 2, p. 42.
30. Ibid., p. 43.
31. The details of this conflict, because it involves the participation crisis, will be presented in that section.
32. Livermore, A New History of Portugal, pp. 319-320.
33. Marques, History of Portugal, Vol. 2, p. 180.
34. Ibid., Vol. 1, pp. 83-84.
35. Livermore, A New History of Portugal, p. 73.
36. Ibid.
37. Ibid., p. 83.
38. Marques, History of Portugal, Vol. 1, p. 98.
39. Nowell, A History of Portugal, p. 48.
40. Livermore, A New History of Portugal, p. 123.
41. Nowell, A History of Portugal, pp. 51-52.
42. Marques, History of Portugal, Vol. 1, pp. 176, 186, 188.
43. On the concept of the administrative state see Dwight Waldo, The Administrative State (New York: Ronald Press, 1948); Fritz Morstein-Marx, The Administrative State: An Introduction to Bureaucracy (Chicago: University of Chicago Press, 1957); and S. N. Eisenstadt, The Political System of Empire (New York: Free Press, 1963).
44. This distinction has been pointed out by Gordon Smith, Politics in Western Europe (New York: Holmes and Meir, 1973), p. 124.
45. Payne, A History of Spain and Portugal, p. 277.
46. Marques, History of Portugal, Vol. 1, p. 189.
47. Livermore, A New History of Portugal, p. 266.
48. Ibid., pp. 266-268; and Marques, History of Portugal, Vol. 2, pp. 87-90.
49. Marques, History of Portugal, Vol. 2, p. 88.
50. Marcello Caetano, História Breve das Constituições Portuguesas (Lisbon: Editorial Verbo, 1971), p. 41.
51. Marques, History of Portugal, Vol. 2, p. 90.
52. Livermore, A New History of Portugal, p. 274.
53. Ibid., pp. 274-278.
54. Caetano, História Breve das Constituções Portuguesas, pp. 49-51.
55. J. Vaz de Carvalho, "As Constituições Portuguesas," Economia e Sociologia: Nova Leitura das Eleições--1975, p. 21.
56. Livermore, A New History of Portugal, pp. 287-288; and Caetano, História Breve das Constituções Portuguesas, pp. 60, 68-70.

57. Livermore, *A New History of Portugal*, p. 297.
58. Marques, *History of Portugal*, Vol. 2, pp. 77-82.
59. On the First Republic see V. de Bragança-Cunha, *Revolutionary Portugal (1910-1926)* (London: James Clarke, 1937); and Douglas L. Wheeler, *The First Portuguese Republic* (Madison, Wis. University of Wisconsin Press, 1978).
60. Marques, *History of Portugal*, Vol. 2, pp. 160-162.
61. Payne, *A History of Spain and Portugal*, Vol. 1, pp. 126-127.
62. Raymond Grew, "The Crises and Their Sequences," in *Crises of Political Development in Europe and the United States*, ed. Raymond Grew (Princeton, N.J.: Princeton University Press, 1978), pp. 3-37.

3
The New State: The Instauration and Collapse of Authoritarianism

On April 25, 1974, Portugal experienced a <u>golpe de estado</u> which brought to an abrupt end the authoritarian regime established nearly fifty years earlier by António de Oliveira Salazar.[1] There followed a relatively brief but tumultuous period of exception which lasted until April 2, 1976, when the constituent assembly, elected on April 25, 1975, approved a new constitution and established a West European style pluralist democracy in Portugal. This shift from one type of regime to another is important to analyze because of the light it may shed on the theory of authoritarian regimes, especially their breakdown, and whether the events following the <u>golpe</u> can be considered as a revolution in the strict meaning of the word.

The purpose of this chapter is to examine the first phase of the process of regime change; that is, the collapse of the New State. This is done by examining the New State in terms of the comparative theory extant on authoritarian regimes, especially the phenomenon of regime breakdown. This chapter seeks to explain why the New State, which seemed so monolithic, impenetrable and otherwise impervious to change on the eve of the <u>golpe</u>, collapsed like a house of cards. The second phase of this change in regimes, the establishment of a West European style democracy, will be the subject of the following chapter.

AUTHORITARIAN REGIMES

While there exists considerable social science theoretical literature on the breakdown of democratic regimes, there is very little available on authoritarian ones.[2] The most ambitious attempt to understand authoritarian regimes has been made by Linz. In an early essay, he defined authoritarian regimes as political systems "with limited, not responsible, political pluralism without elaborate and guiding ideology, but with distinctive mentalities, without extensive nor intensive political mobilization, except at some point in their development, and in which a leader or occasionally a small group exercises power within formally ill-defined limits but actually quite predictable ones."[3]

In a more recent work Linz has worked out a typology of authoritarian regimes using two criteria: (1) the character of their limited pluralism and (2) the degree of apathy or demobilization of their citizenry. The first takes into account which particular groups are allowed to participate and the second, the nature and extent of political mobilization. In terms of limits on pluralist participation, authoritarian regimes can range from those controlled exclusively by a bureaucratic-military-technocratic elite to those in which participation is channelled through a single dominant party or a variety of social groups and structures defined by the state. In terms of limits on participation, authoritarian regimes can vary from those in which there are few channels, if any, for mass participation and no interest on the part of the elite to encourage political involvement, to those in which the citizenry is mobilized through well-defined channels created by the elite, such as a dominant political party or functionally organized groups.[4]

Linz calls authoritarian systems dominated by a bureaucratic-technocratic-military elite in which there are few channels, if any, for participation, __bureaucratic-military__ regimes. In such regimes, a __coalition__, most frequently dominated by military officers and civil servants without ideology, gains control of the governmental apparatus and makes decisions purely on the basis of bureaucratic criteria and neither creates nor permits political activity except through an official government sponsored party whose purpose is to control mobilization.[5]

Linz calls authoritarian systems in which there are a variety of groups and institutions established by the state to allow participation and to encourage the mobilization of the citizenry, usually through a dominant party and dependent mass organizations, __organic-statist__ regimes. In such systems, the elite consciously attempt to go beyond bureaucratic-military government by mobilizing and controlling participation through "organic" structures such as the family, parish, municipality, cooperative, professional association, place of work, and the like. The elite of organic-statist systems reject liberalism's stress on the individual and the heterogeneity of group interest as well as Marxism's class conflict and seek a third way through corporatist forms of interest representation.[6]

Although Linz has provided an excellent classificatory scheme, he has not, as yet, paid much attention to the dynamic properties of authoritarian regimes. As

Schmitter has argued, the tendency of most scholars of authoritarian systems is to present them as monolithic, unified, holistic systems of mutually reinforcing institutions, behaviors and ideology which are impervious to change once established; that is, as a "virtually self-sustaining entity, a cohesive, purposeful, demi-urgic, omnipresent, and omnipotent force that molds civil society to fit the state's reproductive and expansive needs, instead of acting as the responsive agent of societal imperatives implied by the liberal-democratic scenario or the agent of revolutionary transformation of productive relations as in the communist-totalitarian situation."[7] The assumption of much scholarship on authoritarian regimes has thus stressed that such systems are inherently different from other types of regimes such as democracies and totalitarian ones because they do not require any participatory linking or mediating structures between themselves and their citizenry. Indeed, in many studies of authoritarian systems this disconnection is seen as a basic source of strength and flexibility rather than weakness because it isolates such regimes from their citizenry.

As Schmitter has pointed out, however, this assumption about the strength of authoritarian regimes is largely an illusion; that is, such regimes are not necessarily monolithic but may contain structural weakness and self-defeating tendencies which can, under certain conditions, lead to regime breakdown. For Schmitter, the most important source of structural weakness of authoritarian regimes can be found within the regime itself; that is, in the internal balance among its functionally differentiated, hierarchically structured, privileged orders, such as the armed forces, industry, commerce, and the like. Schmitter concludes, then, that the cause of the breakdown of an authoritarian regime lies within the regime itself and not outside in its relationship to the broader civil society.[8]

While there is little doubt that within system contradictions are important aspects of authoritarian regime weakness and breakdown, it is the contention here, however, that internal contradictions are not the root cause of the collapse of such regimes. It is the thesis here that authoritarian regimes are not much different from other types of regimes in terms of the necessity of all political systems to resolve the participation crisis; that is, to generate and institutionalize a set of mediating structures which provide some measure of involvement on the part of the citizenry, however slight, in the decisionmaking process. All political systems must have some means of connecting the citizenry to the government which is capable of mobilizing support for the regime from time-to-time, but especially in times of severe crisis. If a regime's political infrastructure is nonexistent, weak, or poorly institutionalized, it will have great difficulty rallying support for itself and its policies. In other words, within-regime contradictions are sufficient but not necessary conditions for regime breakdown, while the failure to resolve the participation crisis by creating effective mediating structures between the regime and its broader civil society is a necessary condition but not of itself a sufficient reason for regime breakdown.

Thus, the ability of an authoritarian regime (or any regime for that matter) to mobilize support and rally its citizenry behind certain policies depends upon the degree to which the elite has resolved the participation crisis in an institutionalized way. Whether or not this can be accomplished depends in large part upon the type of authoritarian regime the system happens to be. To return to Linz's typology, a bureaucratic military-authoritarian regime dominated by a technocratic elite which controls the society through the administrative apparatus of the state and makes decisions purely on the basis of bureaucratic criteria and neither creates nor permits political activity, will not have available to it an effective political infrastructure capable of mobilizing support for the regime and its policies. On the other hand, an organic-statist authoritarian regime, controlled by an elite which has consciously and successfully built up a set of mediating structures, corporatist or otherwise, will have in place a political infrastructure which supports the regime by involving the citizenry in the decisionmaking process on a regular basis and could be used to mobilize them around the regime in times of crisis.

Understanding why the awesomeness of the New State was more apparent than real requires, then, not an examination of its internal contradictions but, rather, an examination of the precise nature of the connection that actually existed between itself and the broader civil society. This will be done by discussing the emergence and instauration of Salazar's New State and the way in which he attempted to resolve the participation crisis; that is, by examining the means by which he attempted to create structures that were meant to mediate between the regime and the citizenry.

THE EMERGENCE AND INSTAURATION
OF THE NEW STATE

The New State emerged from the period of exception that followed the military overthrow of the First Republic on May 28, 1926, which, as was suggested earlier, was the result of the failure of the First Republic to develop a party system capable of mobilizing and controlling popular participation; that is, to resolve the participation crisis. Wheeler has divided the formative period of emergence and instauration into three phases: the military dictatorship (1926-1928); the advent of Salazar and the rise of civilian authoritarianism (1928-1930); and the installation of the New State (1930-1933).[9]

The first of these phases was dominated by a group of young army officers who, when they overturned the First Republic, had no grand design and attempted to govern apolitically. They promised to restore order to social and economic life and bring efficiency to government. To achieve these goals they purged the administrative apparatus of political appointees and replaced them with military officers. Party politics were thus eliminated in favor of a military dictatorship. However, because they lacked technical expertise and were themselves unable to rise above "adventurism, personalism, and empregomania,"[10] these young officers were incapable of setting out politically defined goals and solving Portugal's pressing social and economic problems.[11] As political unrest continued the reputation of the military as saviors of the nation declined. When it finally became obvious to General Óscar de Fragosa Carmona, the leader of the military government, that soldiers could not bring order to the nation, he sought the help of a civilian, Salazar, who was at that time a professor of law and economics at Coimbra University. On April 27, 1928, Salazar was appointed minister of finance and the purely military phase in the establishment of the authoritarian regime which was to endure until April 25, 1974 came to a close.

Although Salazar initially took up the post of finance minister without a clear program or articulated ideology, he did extract from the military an agreement which placed in his hands strict control over the government's budget. Each ministry was to limit its spending to only the amount allocated to it, and no decision could be made which would effect the budget without the express approval of the Ministry of Finance (i.e., Salazar), who was empowered to veto any request for increases. In addition, uniform accounting procedures and principles were introduced to give coherence to the budgetary process and the government's spending program.[12] These simple measures enabled Salazar not only to balance the budget in his first year as finance minister but also to produce a surplus.

With Salazar's appointment, the first step toward the instauration of a civilian regime was taken. Between 1928 and 1932 Salazar began to outline his own program and legitimating ideology. During these years discussions took place between Salazar and the military in which a new civilian political order was gradually defined. This occurred relatively early and smoothly because (1) Salazar, who had by this time become certain of his own intentions, began to articulate his corporative model and had developed concrete proposals for its implementation; (2) the military was sympathetic to the corporatist solution; (3) corporatism had also appeared in Italy, France, and Spain; and (4) corporatism promised a middle way between liberalism and socialism which could be used to coopt the broad middle of the spectrum between monarchists and republicans.[13] Starting in 1929, Salazar began to formulate the ideology which he would use to legitimate the new regime. In two key speeches, one delivered on May 28 and the other on July 30, 1930, he revealed that the new order would be a republic built upon a strong state and grounded in the moral principles of Catholic corporatism.[14]

Portuguese corporatism is eclectic in philosophical background and draws upon the works of utopian socialism, positivism, and Catholic reformism. Developed during the nineteenth century by social theorists concerned with the problems associated with the process of modernization, corporatism sought to merge a tradition of social order based on obedience and hierarchy with the requirements of modernity and the problem of mass man in a way that would prevent class conflict and provide for structured participation rather than rootless alienation. As such, corporatism was clearly an attempt to solve Portugal's crisis of participation by blending traditional and modern elements of social structure into a new institutional form. Participation was to be organized according to a group's natural interest and social function and controlled by the state which had the power to sanction groups and determine when and how much they would influence the decisionmaking process and share in society's benefits.[15]

Thus, Salazar sought to transform Portugal from a bureaucratic-military regime into an organic-statist authoritarian one which he saw as both natural and necessary, ordained by God, based on natural groupings, such as families, parishes, municipalities and the like. The role of the state was to act as moral leader and rationally to order economic and political life by regulating and stimulating the economy (but not owning it) and by organizing and controlling participation. The individual's place in this system was as member of one of its "natural" groups which would define each person's rights and duties. These primary groups were to form the foundation on which the corporatist system of representation was to be constructed.

At the grassroots level were to be families, municipalities, people's and fishermen's houses (<u>Casas do Povo</u> and <u>Casas dos Pescadores</u>), syndicates (<u>sindicatos</u>), and guilds (<u>grêmios</u>). At the regional level there were to be unions (<u>uniões</u>) and federations (<u>federações</u>), which were to encompass the smaller units below them. At the apex of the system there were to be the corporations (<u>corporações</u>), which represented the units in the hierarchy below them and were to be organized according to economic sector: agriculture, fishing, commerce, industry, transportation, and so on. Within each corporation, workers, managers, and owners were to coexist in harmony and equality. Finally, the entire apparatus was represented in a functionally organized Corporative Chamber (<u>Câmara Corporativa</u>), which included representatives from the army, Catholic Church, and civil service, and was to provide the citizenry with a voice in the policymaking process and a formal linkage with the government.[16]

In 1931 Salazar began to implement this corporate system in order to close the gap between the regime and the citizenry. In that year, the General Confederation of Labor was disbanded and all labor activity was reorganized along corporatist lines. Laws were passed enabling Salazar to create a system of employer's guilds (<u>grêmios</u>). Emergency decrees were passed to regulate the economy and a Superior Council of the National Economy was set up with subsections pertaining to the various functional divisions within economic life. On July 5, 1932, Salazar was named prime minister, a post he held until 1968 when he was incapacitated by a cerebral hemorrhage brought on by the collapse of a deck chair at his summer home in Estoril.

The year 1933 was the most important year for the instauration of Salazar's corporatist regime. In that year, on March 19, the constitution defining the new order was approved in a national referendum. Corporatism was expressed in this document most clearly in the section on the Corporative Chamber (<u>Câmara Corporativa</u>), which contained twenty-four sections, one for each of the major social and economic areas of activity as well as moral and spiritual groups. The chamber was to hold hearings on these various activities and prepare advisory opinions for the government. The Labor Statute, which accompanied the constitution, sought to establish a system of labor-owner collaboration along corporatist lines. Strikes and lockouts were prohibited. Disputes were to be settled by discussion and arbitration, not confrontation. A system of labor courts was established as was a structure for government mediation. Several additional decrees were passed in 1933 which created a web of grassroots corporatist organizations. One of these laws established a national system of guilds or employer's associations. They were organized according to branch of production (e.g., wines, cereals), were to be monopolistic in character, and were to represent the entire branch. Another law set up a national system of unions which paralleled the guilds. These were to be organized by administrative district and designed to represent the worker in the Corporative Chamber and to advance the interest of their members in collective bargaining with employers. A third law authorized the creation of the people and fishermen's houses, which were to represent the interests of their members and their families as well as to raise their educational and cultural standards.[17]

In addition to these strictly corporatist structures, Salazar moved to create "collaborative agencies" such as the National Union (União Nacional: UN); the National Foundation for Joy in Work (Fundação Nacional para a Alegria no Trabalho); the Society for the Defense of Family (Sociadade para a Defesa da Família); Work of the Mothers' for National Education (Obra das Maẽs para a Educação Nacional), Portuguese Youth (Mocidade Portuguesa); and the Portuguese (Legião Portuguesa). The most important of these was the UN, which was not a political party but, rather, a nonpartisan "association" designed to help spread corporatist ideology at the mass level and to consolidate all opinions and values into a national consciousness. It was specifically established to stamp out all partisan activity, to eliminate dissent, and harmonize class and regional differences.[18]

By analyzing the occupations of individuals who were elected and selected to sit in the National Assembly (Assembleia Nacional) and Corporative Chamber between 1934 and 1968, Schmitter has determined that the formation of the New State involved the mobilization of Portugal's provincial towns and rural masses, especially in the Catholic north, against the cosmopolitan and secular south, especially Lisbon. This mobilization was accomplished by a new, relatively privileged, northern, rural elite comprising mainly civil servants, engineers, lawyers, and university professors, all of whom were greatly dependent upon public employment.[19]

With the approval of the 1933 constitution, the return to civilian rule was completed and the formal-legalistic framework for what was by that time being called the New State was in place. It was at this juncture that Salazar moved to solidify and flesh out the corporative apparatus. A Secretary of State for Corporations and Social Welfare was established which had as its main goal the extension of the system down to the grassroots. However, for a variety of reasons, this effort was largely unsuccessful and the corporative political infrastructure remained largely unfinished.

FAILURE TO INSTITUTIONALIZE CORPORATISM

Salazar failed to complete and institutionalize the New State's corporative infrastructure for three reasons: (1) resistance within the broader civil society to reorganization into corporative political mediating structures; (2) historical events which diverted scarce resources and Salazar's attention away from the task of institutionalization; and (3) the presence of an already institutionalized, centralized, administrative apparatus which constrained the creation of new, innovative political structures and dominated the policy formation process.[20]

From the outset problems and difficulties were encountered because of the resistance put up by the various social groups the system was intended to benefit. Indeed, few Portuguese were inclined to accept corporatism. They saw it as an abstract and intellectual scheme whose origins and purposes were obscure. Salazar was never able to diffuse the ideology of corporatism very widely. Second, certain groups resisted the government's attempts to organize them into syndicates. The Labor Statute was met with massive strikes, and it required the imprisonment of much of labor's leadership to get the new corporate structure in place. The liberal professions also reacted negatively and much corporate legislation, as it applied to them, had to be watered down to get lawyers, doctors, engineers, and the like to accept the new system. Finally, business and commercial interests at first reacted negatively but later learned how the corporations could be circumvented and used as an instrument to control workers.[21]

Resistance to corporatism came also from the army, Catholic Church, universities, and civil service. In fact, Salazar did not actually attempt to integrate the military into the corporate system and it remained above and beyond these civilian institutions, its command structure paralleling the corporations and directly responsible to Salazar. Although the church had been given seats in the Corporative Chamber, its hierarchy also remained independent, but with special rights and privileges, as defined in the Concordat signed with the Vatican in 1940. The universities too remained outside the system not only because of the great difficulty the integration of these complex organizations into the structure created but also because of resistance from faculty and students. Although the public service was given representation in the Corporative Chamber and individual civil servants were required to join the UN and swear allegiance to the corporatist state, it too remained beyond the corporative umbrella.[22]

Two historical events, the Spanish civil war and the Second World War also inhibited the process of institutionalization because of the exigencies these conflicts placed on the new system. Within the corporations, elections were suspended and leadership was appointed by the government for the duration. The corporations became little more than bureaucratic appendages of the state apparatus, essentially direct agents of the regime, which were used to implement and enforce strict wage and price policies implemented during the war. The use of the corporations to control the citizenry and the

Second World War, which demonstrated the horrors of fascism, led to a general repudiation of corporatism by many Portuguese and, eventually, demands for change.[23]

After much internal debate and rethinking, a corporatist revival was launched during the early 1950s. However, these efforts to revitalize and extend the system also failed. Although the corporations themselves were finally mandated, they remained little more than paper organizations. Salazar himself increasingly lost interest in the corporative system and a new, younger, post-war generation had little enthusiasm for the system which had been discredited and seemed so out of touch with contemporary needs. A final effort to breathe life into the corporate system was launched during the late 1960s by Marcello Caetano, Salazar's successor as prime minister. In addition to a general liberalization of the regime there was a flurry of activity designed to regenerate and extend the corporations. New people's houses were established and greater freedom in choosing their own leadership was allowed the corporations. The social services corporations were made more attractive and benefits extended. However, these efforts were too little and came too late.[24]

Finally, Salazar failed to institutionalize the corporative structure of the New State because of the existence of a powerful, highly centralized administrative system in Portugal. Even in the heyday of the New State during the 1930s, the corporations were not at the center of the policy formation process. Decisional authority was never actually transferred from the powerful state apparatus and public policymaking was limited to the bureaucratic arena. Behind the façade of corporatism, the actual policy process was dominated by a bureaucratic-technocratic elite that made decisions without reference to inputs from the corporations, which were theoretically designed to link the citizens to the decisional process. Moreover, over time government ministers became less important as politicians and more important as administrators and technicians. Gradually, Salazar placed greater and greater emphasis on the technical aspects of running a particular ministry while the concept of minister as politician was progressively downgraded.[25]

For their part, most if not all corporations were principally involved in performing social welfare tasks and did not involve their members in the policymaking process. Moreover, the Corporative Chamber never played a significant policymaking role, nor were members of the corporations ever given a significant voice in running their own organizations. By and large, the corporations were run by civil servants appointed by the government as little more than administrative agencies of the state. What policymaking role they did have was limited to labor relations problems and public assistance questions. Finally, the New State's collaborative agencies did not provide a mechanism for popular involvement in the policy process. The most important of these, the UN, never evolved into a mass organization capable of mobilizing the citizenry. It remained, until Salazar's incapacitation in 1968, a loose patron-client network composed, by and large, of civil servants who were members as a condition of state employment. The UN never functioned to communicate demands and support for the New State. It too had become little more than an administrative arm of the state.[26]

While ostensibly corporatist, then, the reality of Salazar's regime was that of the demobilized, depoliticized, administrative state in which the making and implementing of public policy were dominated by a technocracy and political conflict was consciously limited to the bureaucratic arena. In both law and practice, "the dominant attitude . . . was one that conceived of the roles of central authorities as administrators of public services to a quiescent population, as defenders of public order against the enemies of the state, or agents of a ruling class committed to policies designed to insure the survival of greater Portugal."[27] In the New State, then, decisionmaking was guided by bureaucratic and technocratic considerations not political ones, and the regime's link to the citizenry was principally administrative. Thus, the hallmark of the New State was its highly centralized and rigid administrative system and the predominance of technocrats in the policy formation process and not the corporative infrastructure.

This state of affairs was the result not only of corporatism's philosophical principles which extolled the virtues of the strong state but the early and thorough resolution in Portugal of the penetration crisis. As was shown in the previous chapter, the penetration crisis was resolved by the sixteenth century and since that time there have been a gradual accruing and concentration of power and authority to the central administrative apparatus of the state. This concentration has become so great that it is possible to conceive of the penetration crisis as having been "over-resolved" and the administrative apparatus "over-institutionalized." That is, Portugal's administrative apparatus is "too old, deeply entrenched, and durable"[28] and has stifled change and constrained various political elites who have attempted to organize new patterns of policymaking and a new political infrastructure. Thus, the enormous institutional weight of the administrative system gradually overwhelmed the traditional <u>cortes</u>, prevented the creation of a new political infrastructure during the First Republic, and also inhibited and constrained Salazar's efforts to create a corporative infrastructure during the New State period. Salazar, like other political innovators before him, was unable to break through the confining conditions imposed by the overinstitutionalized administrative state. Indeed, the reliance on the administrative system during the New State period only served to make that system even more durable, inflexible, and deeply entrenched.

CONCLUSIONS

While Salazar was successful in transforming the bureaucratic-military regime into a purely bureaucratic one, he and his successor, Caetano, were unsuccessful in transforming their regime into an organic-statist one. Because of resistance within Portuguese society, historical events and the overinstitutionalized administrative apparatus of the state, they were unable to push the system beyond administrative rule and create a viable political infrastructure of corporations capable of mobilizing the citizenry in support of the regime and its policies. During the New State period, then, the linkage between the regime and the broader civil society was essentially administrative not political in character. Indeed, the regime encouraged apathy, passive acceptance, and bureaucratic politics.

The policy which finally brought the regime down, not by mass protest but from within, was Salazar's decision to maintain Portugal's African empire. The idea that colonies in Africa were an integral part of metropolitan Portugal had been from the beginning intimately connected to Salazar's New State concept. On this issue, as perhaps on others, the regime was rigid and inflexible. The New State's "conception of Portugal's national identity and its survival as an independent polity was linked to the belief that all the overseas possessions had to be retained regardless of the cost. But by total opposition to any dismantling of the imperial edifice built by Salazar [the] . . . governing elite ultimately destroyed its own power base."29

The outbreak of wars of national liberation in Angola in 1961, Guinea (Bissau) in 1963, and Mozambique in 1964 called this conception into question.30 While there had been some debate within the regime about how to deal with these challenges, there was no possibility for open debate without challenging the New State itself. Moreover, there existed no political infrastructure which could be used to mobilize support and rally the citizenry around the war effort. Moreover, the regime was totally incapable of innovating by allowing for a political solution. Therefore, its response was the age old one: the regime fell back on old routines and institutions and attempted to force a solution by consolidating and centralizing control over the colonies even more. Of course, the situation required new, not old, patterns of institutionalization; required a different set of procedures for dealing with the problem which could not be dealt with by recourse to the already established institutions and procedures of the administrative state.

The golpe of April 25, 1974 can be seen then as a turning point requiring new patterns of institutionalization within the system which might not have ever occurred had a viable political infrastructure been in place which could have been used to mobilize and rally the citizenry to the defense of the regime. The autonomy of the New State from the general population was, then, a source of weakness not strength, which made it extremely vulnerable from within.

As shall be discussed in greater detail in the following chapter, a relatively minor complaint by military officers gradually escalated into a challenge to the regime itself and precipitated a factional split at the top of the military establishment itself between senior pro-colonial officers and their civilian allies and junior pro-change officers and theirs.[31] The denouement was, of course, the overthrow of the New State and the search for a new one.

Thus, the key to the maintenance of any regime, even authoritarian ones, seems to be the satisfactory resolution of the participation crisis by creating new institutions that connect the regime to the broader civil society in a way which will allow popular mobilization and support for the system and its policies, especially in times of crisis. Now that the reasons for the breakdown of the New State have been examined, the second phase of Portugal's recent regime change, the period of exception, can be examined.

NOTES

1. Accounts of the golpe de estado can be found in Michael Harsgor, Portugal in Revolution (Beverly Hills, Calif.: Sage Publications, 1976); Neil Bruce, Portugal: The Last Empire (New York/Toronto: Wiley, 1975); Robert Harvey, Portugal: Birth of a Democracy (New York: St. Martin's Press, 1978); and Douglas Porch, The Portuguese Armed Forces and the Revolution (London: Croom Helm, 1977).

2. On democratic regime breakdown, see Juan J. Linz and Alfred Stepan (eds.), The Breakdown of Democratic Regimes (Baltimore and London: The Johns Hopkins University Press, 1978).

3. Juan J. Linz, "An Authoritarian Regime: The Case of Spain," in Cleavages, Ideologies and Party Systems, ed. Erik Allard and Yrjo Littunen (Helsinki: Westermark, 1964), p. 225.

4. Juan J. Linz, "Totalitarian and Authoritarian Regimes," in Handbook of Political Science, Vol. 3, Macropolitical Theory, ed. Fred I. Greenstein and Nelson W. Polsby (Reading, Mass.:

Addison-Wesley, 1975), pp. 269; 277-279.
   5. Ibid., pp. 285-288.
   6. Ibid., pp. 306-313.
   7. Philippe C. Schmitter, "Liberation by _Golpe_: Retrospective Thoughts on the Demise of Authoritarian Rule in Portugal," _Armed Forces and Society_ 2 (1974): 9.
   8. Ibid., p. 20.
   9. Douglas L. Wheeler, _Republican Portugal: A Political History, 1910-1926_ (Madison, Wis.: University of Wisconsin Press, 1978), p. 246. See also Tom Gallagher, _Portugal: A Twentieth-Century Interpretation_ (Manchester: Manchester University Press, 1983), pp. 42-57.
   10. Wheeler, _Republican Portugal_, p. 247.
   11. Tom Gallagher, "From Hegemony to Opposition: The Ultra Right Before and After 1974," in _In Search of Modern Portugal: The Revolution and Its Consequences_, ed. Lawrence S. Graham and Douglas L. Wheeler (Madison, Wis.: University of Wisconsin Press, 1983), pp. 84-85.
   12. Hugh Kay, _Salazar and Modern Portugal_ (New York: Hawthorn Books, 1970), p. 42. See also Gallagher, _Portugal_, pp. 62-75.
   13. Howard J. Wiarda, _Corporatism and Development: The Portuguese Experience_ (Amherst, Mass.: University of Massachusetts Press, 1977), p. 97.
   14. Stanley G. Payne, _A History of Spain and Portugal_, Vol. 2 (Madison, Wis.: University of Wisconsin Press, 1973), p. 666. See also Richard Robinson, _Contemporary Portugal: A History_ (London: George Allen & Unwin, 1979), pp. 32-82.
   15. Wiarda, _Corporatism and Development_, pp. 62-70.
   16. Ibid., pp. 86-87.
   17. Ibid., pp. 100-115.
   18. Ibid., pp. 117-121.
   19. Philippe C. Schmitter, "The 'Regime d'Exception' That Became the Rule: Forty-eight Years of Authoritarian Domination in Portugal," in _Contemporary Portugal: The Revolution and Its Antecedents_, ed. Lawrence S. Graham and Harry M. Makler (Austin: University of Texas Press, 1979), pp. 5-23.
   20. Gallagher, _Portugal_, p. 72, has suggested a fourth reason; that Salazar came to be more motivated by his lust for personal power and desire to remain in office than his ideological commitment to corporatist ideology.
   21. Wiarda, _Corporatism and Development_, pp. 139-140.
   22. Ibid., pp. 122-125.
   23. Ibid., pp. 164-168.
   24. Ibid., pp. 206-208.
   25. Paul H. Lewis, "Salazar's Ministerial Elite, 1932-1968," _Journal of Politics_ 40 (August 1978): 622-647.
   26. Wiarda, _Corporatism and Development_, pp. 122-125; 139-140; 155; 164-175; 179-180; 219; 227-239; 243.
   27. Lawrence S. Graham, _Portugal: The Decline and Collapse of an Authoritarian Order_ (Beverly Hills, Calif.: Sage Publications, 1975), p. 17.
   28. On the concept of "overinstitutionalization," see Mark Kesselman, "Overinstitutionalization and Political Constraint: The Case of France," _Comparative Politics_ 3 (October 1970): 21-44.

29. Graham, *The Decline and Collapse of an Authoritarian Order*, p. 24.

30. A good general treatment of the colonies and the wars for national liberation is Malyn Newitt, *Portugal in Africa: The Last Hundred Years* (London: Longman, 1981).

31. Schmitter, "Liberation by *Golpe*," pp. 24-25.

4
April 25, 1974: The *Golpe* and Period of Exception

    The fact that the New State collapsed overnight with many of its structures reemerging the following day under different, revolutionary names, has led one observer to suggest that the "Portuguese experience may force analysts to break away from the conventional assumption that institutional change is the hallmark of a revolutionary experience, and that there will be a one-to-one correlation between meaning and structure."[1] The purpose of this chapter is to show that an understanding of the *golpe* and the period of exception does not require the abandonment of conventional assumptions about what constitutes a revolution. It does require, however, that the experience of regime change be put within the historical context of such change in Portugal. It also requires that what constitutes a true revolution and what does not be kept squarely in mind.[2] The argument here is that the characterization of the regime change in Portugal, as a revolution, as has been done by numerous observers,[3] is to confuse the rhetoric of revolution with the reality of the events that were actually taking place. Such a characterization amounts to a flagrant misuse and vulgarization of the concept of revolution.[4]

    As was shown in Chapters 2 and 3, revolution has not been the primary method of regime change in Portuguese history. Such changes have resulted from crises within an already existing system rather than the mobilization of broad sectors of society against the regime. Moreover, change in regime type has generally had only a negligible impact beyond the major cities and towns. The collapse of the New State, like that of the monarchy in 1910 and the First Republic in 1926, was not the result of a mass-based, revolutionary movement but purely the work of a military conspiracy which effortlessly overturned a regime that was powerless to defend itself. As Linz has written changes in regimes in Portugal have been "more the result of the disintegration of previous regimes, their loss of legitimacy among the middle classes, shifts in loyalty of the armed forces and other institutions, and the consequent development of a power vacuum to be filled by new active minorities."5

Thus, regime change in Portugal, although often characterized by participants and observers alike as revolutionary, has been more the result of the work of relatively small minorities who have exploited the weakness of extant institutions and appealed to temporarily sympathetic groups for the changes they wanted to effect.

As will be shown below, the golpe and the events of the period of exception were not the result of a broad revolutionary movement but, rather, the result of the activities of various rival, primarily military, elites, frequently led by charismatic leaders using populist appeals, who sought to gain control of the "situation"6 and fill the power vacuum with a regime suitable to them. Moreover, it is argued that there was actually very little in the way of spontaneous, mass-based change oriented activity and what little there was tended to be motivated more by specific instrumental concerns than broad revolutionary goals and was viewed as a threat by competing elites who sought to contain and frustrate such activity.

Before the period of exception and spontaneous action are discussed, the reasons for the shift in loyalty of the Portuguese armed forces need to be analyzed in some detail in order to gain insight as to the meaning of subsequent events.

THE ARMED FORCES MOVEMENT

The golpe of April 25, 1974, was carried out by a group of military officers who called themselves the Armed Forces Movement (Movimento das Forças Armadas: MFA). The MFA was not a homogeneous unit nor was it initially organized to overturn the New State. It began, rather, as a kind of military pressure group which was concerned with specific military grievances and gradually evolved into a conspiracy to bring down the regime. While the direct precipitant of the golpe was a decision taken by the Caetano government to grant regular commissions to conscript officers (milicianos), the underlying cause had much to do with class, educational, and generational differences within the officer corps.

Until World War I, the officer corps of the Portuguese armed forces, especially its higher echelons, was, not unlike their compatriots in other European countries, recruited from the old aristocracy. As the criteria for recruitment had little to do with merit, the officer corps was, by and large, incompetent. This fecklessness was demonstrated by the devastation wrought on the Portuguese expeditionary force in World War I.

As a consequence of this disaster, a modernization program of the armed forces was begun during the 1920s, and accelerated during the 1930s, which not only upgraded the quality of the military's armaments but also changed the social composition of the officer corps. Gradually, graduates of military academies, men recruited from the middle class, replaced older officers from the aristocracy. However, this new class of officers, although better trained and more competent, tended to ape the ways of the old aristocratic officer corps. The colonial wars which began in the early 1960s again wrought changes in the social class backgrounds of the officer corps. As the wars dragged on, many young officers from middle class backgrounds abandoned the armed forces and the prospect of repeated tours of duty in Africa for the safer and more lucrative haven of Lisbon and civilian life. These officers were gradually replaced by men recruited from the lower middle classes for whom a military career represented an opportunity for education and social advancement. In time, these class differences, as well as frustration with the Caetano government's conduct of the African war, created a cleavage within the officer corps that was also generationally based. This cleavage was between field grade officers, largely from middle class backgrounds, who aped the haughty ways of their aristocratic predecessors, and company grade officers who were essentially from lower middle and lower class backgrounds.[7]

The ranks of the MFA were filled almost to a man by officers, none of whom were above the rank of captain, from lower middle and lower class backgrounds. These upwardly mobile officers saw their recently acquired status and future careers threatened by the Caetano government's decision to grant regular commissions to the milícianos, most of whom were from middle class backgrounds and graduates of civilian universities.[8]

In two meetings in 1973, one on September 9 and the second on October 6, documents were signed by about 125 officers protesting the government's policy change on conscripted officers and threatening mass resignations if it were not rescinded. The government's refusal to comply with their demands encouraged the captains to begin discussing more drastic measures. By the end of 1973 secret planning for the golpe was well underway. Even at this stage, however, the goals of the MFA were not revolutionary. Although a few officers saw the golpe as an opportunity to bring about broader social and economic changes, the vast majority of the MFA was composed of essentially apolitical and ideologically unsophisticated officers who were concerned primarily with a specific military grievance.[9]

The final decision to intervene was most likely influenced by a growing sense of insecurity on the part of the MFA that another military faction might act first.

As Pimlott has written, the golpe "was in a sense preemptive: the growing powerlessness of Caetano in the face of competing generals had created an uneasy sense of political vacuum, and the feeling that a coup was coming from some quarter soon was widespread. In these conditions the MFA officers were anxious to get in first before some more repressive and reactionary group did so."[10] Thus, although political questions were increasingly coming to the fore, at the time of the golpe the MFA was still more concerned with the corporate self-interest of upwardly mobile, ambitious, young captains from lower class backgrounds than with broad revolutionary social and economic changes.

Although the officers of the MFA were in essential agreement about the need to overturn the regime, there were nonetheless divisions among them. These divisions, which in a few cases were based on ideology, were more connected to ties of friendship and loyalties (panelinhas) to certain charismatic personalities. These panelinhas, first made in Africa, provided the basis on which many of the rivalries for control of the "situation" during the period of exception turned.[11]

It has been pointed out that the MFA, as it evolved from a narrow military conspiracy, gradually began to manifest features commonly associated with progressive populism: ideological vagueness, loose structure, heterogeneous following, and charismatic leadership.[12] Such populist-charismatic movements are not unusual to Portugal and have appeared over the last several centuries especially in times of crisis. The idea that a charismatic figure would appear to save the nation dates from the sixteenth century when the myth developed that Sebastião, the boy-king who disappeared while on the ill-fated campaign in 1578 at Alcácer-Quivir, would miraculously return to lead Portugal to new heights of greatness. A number of military figures have filled this role beginning with the Duke of Saldanha, in the eighteenth century and generals Gomes de Costa, Sidónio Pais, and Humberto Delgado in this one. The populist aspect of the MFA was demonstrated most clearly during the spring and summer of 1975. During these months the MFA began to define itself as a "liberation movement of the Portuguese people" and attempted to create a left-populist regime by mobilizing the citizenry, especially the urban masses and rural peasantry. Emphasis was placed on popular unity and independence from the political parties which had appeared and were appealing to the population for support.[13]

Although several charismatic personalities emerged from the MFA during the period of exception, perhaps the most successful was Otelo Saraiva de Carvalho who played a central role in organizing the golpe. As commander of the Continental Operations Command (Comando Operacional do Continente: COPCON), a mobile strike force organized by the MFA, Otelo gradually evolved from a democrat into the darling of the far left. Identifying himself with Third World socialism, Otelo attempted to transcend the myriad ideological divisions among the far left by radicalizing popular resentment against the state and to mobilize his followers by using direct appeals to the people.[14]

THE PERIOD OF EXCEPTION

Immediately after the golpe the MFA created the Board of National Salvation (Junta de Salvação Nacional: JSN) composed of seven sympathetic, high-ranking officers chosen to give the movement legitimacy. The JSN was presided over by General António de Spínola, a hero of the war in Guinea (Bissau) Portugal's colony in West Africa and the author of the book, Portugal e o Futuro (Portugal and the Future),[15] which had rocked the Caetano government some months before the golpe by counseling a political settlement in Africa. The JSN was to be the supreme policymaking organ during the period of exception and was to see to it that the objectives of the MFA were carried out. The first and most immediate objective was to dismantle the political apparatus of the New State. Thus, the National Assembly and Corporative Chamber were dissolved; the President of the Republic, Admiral Américo Tomás, and civil governors of the administrative districts on the mainland and in the overseas colonies were dismissed; the PIDE, which had been renamed the General Directorate of Security (Direção-Geral de Segurança: DGS) during the Caetano years,[16] and fascist-style paramilitary organizations such as the Portuguese Legion (Legião Portuguesa), Naval Brigade (Brigada Naval) and Portuguese Youth (Mocidade Portuguesa) were all disbanded. The second objective was to define the political institutions that were to govern the country during the period of exception. The MFA decided that a new president would be chosen from among the membership of the JSN which would also designate a new prime minister and cabinet. The government was empowered to govern by decree (decreto-lei). The third objective was decolonization. Recognizing that the solution to the colonial wars was political not military, the MFA called for a frank and open debate on the overseas question.[17]
According to Graham, the period of exception can be divided into four distinct phases each corresponding to the rise and fall of certain, sometimes charismatic, military personalities supported by a specific military faction and sympathetic civilian groups.[18] The first phase extended from the golpe until September 30, 1974, and corresponded to the rise and fall of General António de Spínola and his followers, called spinolistas, who favored moderate policies and sought to fill the

political vacuum in the manner of de Gaulle. Spinolistas wanted to elevate General Spínola to the position of national leader, dismantle the MFA, return the military to the barracks, and establish a civilian dominated West European style liberal democracy. During the early weeks and months of the period of exception, General Spínola, who had been chosen by the JSN to be the president of the republic, was able to employ his considerable charisma to generate widespread popularity both within and outside of the military and his followers were clearly in the majority on the JSN. The first provisional government was dominated by individuals, mostly civilians, favorably oriented to a spinolist solution.

However, Spínola's political activities and obvious attempt to gain control of the "situation" through populist appeals, generated tensions between the MFA and the JSN. For many MFA officers, some of whom were beginning to appear as radicals, Spínola was viewed as determined to maintain the haughty personalistic and paternalistic upper middle class style of leadership of the old regime's officers. This tension precipitated the collapse of the first provisional government and the formation of the second in which the number of portfolios given to MFA officers was increased from one to seven, and a colonel, Vasco Gonçalves, was named prime minister.

The second phase began in September and ran until March 1975. During this period the tension between the spinolistas and the MFA, which was becoming increasingly radicalized, came to a head. This resulted in the complete displacement of Spínola and his followers from the JSN and the second provisional government and their replacement by radical MFA officers, many of whom were personally loyal to the prime minister, Vasco Gonçalves.

The event that brought the situation to a head was a demonstration in Lisbon which the spinolistas had called for September 28 in order to protest the growing influence within the second provisional government of newly radicalized MFA officers. This sparked rumors that the spinolistas were going to effect a countergolpe. Groups on the left then organized a series of demonstrations against the spinolist activity. Shortly before the 28th, radical MFA officers pressured Spínola to cancel the demonstration. Lisbon was sealed off from the rest of the country, and a small group of officers, led by COPCON's charismatic commander, Otelo Saraiva de Carvalho, took charge. This resulted in Spínola's resignation from the second provisional government. General Costa Gomes, nicknamed "The Cork" because of his tendency to float passively with changing political currents, was named president, and the portfolios of the spinolistas were given to MFA officers.

It was during this phase of the period of exception that the MFA began to envision a more permanent role in

Portugal's future political regime. Dissatisfied with the operation of the JSN, the MFA formed two new military organizations: the Superior Council of the MFA (Conselho Superior do MFA), known as the Council of Twenty, and the Assembly of the Armed Forces (Assembleia das Forças Armadas), informally known as the Council of Two Hundred. The power to take decisions was removed from the JSN and transferred to the Council of Twenty, which became the effective center of power for the military as well as the country as a whole. The Council of Twenty was composed of the president of the republic, Costa Gomes; the prime minister, Vasco Conçalves; the military ministers of his government; and seven officers from the MFA's Coordinating Committee.

These changes almost immediately precipitated divisions within the ranks of the MFA over the nature of the future regime and its economic organization. Three distinct factions each associated with a particular personality and faction within the armed forces, began to emerge. The first faction was that of the remaining spinolistas who were principally cavalry officers, as was Spínola, but some supporters were also to be found in the infantry and artillery. The second faction was that of the left wing of the MFA centered around the prime minister, Vasco Gonçalves. In addition to radical MFA officers gonçalvistas included a number of officers on the JSN, a majority of the MFA's Coordinating Committee, and several military ministers. Within the broader armed forces Gonçalves drew support from his parent unit, the Engineer Corps, and a majority of marine officers. The third faction was led by Major Melo Antunes, a minister without portfolio, who favored MFA collaboration with those political parties which supported the creation of a socialist but West European style democratic regime. While most antunistas were from the air force, there were significant numbers within the army scattered among the various units.

The rivalry for control of the "situation" among these factions culminated in the events of March 11 which mark the end of the second phase of the period of exception and the beginning of the third. On that date the spinolistas attempted a counter-golpe. The attempt was unsuccessful and Spínola and several of his aides were forced to flee Portugal.[19] In the aftermath, all spinolistas were purged from the MFA as well as positions of power and responsibility within the armed forces. With the spinolistas out of the way, the radical faction led by Vasco Gonçalves began to dominate the MFA and the course of events for the next several months.

During this phase the MFA, now purged of spinolistas, began to define itself as a kind of "national liberation movement" for Portugal and sought to create a left-populist regime based on peasant masses independent of the civilian political parties (about which more in Chapter 6). In order to create such a regime, the radicals extensively reorganized the military government. The JSN, MFA Coordinating Committee, and Council of Twenty were merged to form a single body called the Council of the Revolution (<u>Conselho da Revolução</u>: CR), whose twenty-five seats were occupied by those radical officers most influential in bringing about the new organizational structure. The Council of Two Hundred was expanded to 240. Non-commissioned officers and enlisted men were now included in its membership. During this phase, banks, insurance companies, and large-scale manufacturing and commercial firms were nationalized. In addition, in exchange for allowing elections for a constituent assembly to proceed as scheduled, the MFA forced the major civilian political parties to sign a protocol (<u>pacto</u>) in which they agreed to a supervisory role for the MFA over political institutions for a period of three to five years in any future civilian regime.

The elections for the constituent assembly brought to the fore civilian political forces which heretofore had not played a critical role in the events of the period of exception. The constituent assembly election legitimated these forces and brought civilian political elites into the struggle for control of the "situation." Certain of these elites were unwilling to accept the kind of regime that the MFA, now dominated by radical officers, envisioned for Portugal. They wanted a West European style parliamentary democracy. The communist leadership, on the other hand, refused to align itself with the other democratically oriented elites and even reaffirmed their support of the radical MFA faction which they saw as allies in their attempt to gain control of the "situation." This convinced radical officers that the communists were the only civilian group desirous of "liberating" Portugal from capitalism as the African colonies had been liberated from Portuguese imperialism.

It should be stressed that the radicalization of the MFA was not the result of spontaneous mass upheavals of peasants and workers demanding a new social order. Nor was this radicalization the result of the influence of the communist party or other civilian groups. It was, rather, simply the result of the realignment of different military personalities and factions within the various MFA institutions. The activity of civilian political elites was aimed at influencing the direction these various personalities were travelling. A less radical outcome was only possible when less radical officers took charge of the "situation."

Although the radicalization of the MFA was not brought about by mass demands for revolutionary change, it did produce outbreaks of violent anti-MFA demonstrations and attacks on communist party offices in the north during the "Hot Summer" of 1975. These events split the MFA into five factions. Two of these factions emerged within the ranks of the radicals themselves. The dominant of these two was headed by Vasco Gonçalves, and was favorably inclined toward close collaboration with the communist leadership. The second faction was led by COPCON commander, Otelo Saraiva de Carvalho, and favored a revolutionary government of the Third World variety. The third faction was led by Major Melo Antunes and Brigadier Vasco Lourenço. This faction favored a socialist but democratic future for Portugal. The fourth faction was led by the president, Costa Gomes, and was composed of independent officers who favored a non-socialist, democratic regime.

In addition to these four factions within the MFA there was the existence of a fifth military faction comprised of various officers who identified themselves with the extreme left. This group was important not because of its activities within the MFA but because of its connections with the extreme left civilian parties outside. In an attempt to gain control of the "situation," these parties organized the United Revolutionary Front (Frente Unida Revolucionária: FUR), whose objective was to instigate a rebellion within the ranks of the military in order to promote a mass movement of enlisted men which could then be joined to radicalized workers and peasants. With the help of those officers who identified with this strategy, the FUR was able to organize a movement among enlisted soldiers called Soldiers United Will Win (Soldados Unidos Vencerão: SUV). Because the MFA was highly factionalized, the SUV soon challenged the military command structure itself and troop discipline began to decline at an alarming rate.

The problems created by the collapse of military discipline were matched by those created by the fall of the fourth provisional government and the instauration of the fifth. The fourth provisional government fell when socialist and social democrat members resigned over what they considered to be the excessive influence of the communists on the prime minister, Vasco Gonçalves. The radical dominated CR sought to regain control over the "situation" by creating a triumvirate comprised of the president, Costa Gomes; the prime minister, Vasco Gonçalves; and COPCON commander, Otelo Saraiva de Carvalho. The council's aim was to bring some order to the "situation" so that a fifth provisional government could be organized.

This was accomplished on August 8, 1975. However, this government was even more openly and closely linked through the personage of the prime minister to the communist party. Again socialists and social democrats protested the attempt by the gonçalvistas to unite the provisional government with the communist party. At the height of this dispute, the faction led by Major Antunes and Brigadier Vasco Lourenço decided to attempt to gain control of the "situation." On August 7 they handed over to President Costa Gomes a manifesto which defended the concept of a democratic and socialist Portugal, demanded an end to the links between the gonçalvistas and the communists, and called for an alliance between the MFA and "progressive" democratic parties.

Having followed a strategy of gaining the widest possible support within the MFA for their position, the Group of Nine (Grupo dos Nove), as this faction came to be called, presented the gonçalvistas with a fait accompli. Seeing that they did not command wide support within the MFA, Gonçalves, Otelo, and other radical officers accepted defeat and announced that henceforth the CR would abandon much of its executive functions and permit the organization of a sixth provisional government dominated by civilians and military officers who wanted a socialist but democratic regime for Portugal. At this point the MFA essentially agreed to underwrite a pluralist democracy of the West European type. The ascension of the Group of Nine marks the end of the third phase of the period of exception and the beginning of the fourth and final stage.

Throughout the autumn of 1975 control over the "situation" shifted toward the Antunes-Lourenço faction as support among the military for a pluralist democratic solution widened. The sixth provisional government, which was formed on September 19, was dominated by socialists and social democrats. For the first time since April 25, a faction favoring a return to the barracks and the relinquishing of power to a civilian government gained control of the "situation." Control of the armed forces was returned to the Chief of the General Staff of the Armed Forces (Chefe do Estado-Maior General das Forças Armadas: CEMGFA), first under Costa Gomes and later under Ramalho Eanes, and military discipline was restored. Gradually, Eanes, Portugal's present president, emerged as the leader of this faction.

The final defeat of the radical faction came on November 25, 1975, when extreme left groups attempted a golpe by instigating an uprising of military personnel at several air force bases in the Lisbon area. The attempt collapsed when no other units followed suit and was crushed by units loyal to Eanes and the Group of Nine. Implicated in the attempt, Otelo, Gonçalves, Fabião and others of the radical faction were removed from positions of power, and complete control over the "situation" was achieved by the novistas. During this final phase of the period of exception, support for a pluralist democratic regime of the West European variety solidified and the MFA gradually began to play a secondary but supervisory role.

THE CONTAINMENT OF SPONTANEOUS ACTION

At the same time that the various factions within the MFA were maneuvering to gain control of the "situation," a wave of spontaneous, non-elite activity broke over Portugal. This activity took four primary forms: strikes, factory takeovers, the formation of urban residents' commissions, and dwelling occupations. It should be stressed that these activities were "not, however, the product of any form of political agitation or mobilization, but of social tensions and pressures already existent within Portuguese society."[20] Moreover, most if not all of these "spontaneous" activities were, on the one hand, encouraged from above, and on the other, eventually contained and frustrated by various provisional governments, the communists, and the bureaucratic apparatus of the state.

As was mentioned in the previous chapter, Caetano, Salazar's successor as prime minister, sought to revitalize the corporate structures of the New State by making them more representative of workers' interests in order to coopt support for the regime. The general policy was to attempt to create an independent trade union movement which would remove the state from a direct role in wage bargaining. Several decree-laws were passed which strengthened the position of workers against employers and allowed workers to select their own leadership and organize themselves more effectively. Much of the union leadership that emerged during this period was clandestinely connected to the communist party. In October 1971 a blanket labor organization composed of about twenty unions called Intersindical was formed. Hence, the communists were able to gain control of the labor movement as it gradually emerged during the last years of the New State.[21]

During the first months of the period of exception numerous spontaneous strikes were held by workers not integrated within the Intersindical framework. Although in some cases these strikes sought fundamental changes, for the most part they were carried out to achieve instrumental demands such as higher wages, better working hours and conditions, and paid vacations. From the outset of the period of exception the various provisional governments, from those dominated by the spinolistas to those by the gonçalvistas, pursued a policy of containing spontaneous strike actions. The main vehicle of this policy was a decree-law (No. 392/74) which, while guaranteeing the right to strike, authorized the use of the "lockout" by employers if the strikers exceeded the limits of the law. The law prohibited politically or religiously motivated strikes, solidarity strikes, work stoppages by isolated groups of workers in strategic sectors of the economy, and attempted to incorporate such activity into a formalized bureaucratic process involving unions or a majority of the work force in a particular sector.[22]

As spontaneous strikes represented a threat to the control of the labor movement by the communists, the party went to great lengths to contain such activity and subsume it beneath the <u>Intersindical</u> umbrella. The communist strategy was to help the various provisional governments suppress outbreaks of worker unrest. To this end, they organized demonstrations against "wildcat" strikes, denounced "strikes for strikes' sake," and condemned such strikes as "unauthorized," "unrealistic," and "irresponsible." In like fashion, <u>Intersindical</u> collaborated with the efforts of the various provisional governments to quash spontaneous worker activity and sought to coopt such workers into its own apparatus. During this period, <u>Intersindical</u> expanded its membership to over 200 unions.[23]

The temporary domination of the "situation" by the radical <u>gonçalvistas</u> military faction did not change the provisional government's view of spontaneous strikes. If anything, it led to an even more repressive and authoritarian approach because of the close connection between Gonçalves and the communists. Thus, the main feature of spontaneous worker mobilization during the period of exception was the "relative ease with which repression by a corporatist state, in which workers were not represented, was replaced by the subordination of workers' perceived needs to the requirements of the organizations that purported to represent them . . . [and] the manipulation of the labor movement through means not dissimilar in substance (though quite different in ideological content) from those used by Caetano's state."[24]

Another area of spontaneous activity was the interrelated formation of urban residents' commissions (<u>comissões de moradores</u>) and the occupation of vacant urban dwellings. The residents' commissions were an attempt by neighbors to organize themselves with the aim of solving local problems such as the lack of adequate and decent housing, schools, sewers, electricity, trash collection, telephone booths, pharmacies, transportation, parking lots, and child care facilities in poorer neighborhoods (<u>bairros</u>). The occupations occurred principally because of the pressing need for housing.

Four phases in the formation of residents' commissions have been identified, each corresponding to the ebb and flow of events at the national level during the period of exception. The first phase began immediately after April 25 and ran until November, 1974. During the first two months of this phase residents' commissions sprang up in many of the bairros of Lisbon, Porto, and Setúbal, especially in the shantytowns (barracas). Few others were organized until mid-August when some bairros began forming commissions in response to pressure by the Mobil Local Support Service (Serviço Ambulatório de Apoio Local), which, in the meantime, had been created at the national level to encourage local initiative in solving neighborhood problems. In order to receive support from this service, local residents had to be organized into a residents' commission or some other type of local organization. The second phase began in November and extended until March, 1975. During this phase the MFA began to conceive of itself as a "national liberation movement" and began its program of mobilizing the population (dinaminazação), especially the rural peasantry and poor urban masses. During this phase great emphasis was placed on self-help organizations to solve local problems. Those bairros without residents' commissions were encouraged to organize them, and, in those where the already extant commissions had become coopted by local government (juntas de frequesia), alternative, independent organizations called occupants' commissions were encouraged. The third phase ran from March to November, 1975, and was marked by the formation of many additional commissions as well as workers' commissions (comissões de trabalhadores) as the MFA fell increasingly under control of the radical faction. During this phase, the MFA called for the establishment of a socialist state based on non-bourgeoisie forms of popular participation, such as the local residents' commissions. The fourth and final phase began after November 25, the day when the attempted golpe by the far left was routed, and ran until the end of the period of exception. During this phase, very few local residents' commissions were formed, as they were no longer encouraged by the national government.[25]

The phases in the formation of residents' commissions were paralleled by successive waves of housing occupations. The first wave began immediately after the golpe and involved the occupation of completed and partially completed government-owned housing. This phase lasted only two weeks, just long enough for the government-owned housing available to be fully occupied. In response to these occupations the first provisional government passed a decree-law requiring landlords to rent all vacant property within 120 days, after which time it would be rented for them by local government authorities. After the expiration of the 120 day grace period, a second wave occurred as many unrented, single-family, private dwellings were occupied. This wave lasted until April 1975. With most of the vacant single-family dwellings now occupied, many residents' commissions announced that all apartments still vacant would be systematically taken over and distributed to those most in need. This announcement was followed by a third wave of occupations as newly constructed private apartment buildings were occupied. These occupations were well organized, having been orchestrated by residents' commissions and groups of the far left. After November 25 and the fall of the radicals, no further housing occupation took place.[26]

What is clear from this brief outline of local activities during the period of exception is the extent to which "spontaneous" action was actually sensitive to the ebb and flow of the elite competition for control of the "situation" at the national level and the degree to which such action was actually generated by entities created for that purpose at the national level, such as the Mobil Local Support Service. Moreover, the spontaneity of local autonomous organizations was eventually contained by the traditional local governmental authorities (about which more in Chapter 8) on whom they were dependent. After November 25, the residents' commissions were gradually absorbed by the local authorities and many occupations were declared illegal and squatters were evicted.[27]

The third area of spontaneous activity during the period of exception was factory and business takeovers by workers and the establishment of worker-managed firms. Such firms came into existence in two ways. First, some firms were initiated by unemployed workers in activities not requiring large amounts of start-up capital, such as civil construction and domestic service. Second, firms which had been in private hands before the golpe were taken over by their employees. These takeovers were not, however, the result of a broadly-based revolutionary impulse on the part of workers but rather the result of the desire of employees to remain employed. After April 25, market instability and the immediate increase of wages by 30 percent put many firms in a state of financial crisis. Proprietors who could not or would not meet these new higher costs of doing business responded by either dismissing workers or going out of business altogether. Seeing their livelihoods evaporate, workers in many firms responded by taking over the management, in most cases, however, only after the original owners had completely abandoned the business or factory. Thus, most worker-managed firms came into existence as a result of passive transfers of ownership, that is, when employees had no other choice in order to maintain their jobs.[28]

In sum, then, the great bulk of the non-elite spontaneous activity which took place was not revolutionary; that is, it was not a broadly-based attempt by the masses to consciously attempt to transform social and economic relationships. Workers went on strike for higher wages, better working conditions, and paid vacations. Urban dwellings were occupied because of the pressing need for housing, and local commissions were organized to bring pressure to bear on the authorities for improvements in specific local public services such as electricity, transportation, and trash collection. Businesses and factories were taken over to keep them open and to maintain employment and wages. Moreover, much "spontaneous" activity frequently occurred as a consequence of decisions and policies made at the national level by elite factions which were vying with one another for control of the new regime.

A similar conclusion can be drawn about the agrarian reform movement in the Alentejo. During the first year of the period of exception, the demands of rural workers were restricted to the right to form unions and higher wages. The first occupations of land did not occur until January 1975, a full nine months after the golpe, and involved the seizure only of uncultivated land. The movement to occupy land did not become widespread until toward the end of September when the Ministry of Agriculture agreed to provide funds to pay workers on cooperatives. As in the case of factory workers, the communist-dominated agricultural workers' unions encouraged the state to quash any independent attempts to occupy land or hold "unauthorized" strikes.[29]

Finally, all of these spontaneous activities were in one way or another contained, frustrated, and otherwise absorbed by the provisional governments in some cases, the communists in others, and the administrative apparatus of the state in yet others. This fate eventually befell worker-managed firms, although after the period of exception.[30]

CONCLUSIONS

As was shown in the previous chapter, the collapse of the New State was the result of the failure of Salazar and his successor, Caetano, to resolve the participation crisis by institutionalizing the regime's corporatist political infrastructure. A major source of weakness of the New State was the lack of effective political linkages with the broader civil society which could have been used to mobilize support for the regime and its policies. The failure to resolve the participation crisis was due to resistance within the broader civil society at being reorganized into corporatist mediating structures, historical events which diverted resources away from the corporations, and the presence of a highly centralized, bureaucratic state apparatus which constrained the creation of new, innovative linking structures and dominated the policymaking process.

The period of exception can be seen as the reemergence of this crisis as well as the crisis of distribution and a new search for solutions by elites. Although the precipitant of the golpe which brought down the New State on April 25, 1974, was a professional military grievance, it created a political vacuum which required filling. The swirl of events during the period of exception was not the result of a broad revolutionary movement led by the MFA or any other broadly-based revolutionary party, but, rather, the intense maneuverings of various elite factions, led frequently by charismatic leaders, as they sought to gain control of the "situation" and impose on society a new regime. These rivalries, frequently based on personal connections and friendships, were intensified by the differing models of new regimes that were being put forward: pluralist democracy of the West European variety, East European socialist, or Third World revolutionary. Thus, the period of exception was not a revolution in the true sense but a struggle among military elite factions over the nature of the new regime. As in the past, spontaneous demand making was contained, frustrated, and otherwise coopted by the various provisional governments, the communists, who saw them as a threat to their power, and the bureaucratic apparatus of the state.

This is not to say that there was no change in social, economic, and political arrangements. There certainly were, and many, such as the nationalization of the commanding heights of the economy, the redistribution of land, and the establishment of a new set of political institutions, were major innovations. It is only to say that these changes were not the result of the actions of a broadly-based revolutionary movement. At best, the events surrounding April 25, 1974 and the period of exception might be characterized as something of an "elite revolution"; that is, a change in regime which was (1) generated by conditions external to the society (i.e., the African wars); (c) carried out by elites from within the regime itself (i.e., the military); and (3) did not involve the mass mobilization of the citizenry before or after the takeover of power.[31]

With the election of a constituent assembly and the victory of the military faction committed to a West European style regime, the conflict over the precise way in which the participation and distribution crises would be resolved shifted to civilian political elites charged with providing a new political infrastructure. To this struggle the book now turns.

NOTES

1. Joyce Firstenberg Riegelhaupt, "Introduction," in In Search of Modern Portugal: The Revolution and Its Consequences, ed. Lawrence S. Graham and Douglas L. Wheeler (Madison, Wis.: University of Wisconsin Press, 1983), p. 6.

2. For a discussion of what revolution is and is not, see Mark N. Hagopian, The Phenomenon of Revolution (New York: Dodd, Mead, 1974).

3. The number of books and articles which characterize the events of the period of exception as a part of a broad revolutionary process is legion. See, for example, "A Revolution Tamed: Survey of Portugal," The Economist 263 (May 28, 1977): 3-30. Jean Pierre Faye (ed.), Portugal: The Revolution in the Labyrinth (London: Spokesman Books, 1976); Rona Fields, The Portuguese Revolution and the Armed Forces Movement (New York: Praeger, 1976); Jane Kramer, "A Reporter at Large: The Portuguese Revolution," The New Yorker, December 15, 1975, pp. 92-131; Kenneth Maxwell, "Portugal: The Hidden Revolution," New York Review of Books, April 17, 1975, pp. 29-35; and "The Thorns of the Portuguese Revolution," Foreign Affairs 54 (January 1976): 250-270; Lawrence Nevils, "The Portuguese Revolution," Worldview, July-August 1975, pp. 40-47; and Douglas Porch, The Portuguese Armed Forces and the Revolution (Stanford: Hoover Institution Press, 1977).

4. On the vulgarization of the concept of revolution, see Jacques Ellul, Autopsy of Revolution (New York: Alfred A. Knopf, 1971), Chap. 8.

5. Juan J. Linz, "Spain and Portugal: Critical Choices," in Western Europe: The Trials of Partnership: Critical Choices for Americans, Vol. 3, ed. David S. Landes (Lexington, Mass.: Lexington Books, 1977), p. 242.

6. "Situation" (a situação) is the word given by Portuguese to the prevailing regime or government at a particular time. For a discussion of "situationalism" see Richard Robinson, Contemporary Portugal (London: Allen & Unwin, 1979), pp. 33-34.

7. Howard J. Wiarda, "The Portuguese Revolution: Towards Explaining the Political Behavior of the Armed Forces Movement," Iberian Studies 4 (Autumn 1975): 53-54.

8. On the movement itself see Avelino Rodrigues et al., O Movimento dos Capitães e o 25 de Abril (Lisbon: Moraes, 1974).

9. Ben Pimlott, "Were the Soldiers Revolutionary? The Armed Forces Movement in Portugal, 1973-1976," Iberian Studies 7 (Spring 1978): 16. See also Ben Pimlott, "Socialism in Portugal; Was It a Revolution?" Government and Opposition 12 (Summer 1977): 332-366.

10. Pimlott, "Were the Soldiers Revolutionary?" p. 16.

11. Wiarda, "The Portuguese Revolution," pp. 54-55.

12. David L. Raby, "Populism and the Portuguese Left: From Delgado to Otelo," in In Search of Modern Portugal, ed. Graham and Wheeler, p. 64.

13. Ibid., p. 74.

14. Ibid., p. 75.

15. António de Spínola, Portugal e o Futuro (Lisbon: Arcádia, 1974).

16. On the operations of the PIDE during the New State see Tom Gallagher, "Controlled Repression in Salazar's Portugal," Journal of Contemporary History 14 (July 1979): 385-402.

17. Emídio de Veiga Domingos, Portugal Político: Análise das Instituições (Lisbon: Edições Rolim, 1980), pp. 43-47.

18. Lawrence S. Graham, "The Military in Politics: The Politicization of the Portuguese Armed Forces," in Contemporary

Portugal: The Revolution and Its Antecedents, ed. Lawrence S. Graham and Harry M. Makler (Austin and London: University of Texas Press, 1979), pp. 221-256. The following discussion of the period of exception closely follows that of Graham, see especially, pp. 232-251.

19. There is some question as to whether Spínola was actually involved in the plotting. It was probably more a case of guilt by association.

20. Bill Lomax, "Ideology and Illusion in the Portuguese Revolution: The Role of the Left," in In Search of Modern Portugal, ed. Graham and Wheeler, p. 114. See also Phil Mailer, Portugal: The Impossible Revolution (New York: Free Life Editions, 1977).

21. John R. Logan, "Worker Mobilization and Party Politics: Revolutionary Portugal in Perspective," in In Search of Modern Portugal, ed. Graham and Wheeler, pp. 138-140.

22. Ibid., p. 143.

23. Lomax, "Ideology and Illusion in the Portuguese Revolution," pp. 114-117. For a good discussion of the activities of the communists during this period see Kenneth Maxwell, "Portuguese Communism," in Eurocommunism: The Ideological and Political-Theoretical Foundations, ed. George Schwab (Westport, Conn.: Greenwood Press, 1981), pp. 269-302; and Thomas C. Bruneau, "The Left and the Emergence of Liberal Democracy," in Eurocommunism and Eurosocialism: The Left Confronts Modernity, ed. Bernard E. Brown (New York and London: Cyro Press, 1979), pp. 114-178.

24. Logan, "Worker Mobilization and Party Politics," p. 145.

25. Charles Downs, "Residents' Commissions and Urban Struggles in Revolutionary Portugal," in In Search of Modern Portugal, ed. Graham and Wheeler, pp. 157-160.

26. Ibid., pp. 162-167.

27. Ibid., p. 175.

28. Nancy Bermeo, "Worker Management in Industry: Reconciling Representative Government and Industrial Democracy in a Polarized Society," in In Search of Modern Portugal, ed. Graham and Wheeler, pp. 182-186.

29. Lomax, "Ideology and Illusion in the Portuguese Revolution," p. 120.

30. Bermeo, "Worker Management in Industry," pp. 186-192.

31. Ellen Kay Trimberger, "A Theory of Elite Revolutions," Studies in Comparative International Development 7 (Fall 1972): 191-207.

5
The Party System: The Political Archaeology of Portuguese Parties

In the months immediately following the golpe of April 25, 1974, more than fifty groups sprang up in Portugal calling themselves political parties. A year later, when elections were held for the constituent assembly, fourteen of these had been certified by the electoral commission and seven won seats. Now, one constituent, three general, three local, and two presidential elections later, Portugal has what can only be described as a multiparty system in the classic West European tradition. Today, the political spectrum runs from Trotskyists and Maoists on the extreme left to neo-fascists and monarchists on the extreme right. The spectrum between these two extremes is occupied by Christian democrats, social democrats, socialists, and communists. This great proliferation of political parties can be seen as the birth of the political infrastructure of popular control. As such, it represents an attempt to break through the confining conditions of the New State and to resolve the participation crisis which Salazar's corporative infrastructure had failed to do. The questions with which this chapter is concerned are: why has this institutional void been filled with a multiparty system and from where did these parties come?

According to Smith, the many answers which have been offered to the question of why multiparty systems such as Portugal's develop can be grouped under two broad headings: social forces explanations and constitutional explanations.[1] Proponents of social forces explanations argue that multiparty systems are produced by or reflect a particular society's linguistic, religious, regional, and class cleavages. By definition, those political systems with only two parties must not be riven by such cleavages because they do not have a fragmented political spectrum.[2] Proponents of constitutional explanations, on the other hand, maintain that the form a government takes, legal constraints on party activity, and the electoral system are determinative of the political party system. Of constitutional factors, the electoral system has been singled out as the most decisive. It is argued that single-member, "first-part-the-post," "winner-take-all" electoral systems, as found in Great Britain and the United States, limit the polity to only two parties by encouraging the coalescence of voters into two large, opposing blocks to the immediate right and left of the center of the political spectrum. This discourages third parties which have little chance of representation under such conditions. It is further argued that multimember, proportional representation (PR), as is found in Portugal and many other West European democracies, encourages a multiplicity of parties. In PR systems, the rules of the game do not require a coalescence of voters toward the center of the spectrum and, as seats are allocated in rough proportion to the number of votes each party receives, smaller "third" parties stand a good chance of achieving some representation.[3]

Recently, a third set of answers to the question of party system development has appeared in the literature that, for want of a better term, can be placed under the rubric "political." An early example of such writing is Loewenberg's analysis of the evolution of the German party system which shows that the "sharp discontinuities in the development of the German party system do not seem to correlate readily either with socio-economic or with 'cultural' change, nor in any simple manner with the advent of proportional representation."[4] He concludes that the marked changes in the German party system are closely connected to dramatic political changes, especially those of 1933 and 1945. Additional evidence for the importance of political factors such as the specific decisions of leaders and a particular policy of a political party has been found for Scandinavia[5] and Imperial Germany.[6]

The purpose of this chapter is to examine the development of Portugal's system of political parties with the aim of shedding light on the dispute concerning the origins of party systems. The method will be what Berger calls "political archaeology,"[7] that is, the unearthing of successive strata of political party development to determine if there is any correlation between the configuration of the party system and the method of election. The next chapter will examine correlations between socio-economic cleavages and voting behavior, especially since 1974.

ORIGINS OF THE PARTY SYSTEM

Portuguese politics during the nineteenth century, as has already been shown in Chapter 2, involved severe crises of legitimacy and participation. Political parties, as they are known today, did not exist. Politics until the final defeat of absolutism in 1834 was essentially a struggle for control of the state by rival elites. The first was the absolutists, who were supported by the old nobility, the hierarchy of the Catholic Church, and the conservative mass of the Portuguese peasantry. The second elite was the liberals who stood for constitutional monarchy and were supported by the newly emergent upper commercial bourgeoisie in major port cities, educated bureaucrats, some of the petty nobility in the central and southern regions, some military officers, and some of the lower clergy.[8]

Following the victory of liberalism, factions appeared among liberals over the particular document on which the new constitutional monarchy was to be based. One faction, the most radical, was called the "twentiethists" (vintistas) because they advocated a return to the Constitution of 1822. The other faction, the moderates, wanted to found the regime on the Charter of 1826. The conflict between these two factions produced the Constitution of 1838, which attempted a compromise between the Constitution of 1822 and the Charter of 1826. The liberal regime was based on the 1838 document until the Charter was restored by the moderates in 1842 by a bloodless coup.

The conflict between radicals, who came to be called "Septemberists" after the revolt in Porto in September 1836, and the moderates, who became known as "Chartists" because of their support for the Charter of 1826, was essentially a battle between elite factions within the liberal movement over the issue of participation. Septemberists drew significant support from Portugal's nascent industrial and artisan sectors who saw in the direct election of parliament, as required by the 1822 and 1838 constitutions, an opportunity to coopt a broader base of support for the liberal order and to consolidate their control over the regime. The moderates, on the other hand, believed that the new order could best be institutionalized and their control over it maintained by restricting the suffrage and granting to traditional sectors significant representation in an upper house composed of life and hereditary peers as well as clergy.[9]

Despite the restoration of the Charter, Septemberists continued to advocate the direct election of parliament. Gradually, Chartists, who became known as "Regenerators" during the 1850s, recognized that the Charter had to be modified to allow more participation. Beginning in 1852, three amendments to the Charter, called Additional Acts (Actos Adicionais), introduced electoral reforms. The first act introduced direct election of the House of Deputies and reduced income qualifications for voting; the second, passed in 1885, eliminated hereditary parity, limited the number of life peerages to 100, and created fifty elected peers. The third act, passed in 1896, modified the 1855 act by restoring hereditary peerages.[10]

During the 1860s a new elite faction known as the "Historic Progressives," later shortened to simply "Historics" (históricos), because of their claim to be the true heirs of liberalism's radical tradition, arose and shared seats in parliament and government portfolios with the Regenerators. At the beginning of the 1870s, a second oppositionist elite called the "Reformists" appeared. In 1876 the Reformists coalesced with the Historics to form the "Progressives." For the next fifty years, until the collapse of the constitutional monarchy, Progressives and Regenerators rotated in and out of office with such regularity that the system was dubbed Rotativism (rotatavismo). Although the Historics wanted to broaden the suffrage beyond the Additional Acts and hold more honest elections, their policies and programs were virtually indistinguishable from those of the Regenerators. Both Historics and Regenerators were essentially loose coalitions based on outstanding personalities who were willing to play the role of royal opposition.[11]

Elections in Portugal started soon after the victory of liberalism. "Instructions" on how to vote and on the way the first elected cortes should be constituted were the first Portuguese electoral code. Over the next ninety years fifteen electoral laws were passed. These laws were primarily concerned with delineating the size and boundaries of voting districts and determining the number of representatives each should have. Although several of these laws introduced single-member districts, the limited vote, minority system with two to six representatives per constituency was typical. Except for two brief periods (the first during 1822 and the second between 1838 and 1842), elections up until 1852 were indirect. Qualified voters would choose a number of electors from their parishes who, in turn would choose electors for each of the parliamentary constituencies. These electors then elected deputies to the parliament. A plurality decided the election of candidates. Throughout the first half of the liberal era voting laws greatly restricted the franchise by imposing high income qualifications. To be elected to parliament an individual had to have an annual income of 400,000 reis, and to be a voter, 100,000. After 1852, however, and until the end of the constitutional monarchy, deputies to parliament were elected directly and electoral laws gradually expanded the franchise by lowering income and literacy qualifications. The 1878 law enfranchised all who could read and write or had a minimum income of 100,000 reis, or were heads of families and lowered the voting age from twenty-five to twenty-one. The 1895 law lowered the income requirement by half for illiterates.[12]

Between 1843 and 1910 there were forty-three general elections in Portugal. However, these elections had little meaning outside of the major towns. Electoral corruption was widespread and, unlike well-entrenched constitutional systems elsewhere in Europe where elections produced governments, Portugal's governments during the constitutional monarchy produced elections. When a new prime minister was appointed by the king, a government would be formed and then elections would be held to obtain the required parliamentary majority. This was possible because power did not emanate from the people to the government but from the government to the people. Even the Regenerators and Progressives, the two best organized groups, were not parties in the modern sense of the term. They were, for the most part, elite factions whose support base existed principally in the towns and cities, especially Lisbon and Porto, and were manipulated by local bosses, called caciques, who controlled the politically relevant, local population. Thus, the parties were essentially elaborate patron-client networks capable of organizing the vote in exchange for money, political favors, jobs, and the like, and allowed government and politics to be dominated by elite factions who occupied the apexes of these networks. Politics, therefore, functioned on the basis of personal authority and charisma with little relationship to the wishes of the citizenry.

Dissatisfaction with constitutional monarchy as well as the gradual decline of the monarchy itself, brought to the fore new political elites who wanted to change the system and put in its stead a new order. These new elites were heavily influenced by the beliefs of utopian socialism which spread among the Portuguese intelligentsia between 1840 and 1860. One of these elites was the socialists and the other the republicans. Gradually, republicanism lost its socialist elements as the founding of a socialist republic began to be considered impractical in a country like Portugal where, at that time, the working class was a very small minority. Although, at first, republicanism was a movement among the intelligentsia, it began to command a considerable following after 1881 when a formal party apparatus was organized. Republicanism became a vehicle of the urban petty bourgeoisie and a rural middle bourgeoisie in their struggle against the upper middle class oligarchy which had dominated the constitutional monarchy. The majority of republican leaders came from the urban lower middle class. Many were lawyers, doctors, pharmacists, engineers, teachers, journalists, and military officers. By 1900 the movement had gained so much momentum that it enveloped the socialists, anarchosyndicalists, and other anti-establishment groups who saw republicanism as a means of bringing down the monarchy.[13]

The Portuguese Republican Party (Partido

Republicano Português: PRP) was, perhaps, Portugal's first political party in the modern sense of the term. Although its base of support was primarily urban, the PRP had a nationwide organization that extended into the rural areas. In 1904 the party was reorganized to provide a coherent organizational structure by linking republican centers (centros republicanos), which recruited new members, and republican revolutionary boards (juntas revolucionários), in almost every parish, municipality, and district throughout the country. After the revolution was proclaimed in Lisbon, the previously organized boards assumed power in local government.[14]

The PRP did not, however, remain unified. In 1911 a split emerged between moderate and radical republican deputies over the election by the constituent assembly of the president of the republic. The candidate of the radical republicans, led by Afonso Costa, was defeated by the candidate of the moderates, led by Brito Camacho and António José de Almeida, who opposed Costa's radical and intransigent republicanism and feared that he would gain control of the new government. The split widened at the PRP congress in October 1911 when the moderates were hooted down and left in disgust. The moderates then organized the Republican National Union (União Nacional Republicana: UNR) with the directorate consisting of Camacho, Almeida, and Aresta Branco. The UNR was essentially a personal clique of several moderate leaders whose purpose was to get through parliament a program which would mitigate the impact of the more radical republican government. After this split the PRP became known as the Democratic Party (Partido Democrático).[15]

In February, 1912, the UNR itself developed a leadership split producing two republican splinter parties. The immediate cause of the split was disagreements over the UNR program, drawn up by Camacho, but also involved personal ambitions for office between Camacho and Almeida. The rump, led by Camacho, was renamed the Republican Union (União Republicana: UR) and became known as "Unionists." The other group, led by Almeida, was called the Republican Evolutionist Party (Partido Republicano Evolucionista: PRE). The program of the PRE was quite similar to that of the UR but urged a policy of moderation and conciliation, advocated proportional representation, and revision of intolerant anticlerical laws.[16]

From 1912 until 1926, when the First Republic was toppled by a military coup, the original republican party continued to fragment. In addition to these splits, fragmentation was enhanced by the founding of several rival parties within the republican fold, such as President Sidónio Pais' National Republican Party (Partido Nacional Republicano: PNR), the Centrist Party (Partido Centrista: PC), an alignment that combined the right wing of the Evolutionists and the liberal wing of the Monarchist Progressives led by physician Egas Moniz; the Reformist Party (<u>Partido Reformista</u>: PR), another small group of moderates led by independent Machado Santos; and the Liberal Party (<u>Partido Republicano Liberal</u>: PRL), a coalition of Evolutionists, Unionists, Centrists, and Independents who hoped to form an effective front to oppose the PRP.[17] In addition, new parties with no connection to the existing republican movement, such as the socialists and the Portuguese Maximalist Federation, the precursor of the communists; and the Seara Nova (New Harvest) group on the left, and the Academic Center for Christian Democracy (<u>Centro Académico de Democracia Cristã</u>: CADC), the Legitimist Party (<u>Partido Legitimista</u>), the Monarchist Cause (<u>Causa Monárquica</u>) and the Nationalist Party (<u>Partido Nacionalista</u>), which was a fusion of liberals and an earlier moderate offshoot of the Democrats, on the right, continued to exist or appeared. Hence, in 1911, there was only one party, the PRP; in 1919, there were ten; and in 1926, there were twenty-two parties, factions, and coalitions on the political spectrum.

Only the original PRP managed to achieve and maintain any semblance of a mass following down to the grassroots. The others were, not unlike during the previous constitutional monarchy, elite factions with little or no support base even among the generally narrow politically aware public in Lisbon, Porto, and the other major towns. Again, politics functioned on the basis of personal authority and charisma rather than issues and ideas. Both houses of the congress did much to aggravate the immobilism of the First Republic with frequent votes of no confidence, sometimes violent and frequently tumultuous sessions, and a failure to generate a coherent program for dealing with Portugal's economic ills.

In its fifteen years and eight months of life there were seven parliamentary elections and eight for the presidency. Although republicans advocated universal male suffrage, only one election, that of 1918, took place with no voter qualifications. The other elections were governed by electoral laws that imposed requirements that restricted the franchise to males twenty-one years or older who could read and write or were heads of households. These electoral laws continued the limited vote, minority system for all constituencies except for Lisbon and Porto where the d'Hondt proportional method was applied. A list system of proportional representation for the entire country had been proposed in 1915 but failed to be adopted. The size of the percentage of seats in the congress granted automatically to minorities as well as the allocation of parliamentary seats to the various constituencies, especially in key districts like Lisbon and Porto, were major political issues during these years.[18]

Portugal's First Republic was the most unstable in modern European history. This is surprising in view of the fact that the various republican factions had a virtual monopoly of political power throughout the period and were not significantly different in their ideological beliefs. Initially, the major source of difference was the church-state issue which was gradually resolved on a moderate basis. Later, the major sources of discord were personalism and status rivalry. Sharp personalistic and factional lines prevented the growth of larger cooperative groups. Republican factions did not represent broad societal interest, but, narrow, personal political ambitions. The rural population, as before, was largely bypassed by political events in the capital. The radical, urban, youthful intelligentsia of central and southern Portugal gained the most from the First Republic. The conservative north was greatly underrepresented.[19]

By 1925 politicians and parliament had become the butt of ridicule and cynicism. The authoritarian regimes recently established in Spain, Italy, and Greece were becoming attractive alternatives to greater and greater numbers of Portugal's elite. During the last thirteen months of the First Republic there were four major attempts by the army to overturn the system. The fourth of these attempts, on May 28, 1926, was successful. However, the ensuing military dictatorship was faced with many of the same problems of the First Republic: economic stagnation, violence, labor unrest, and political factionalism. As was discussed earlier, the soldiers, like the civilian elite before them, were unable to create a stable regime (there were twelve organized revolts between 1926 and 1931) and turned to Salazar who was offered the portfolio of the Ministry of Finance and given carte blanche to take measures necessary to remedy the economic situation.

THE EMERGENCE OF MODERN POLITICAL PARTIES

As was already mentioned in Chapter 3, when Salazar's constitution went into effect in 1933 all political parties were suppressed, and an official government "collaborative agency," called the National Union, was established. The UN was the direct heir of the various conservative, traditionalist, and "counter-revolutionary" monarchist groups which sprang up during the First Republic. The primary link with the old order was through the Portuguese Integralist Movement (<u>Integralismo Lusitano</u>), an amalgam of monarchists, conservatives, Catholics, and nationalists. Other links were the Monarchist Cause and elements from the CADC, of

which Salazar had been a member.
The UN was to be an association without partisan character, independent of the state, and the organization that was to implement Salazar's corporate ideology among the citizenry. Its objectives were to integrate the nation, build national consciousness, eliminate dissent, and combat partisan activity. The association was organized according to the principles of discipline and hierarchy, and its structure closely paralleled that of the state's administrative subdivisions. It had district, municipal, and parish branches and was directed in its activities by an executive committee, whose president was Salazar. The UN was not, however, a mass movement nor very well run. Its membership was never more than 100,000, many of whom were government bureaucrats who were obliged to join and pay dues as a condition of employment. Outside of the government, the UN was a loose collection of local notables (caciques), personally loyal to Salazar. The UN's principal activity was screening candidates for government positions and elected offices and indoctrinating the citizenry concerning government policy. In 1969, Marcello Caetano, Salazar's successor as prime minister, changed the UN's name to the National Popular Action (Acção Nacional Popular: ANP) and attempted to broaden its base of support, which he accomplished with only very limited success.

A year after the 1933 plebiscite ratifying Salazar's constitution, elections were held for parliament, the National Assembly (Assembleia Nacional). For the duration of the dictatorship the size of the electorate did not change significantly even though college educated women and female heads of households were given the franchise in elections subsequent to the first (in which only male heads of households could vote), the population grew by two million, and the people who met the literacy qualifications increased by 50 percent. A considerable number of those citizens who qualified to vote simply did not bother to register.[20] Electoral registration was never encouraged and abstention rates were high. All partisan political activity was prohibited; therefore, only the UN was permitted to nominate candidates to stand for the National Assembly. Representatives to the Corporate Chamber were hand picked by the government, probably by Salazar himself.[21]

After 1945 Salazar began to allow a certain amount of partisan political activity during (but only during) elections. Designed to dissipate political tension and to appear more democratic in the aftermath of the allied victory over fascism, these concessions consisted chiefly of a partial lifting for the month prior to the election the regime's restrictions on freedom of the press, assembly, and the like. The pressure that those opposed to the New State were able to put on the regime during such intervals was greatly limited, however, In addition to harassment by the PIDE and the disqualification of candidates on legal technicalities, the opposition was contained by the fact that these brief periods of political activity tended to encapsulate and use up oppositionist energy in discrete episodes without opportunities to regenerate or sustain it beyond the election.[22]

Continuity such as there was from election to election came from a loose aggregation of individuals representing diverse ideological orientations such as socialists, dissident monarchists, anti-regime Catholics, and left-over republicans. The basic goal of this democratic opposition was the Europeanization of Portugal through the reconstruction of liberal democratic political institutions. These groups, as well as clandestine organizations, would serve as the basis of the party system which emerged after 1974. The first manifestation of this type of opposition came in October 1945, when the Movement of Democratic Unity (<u>Movimento de Unidade Democrática</u>: MUD) was organized by Teófilo Carvalho Santo and Mário de Lima Alves. The MUD brought together liberals, socialists, communists, republicans, and anarchists and called for freedom of the press, speech, and assembly, as well as the right to organize groups of a partisan nature. Although the MUD had been granted a semi-legal status, its activities were closely monitored and leadership harassed by the PIDE. In March, 1948, it was officially suppressed.[23]

Shortly thereafter another oppositionist aggregation appeared in Porto called the National Democratic Movement (<u>Movimento Nacional Democrático</u>: MND). Although much of the leadership of the MUD reappeared in the MND, this new group was much more leftist in orientation, many of its adherents being members of the underground Portuguese Communist Party (<u>Partido Comunista Português</u>: PCP). The MND supported Admiral Quintão Meireles in a special presidential election in 1951 occasioned by the unexpected death of General Carmona, who had been president of Portugal since 1926. After the defeat of their candidate, the MND died a slow death as its organizational and political force dissipated.[24]

Organized opposition during the month preceding elections did not appear again until the 1969 and 1973 elections and was a response to the limited liberalization that Marcello Caetano, Salazar's successor had encouraged. This time, three aggregations appeared which prefigured the division of Portugal's post-1974 political spectrum into three primary blocs. One of these was the Democratic Electoral Committee (<u>Comissão Democrática Eleitoral</u>: CDE) which represented left-wing Catholics and communists. In 1973 the CDE renamed itself the Portuguese Democratic Movement (<u>Movimento Democrático Português</u>: MDP) and became known as the CDE/MDP. A second aggregation was the Electoral Committee for Democratic Unity (Comissão Eleitoral para a Unidade Democrática: CEUD) which brought together socialists and social democrats. The third was the Monarchy Electoral Committee (Comissão Eleitoral Monárquica: CEM), an amalgamation of radical monarchists which had evolved within the UN from the Monarchist Cause.[25]

Opposition during the dictatorship was not, however, confined to these semi-legal electoral fronts. Between 1945 and 1970, the year of Salazar's death, there were at least ten military conspiracies, two of which actually led to open uprisings, one in 1946 and the other in 1962.[26] The first was an abortive attempt by the National Unified Antifascist Movement (Movimento de Unidade Nacional Antifascista: MUNAF) which had been organized in 1942 by General Norton de Mattos, a former high commissioner for Angola, ambassador to Britain, and the author of numerous books on colonial administration. The MUNAF, which predated the MUD and clandestinely brought together surviving republicans, socialists, and communists, called for the end of the New State and the establishment of a democratic regime. The MUNAF effectiveness was sapped, however, by the significant differences of opinion among its leadership about how the New State was to be brought down. The republicans and socialists thought that a military golpe would succeed while the communists argued for a mass uprising. The communist strategy prevailed, and, in August 1945, an uprising was attempted without success. Following this attempt, MUNAF was ruthlessly suppressed and further paralyzed by internal squabbles. It finally dwindled and died in 1949.[49]

The second and probably more significant military conspiracy was led by General Humberto Delgado and was attempted on New Year's Day at a military base in Beja. Although the uprising was suppressed by troops loyal to the New State, Delgado and his followers who escaped continued to harass the regime from bases outside Portugal. In 1963, Delgado and others who had fled Portugal organized the Patriotic Front for the Liberation of Portugal (Frente Patriótico de Libertação de Portugal: FPLP) and situated themselves in Algeria. The FPLP, like the MUNAF, was made ineffectual by internal differences of opinion over tactics and infiltration by PIDE. Delgado, who was president of the FPLP's revolutionary board, insisted on immediate armed rebellion and urban guerrilla struggle, while other leaders advocated a more cautious and disciplined approach. The PIDE took advantage of these differences and Delgado's subsequent isolation and infiltrated PIDE agents were able to lure Delgado and his secretary to a supposed secret conference with Portuguese supporters at the Spanish border town of Badajoz where both were murdered.[28]

After 1870 clandestine resistance to the New State

was provided primarily by several underground urban guerrilla groups. These groups harassed the regime with random violence in the hope of crippling Portugal's capacity to wage war against the liberation movements in the African colonies. The most important of these was led by a woman, Isabel do Carmo, and was called the Revolutionary Brigades (Brigadas Revolucionárias: BR).[29]

Toward the end of the New State, during Caetano's liberalization, a certain amount of opposition came to be tolerated within the regime itself. The key organizational framework for this opposition was called the Society for Economic and Social Development (Sociadade para o Desenvolvimento Económico e Social: SEDES). The SEDES represented a new elite of young men who had been youth leaders in several of Portugal's Catholic schools, universities, and labor groups during the 1950s and who had been profoundly affected by Pope John's encyclical, Pacem in Terris. In addition to its principal aim of democratizing the regime, SEDES sought to increase the level of public involvement in discussions of the major social and economic issues facing Portugal. This was done by sponsoring seminars and panel discussions on these issues. SEDES still exists and has striven to maintain its image as a non-partisan civic group whose task is to stimulate public opinion on the most important social and economic questions facing the nation. SEDE's membership has never been very large and has concentrated its activities in Lisbon and Porto. Its charter members were by and large professionals: engineers, economists, lawyers, and managers of some large businesses.[30]

Thus, despite the efforts by the New State to suppress partisan activity such activity did take place in a limited way. The oppositionist movements and electoral fronts encompassed socialists, republicans, communists, and social democrats. Moreover, the UN/ANP itself encompassed within its structure a variety of dissident Catholics, monarchists, and liberals. It was these groups within the opposition and government "party" as well as various underground, urban guerrilla movements that were the direct precursors of the parties that emerged after the collapse of the New State in 1974.

POLITICAL PARTIES AFTER
APRIL 25, 1974

In the aftermath of the 1974 golpe political exiles returned, underground groups emerged from clandestinity, and the opposition as well as the UN/ANP began to fragment into discrete parties as the conditions for open partisan activity were created by the MFA. The first post-golpe electoral law was decreed by the second provisional government. This law granted the franchise to all citizens over the age of eighteen and implemented true proportional representation for the first time in Portuguese history. At first the political spectrum lacked clarity because of the newness of the parties, the extremely rapid shift of events, and the uncertainty of many leaders of their position on the ideological spectrum. Since then, some ten years later, the party system has been clarified and the major parties have arranged themselves in fairly distinct fashion. The party system that has emerged resembles other multiparty systems in Western Europe and the parties can be classified according to their size and electoral significance in parliamentary elections.[31]

There are four parties which can be considered mass parties; that is, they attract a large number of voters, have bureaucratic structures extending down to the grassroots, conduct their activities on a continuous basis, and have consistently won seats in parliament, the Assembly of the Republic (Assembleia da República: AR). The first of these is the Socialist Party (Partido Socialista Português: PS). As has already been discussed, there have been socialists in Portugal since the 1860s, but the party has had an intermittent existence. Founded by intellectuals, such as Antero de Quental, the early socialists failed to organize themselves and were gradually displaced by the republicans as the focus of opposition to the constitutional monarchy. The period of the New State was particularly difficult for socialists because the party's leadership, drawn mostly from bourgeois backgrounds, was never able to adjust well to a life of clandestine political activity. There were various efforts during the 1930s, 1940s, and even the 1950s to create a socialist underground. These efforts brought into existence such shortlived organizations as the Republican and Socialist Alliance (Aliança Socialista, 1932-1934), and the Socialist Union (União Socialista, 1950-1954); but no continuous structure emerged. Although disorganized, socialists did support and participate in the various semi-legal, anti-regime electoral coalitions that were permitted during official campaign periods such as the MUD, MND, and the CEUD.

Only the New Harvest (Seara Nova) study/action group provided a continuous source of support for socialism during these years. Founded in 1921 by Jaime Cortesão and other intellectuals, the New Harvest group advocated non-partisan reforms and the regeneration of society and economy through the implementation of socialism. The group published an intellectual monthly journal called New Harvest from which the group received its name. Harvesters (Seareiros), as members of the group were called, provided active, but non-violent, opposition to the New State and were the only continuous source of socialist ideology and inspiration until the emergence of Portugal's present socialist party.

The present socialist party was founded in Bonn in 1973 by exiled intellectuals who had been inspired by an earlier attempt, in Rome in 1964, to organize a socialist movement called the Portuguese Socialist Action (Acção Socialista Português: ASP). Elements of the ASP were actively involved in the CEUD. The guiding spirit of Portugal's present-day socialists is Mário Soares, one of the party's founders and the first prime minister (1976-1978) under the new democratic system. One of Portugal's best-known political figures, Soares had been an active opponent of the New State since his student days as the organizer of the Board of Patriotic Action (Junta da Acção Patriótica: JAP) and as a lawyer who defended numerous political dissidents in a series of celebrated trials.[32]

At the time of the collapse of the New State, PS was little more than an elite faction, organizationally weak and with little grassroots structure and support outside of Lisbon, Porto, Coimbra, and other large towns. The party did not develop its organizational apparatus until 1975 as the date for the election of a constituent assembly approached. This apparatus has proved to be less well-organized and structured than that of other parties and has not submerged the tendency that has existed within the party from its earliest days to depend upon ties of friendship and personal contacts among the urban based intellectual leadership and the rural countryside.[33]

In the period immediately after the golpe, the socialists pursued an alliance with the communists and social democrats within the organizational framework of the CDE/MDP. When, in the months after the golpe, the leadership of the CDE/MDP, which had become dominated by the communists, decided to transform the CDE/MDP into an officially recognized political party, a crisis was precipitated which resulted in the socialist and social democratic components separating themselves in May 1974. The CDE/MDP rump then became a communist support organization, which disguised this connection in the hope of broad electoral support.

This split among socialists, communists, and social democrats gradually widened, especially between socialists and communists. As successive provisional governments were pressured leftward by radical MFA officers, Portuguese parties were polarized into two camps. On one side were the communists and their allies, especially the CDE/MDP. On the opposite side were the PS and the other democratic parties to its right. Soares increasingly found himself to be the spokesperson for all democratic opponents to the communists, and by late 1975 the PS was seen as the last barrier against a communist system which could be erected without abandoning Portugal's need for major economic, social, and political restructuring.[34]

Campaigning under the slogan "Socialism, yes; dictatorship, no" ("<u>Socialismo, sim; ditadura, não</u>"), a reference to the type of regime Portugal would have if the communists were victorious, the PS offered the voters a broad program for social and economic change. In the social sphere the party advocated women's rights and legalization of abortion and birth control programs. In the economic sphere, they sought the nationalization of banks, petrochemicals, steel, shipbuilding, communications, cement, transportation, and automobile assembly. In the political sphere they supported individual liberties, universal suffrage, and democracy. In the 1975 constituent assembly election and the 1976 elections for the AR, the PS won a plurality of the votes and seats.[35] These elections showed the socialists to have received strong support among all social groups and in all regions of the country. Only the PS was able to elect deputies from every one of Portugal's twenty-two electoral districts and therefore was considered by many observers as a true national, mass party. As the "winner" of the 1976 election, Soares was called upon by the president of the republic, General Ramalho Eanes, to form a government. Honoring a campaign pledge not to enter into any coalitions with parties either to the right or left should they receive the most votes, the socialists organized, in July 1976, Portugal's first democratically elected government in almost fifty years.

By seeking support from both left and right within the AR, the socialist government was able to survive for sixteen months. However, by summer, 1977, Portugal's economic situation had deteriorated sufficiently that the government was obliged to seek a loan from the International Monetary Fund (IMF) for 750 million dollars. In exchange, the government was required to implement stiff austerity measures and seek broad parliamentary support for them. The PS was unable to gain this support and the government fell on December 9, 1977. After a period of negotiation, the socialists organized a second government, this time a coalition with the small but electorally significant conservative Party of the Social Democratic Center (<u>Partido do Centro Democrático Social</u>: CDS). However, because of strong ideological differences between the two partners and agitation for a quick end to the coalition by the CDS's most conservative members, this government collapsed six months later, in June 1978.[36]

After the fall of the second PS government, the socialists began to experience a gradual decline in electoral popularity and support which, however, as will be discussed in the following chapter, has proved to be temporary. There were many reasons for this decline and one is internal leadership quarrels which temporarily split the party and left it directionless and incohesive. The first such quarrel came in January 1975 when

Manuel Serra, the radical Catholic who joined PS in June 1974, bringing with him the Popular Socialist Movement (Movimento Socialista Popular: MSP), bolted from the party and subsequently organized the Popular Socialist Front (Frente Socialista Popular: FSP).[37] A second though less serious quarrel came in 1977 when the PS expelled two of its parliamentary deputies who had dissented against the party's proposed budget. These dissidents later organized the unsuccessful Unified Socialist Worker's Party (Partido Operário Unificado Socialista: POUS).[38] The third quarrel occurred in January 1978 when Lopes Cardoso split with the PS over its governmental programs. He accused the socialist leadership, especially Soares, of abandoning the working class and of pursuing what amounted to social democratic policies. Cardoso and a radical faction within the PS called the Association of Socialist Culture-Worker's Brotherhood (Associação de Cultura Socialista-Fraternidade Operária) left the PS and organized a group called the Democratic and Socialist Left (Esquerda Socialista e Democrática), which later, in August 1979, transformed itself into a full-fledged political party, the Left Union for Social Democracy (União de Esquerda para a Democracia Social: UEDS). A fourth quarrel came when a group led by António Barreto and Madeiros Ferreira called the Reformers (Reformadores) left the PS and affiliated themselves with Sá Carneiro's Democratic Alliance (Aliança Democrática: AD), about which more below.[39]

The departure of Serra, Cardoso, Barreto, and other leaders did not settle the issue of socialist ideological identification and the PS leadership continued to quarrel. The party's "establishment"--led by Soares, Jaime Gama, Manuel Alegre, and Maldonado Gonelha--remained under fire by another group called the "Historics" (Históricos) composed of Tito de Morais, Jorge Campinos, Marcelo Curto, and Alfredo Carvalho. This group accused the socialist party of having abandoned its historical identity and ideological purity. The establishment was also buffeted by a second faction called the New Socialists (Socialistas Novas) composed of Vítor Constâncio, António Guterres, Sousa Gomes, Eduardo Pereira, Vítor Hugo Sequeira, and Rui Vilar, who hoped to make the party less ideological and more pragmatic and efficient. The Históricos saw the Socialistas Novas as little more than social democrats and technicians who wanted to dilute the party's democratic socialism to social democracy thereby making the PS indistinguishable from the social democrats.[40]

After the victory of the AD in the interim elections of 1979, the PS organized an electoral coalition called the Republican and Socialist Front (Frente Republicana e Socialista: FRS) in the hope of regaining the electoral momentum that had clearly shifted to the

Alliance. The FRS included the UEDS and a social democratic splinter group called the Independent Social Democratic Association (Associação Social Democrata Independente: ASDI). This front did not, however, immediately reverse the fortunes of the socialists who ran well behind the AD in the regular parliamentary elections of October 5, 1980.

The quarrel among these factions wracked the PS until April 1981 when in a series of brilliant political maneuvers in the weeks before the party's annual congress, Soares, utilizing his personal connections within the party and considerable charisma and popular appeal, was able to silence his critics and regain control of the party by taking his case directly to the rank-and-file. When the congress convened between 60 and 70 percent of the delegates were already pledged to Soares for the post of secretary-general of the party and the continuation of his leadership. Soares emerged from the congress as the party's absolute master.[41]

Although Soares had regained clear control of PS, it was not until another electoral defeat at the hands of AD--this time a by-election in the municipality of Loures in 1981--that the party began to develop a more vigorous opposition strategy. This strategy, which was revealed in November in a document called the PS Answer (Resposta PS), outlined a three-pronged attack against those the party thought responsible for Portugal's poor state of affairs. The first was against the AD government for failing to resolve Portugal's economic crisis; the second, against the president of the republic for not dismissing the government because of its failures; and, the third, against the communists for what were considered by the socialists as that party's various attempts at destabilizing Portugal's new democracy. This "Winter Offensive," as the party called it, was not, however, to have as its immediate objective the dismissal of the AD government nor was it to interfere with the agreement arranged previously with AD on revisions to the 1976 constitution, about which more in Chapter 7. Calls for dismissal and fresh elections were not to come until after the constitutional revision process was completed.[42]

These calls for a vote of no confidence never had to be made, however, because the AD collapsed from within a year later, about which more below, and Portugal's third parliamentary elections were held on April 25, 1983. The unified PS mounted a much more personalized and less ideological campaign which exploited brilliantly Soares' charm, charisma, and ability to "press the flesh" American-style. Faced with a badly disorganized and demoralized AD, which had broken down into its constituent parties, the PS emerged the victor with 36 percent of the vote, a result which was equal to the party's support in the 1975 and 1976 elections. Having made it clear before the election that the PS would not again try to govern alone, Soares invited the runner-up in the election, the social democrats to form a coalition. This was accomplished on June 4, 1983. At this writing Portugal is governed by this coalition with Soares as prime minister.

Portugal's second major party is the Social Democratic Party (Partido Social Democrata: PSD). Originally founded under the name Popular Democratic Party (Partido Popular Democrático: PPD), the PSD was established by Francisco Sá Carneiro, a wealthy Porto lawyer; Francisco Pinto Balsemão, the owner-editor of the influential Lisbon weekly newspaper, Expresso; and Magalhães Mota. These individuals had been elected to the National Assembly on UN/ANP lists during the early 1970s but resigned in protest when Caetano's liberalization failed to go as far as originally promised. In addition to Sá Carneiro, Pinto Balsemão, and Magalhães Mota much of PSD's leadership had been members of the SEDES study group.

After an initial flirtation with socialism in the first months following the 1974 golpe, the PSD has come to be a party of social democracy. It now rejects what it calls the utopianism of socialism and advocates a program of reform, pragmatism, and realism. The party's position is that Portugal can achieve economic development and social justice by guaranteeing civil rights and individual liberties. Although the PSD is firmly committed to rebuilding Portugal's private sector, which it believes has been stifled by an excessive number of nationalizations since 1974 and which it believes holds the key to Portugal's economic future, the party still sees some role for state ownership in certain key sectors of the economy.

Since its founding, the PSD has experienced three major internal leadership quarrels. The first of these broke out in 1975 when the party's left wing--composed of twenty-two constituent assembly delegates, one minister, and four secretaries of state in the first provisional government--split with the moderate PSD leadership and bolted from the party at its second annual congress. This group of dissidents subsequently organized the Social Democrat Movement (Movimento Social Democrata: MSD).[43]

The second major quarrel involved a split between what can be called the "populist" and "technocratic" tendencies within the PSD. The populist wing was led by Sá Carneiro and had a strong base of support in northern rural areas and on the archipelagoes of the Azores and Madeira. The technocratic wing was led by António Sousa Franco and received its support from managers, technicians, and businessmen. The difference between the two wings came to a head in April 1979 over Sá Carneiro's decision, as president of the party, to withdraw all PSD

support in parliament for the Mota Pinto government, a
non-party government of technocrats appointed by President Eanes. The technocratic wing refused to go along
and continued to support this government. After being
publicly berated for breaking party discipline, Sousa
Franco, António Rebelo de Sousa, and thirty-five other
PSD deputies withdrew from the party, but remained in
the AR calling themselves the Social Democratic Action
(Acção Social Democrata: ASD). In September 1979, the
ASD declared itself to be a political party and was renamed Independent Social Democrat Association (Associação
Social Democrata Independente: ASDI).[44]

These early schisms served to strengthen and consolidate the party around Sá Carneiro's leadership.
Having shed its more liberal leadership, Carneiro was
free to initiate contacts early in 1979 with two parties
to the party's right in order to form an alliance for
the interim parliamentary elections which had been set
by President Eanes when several of his governments of
presidential initiative failed to receive the approval
of parliament. In July 1979, AD was formed, comprising
the PSD, CDS, and a small monarchist party, about which
more below. This alliance, which had in the meantime
also picked up support from Barreto's Reformadores, won
both the 1979 interim election and the regular parliamentary election the following year. Sá Carneiro became prime minister, a post he held until his untimely
death in an airplane crash in December, 1980.

The third quarrel, however, unlike the earlier two,
left the PSD leaderless and disorganized, and eventually
led to the demise of the AD. This quarrel was sparked
by Francisco Pinto Balsemão's becoming the party's
leader and prime minister after Carneiro's death. The
first sign of trouble appeared at the party's seventh
congress in 1981, the first to be held without Carneiro.
During the congress, Balsemão was criticized by a group
variously called the "hardliners" (duros) or "critics"
(críticos) led by Eurico de Melo and Cavaco Silva, who
saw his leadership of the AD and government as too compromising and conciliatory, especially in its dealings
with President Eanes.

Although Balsemão survived this early challenge to
his leadership and continued as PSD's president and
prime minister, the hardliners were not to be denied.
At the party's eighth congress the following year, they
again criticized Balsemão's leadership and policies, focussing their attack this time on the poor state of the
economy which had shown no signs of improvement since
the last congress. Although Balsemão again survived the
challenge of the hardliners, criticism of his handling
of the economy also began to come from the PSD's main
alliance partner, the CDS. The CDS demanded a remodeling of the government, wishing especially to see Balsemão's finance minister, João Salqueiro, who was

thought to be indecisive, replaced by an economist with a "strong personality."45 Tensions between the PSD and CDS were exacerbated by a dispute over the presidency of the AR. The CDS refused to accept the individual proposed by the PSD and the PSD refused any other choice. Faced with these challenges, Balsemão declared that local elections, which were scheduled to be held on December 12, 1982, would be a kind of plebicite on the AD and his leadership. Despite the fact that the AD slipped only 4 percentage points from their 1980 return of 47 percent, the results, which also saw the PS increase their share of the vote from 27 to 31 percent, were interpreted as a loss of public confidence in the AD and Balsemão's leadership and led to his resignation as prime minister two weeks later.

Following Balsemão's resignation, the AD gradually disintegrated as PSD and CDS were unable to reach an agreement on a new prime minister to lead the alliance. The PSD put up Vítor Crespo, but the CDS refused to accept him. They then suggested Mota Pinto but he too was refused by CDS. As the AD could not form a new government President Eanes called for fresh elections on April 25, 1983. Unable to agree on combined lists of candidates for these elections, the AD was declared dead and the PSD, CDS, and PPM ran alone. After considerable internal uncertainty over who was going to lead the party, Mota Pinto was chosen to take PSD into the elections. Unfortunately, the campaign was poorly organized and lackluster, and the party slipped to second place with 27 percent of the vote. As was already mentioned, the PSD agreed to a coalitional government with the PS on June 4, 1983, and Mota Pinto became vice-prime minister and minister of defense.

The third major party is the already mentioned Party of the Social Democratic Center (CDS). It was founded in July 1974 by Diogo Freitas do Amaral, a professor of law, and Adelino Amaro da Costa. The party brings together former members of the conservative wing of the SEDES study group; disaffected conservatives from the New State's UN/ANP; as well as some ultra-conservatives who, in the very early days after the golpe of 1974, organized the Party of Christian Democracy (Partido da Democracia Cristã: PDC).46 The ideology of CDS is a mixture of intellectual conservatism, progressive capitalism, and Christian democracy. The party is affiliated with the European Christian Democratic Union and in March 1981 Freitas do Amaral was elected president of that organization. The party is well-implanted in the rural areas of northern Portugal where it enjoys the support of the church hierarchy and the local gentry. As already mentioned, the CDS coalesced with the PSD and the monarchists in July 1979 to form the AD.

Unlike the PS and the PSD, the CDS, a much more homogeneous grouping, has not experienced any serious

leadership quarrels which have led to schisms within
the party. However, Freitas do Amaral's decision in the
autumn of 1982 to quit the party ostensibly to prepare
himself to become a professor catedrático (full professor),[47] precipitated a struggle for control of the CDS
among its top leadership, especially between Lucas Pires
and Luís Barbosa. After a brief period of uncertainty,
Pires emerged as the leader of the party. This struggle
also contributed to the collapse of the AD.

Portugal's fourth major party is the Communist
Party (Partido Comunista Português: PCP).[48] Beginning
in 1919 as the Portuguese Maximalist Federation, the PCP
was founded in 1921 but had little support. Until the
mid-1930s, the party was dominated by anarchists, anarchosyndicalists, and libertarians who had little interest in organizing the working class, which at that time
was quite small in Portugal but increasingly active. In
1941, the PCP's present secretary-general, Alvaro Cunhal,
reorganized the party into a highly disciplined organization with a clandestine network of cells throughout
the country. Illegal during the New State, the party
was continually being persecuted by the PIDE. On several occasions the party's underground was smashed and
its leadership arrested. Cunhal was himself first arrested in 1937 and in the ensuing years spent a total of
fourteen years in prison, eight of these in solitary
confinement.

In the early 1960s, the PCP experienced schisms between its established leadership and younger more radical members who saw Cunhal and those around him as too
Stalinist and removed from Marxist-Leninist orthodoxy.
Many decried the leadership's willingness to participate
in electoral fronts rather than concentrating on achieving the revolution through direct and even armed conflict. The first split came in 1964 when a group of
dissidents left the party to form the pro-Chinese Popular Action Front (Frente de Acção Popular: FAP), and a
second dissatisfied group organized the Marxist-Leninist
Communist Party of Portugal (Partido Comunista de Portugal, Marxista-Leninista: PCP, M-L), a party which itself
soon suffered many splits and factions throughout the
1970s.

The 1974 golpe and the instauration of a democratic
regime in Portugal have not modified the PCP's Stalinist
outlook because the party's leadership does not believe
that the advent of democracy has created the conditions
for worker control of the economy. In the party's view,
Portugal's social structure, with its small middle class,
cannot support capitalism and broad political democracy
simultaneously. The PCP believes that under such conditions the monopoly capital that ruled the country during
the New State can easily regain, if it has not already,
its domination without violence and establish a new
"fascist dictatorship." This view that political power

but not economic power has passed to the democratic forces has led to a two-pronged, PCP political strategy since the return to constitutional government in 1976. The party, on the one hand, vigorously engages in political activities within the framework of elections and parliament and, on the other, confronts various governments with strikes and street demonstrations through its control of Portugal's major labor organization, the General Confederation of Portuguese Workers (Confederações Geral de Trabalhadores Portugueses: CGTP).[49]

The PCP has functioned as a highly centralized organization whose leadership has tolerated little internal dissent. The leadership has been small; only thirty-six individuals until expanded to ninety in 1976 were members of the party's central committee. Party membership is about 150,000, the great majority being industrial workers living in the area around Lisbon and an agricultural proletariate from the Alentejo. Like the PS and PSD, PCP also organized an electoral coalition called the United People's Action (Acção Povo Unido: APU) which included the MDP/CDE.

Like most West European party spectrums, Portugal's has a host of small groups calling themselves parties which cluster at the left and right extremes but fail to win representation in parliament. Of the two parties occupying the extreme right, the most important is the Party of Christian Democracy (Partido da Democracia Cristã: PDC), organized in 1974. In preparation for the constituent assembly election of 1975, the PDC joined with the CDS in an electoral coalition called the Union of the Christian Democratic Center (União do Centro Democrática Cristã: UCDC). This coalition lasted little more than a month, because PDC's violent campaign practices caused the party to be banned from the elections. The ban was lifted, however, for the parliamentary election of 1976. In preparation for this election the PDC received substantial support from a separate but related ultra-right coalition called the Social Democratic Union (União Social Democrático: USD), which was composed of two small radically conservative groups: the Christian Social Democratic Party (Partido Cristão Social Democrático: PCSD) and the Independent Social Democratic Party (Partido Social Democrático Independente: PSDI). For the regular parliamentary elections of 1980 the PDC coalesced with the Party of the Portuguese Right (Partido da Direita Portuguesa: PDP), but won no seats.

The PDP is the second most important ultra-conservative party in Portugal. It was originally organized in June 1977 by Kaulza de Arriaga, an army general who had won recognition as an innovative and aggressive guerrilla fighter during the colonial war in Mozambique, as the Independent Movement of National Reconstruction (Movimento Independente da Reconstrução Nacional: MIRN). Arriaga's goal was to create a reassemblement of the

Portuguese right. This did not happen, however, because MIRN never created an organizational apparatus nor sustained more than sporadic political activity. In addition, most of the right wing is already coopted into the CDS. Converting the MIRN into the PDP and coalescing with the PDC has not altered this state of affairs and the party of the far right has failed to win seats in parliament.

Monarchist sentiments are represented by the Popular Monarchist Party (Partido Popular Monárquico: PPM). The PPM is the continuation of the Monarchist Cause and the Monarchy Electoral Committee which appeared in 1969. From the specific desire to restore the Portuguese throne to Manuel II, the movement has evolved into a political party which attempts to unite modern and conservative anarchist traditions. In its early campaigns the PPM stressed the dignity of rural life and the value of the land and the reorganization of Portugal into autonomous communes. The monarch, who would be elected, would have responsibility for overall planning and providing technical assistance to these decentralized communal units. In recent campaigns this emphasis on the land had evolved into a concern with ecological problems in general. The PPM won 0.6 percent of the vote in the constituent assembly election of 1975. Electoral support dropped to 0.5 percent in the parliamentary elections of 1976. In 1979 PPM joined the AD. This resulted in the seating of five PPM deputies in 1979 and six in 1980. Forced to run alone after the collapse of the AD, the PPM again failed to win a seat in parliament.

The ultra left in Portugal can be subdivided into four categories: radical socialists, radical communists, Trotskyists, and Maoists. Four parties fall within the radical socialist rubric. The most important is the Popular Socialist Front (Frente Socialista Popular: FSP). Originally named the Popular Socialist Movement (Movimento Socialista Popular: MSP), FSP, as was already mentioned, was led by Manuel Serra, a radical Catholic socialist and former merchant marine officer. During the New State, this group supported Humberto Delgado's FPLP. In June 1974 Serra led the MSP into a merger with the PS. Because of leadership differences Serra and his group withdrew from the PS in January 1975 and renamed themselves the FSP. In April 1978, after unsuccessfully contesting two parliamentary elections alone, the FSP coalesced with the Revolutionary Party of the Proletariat (Partido Revolucionário Proletariado: PRP) to form the United Organizations of Workers (Organização Unida de Trabalhadores: OUT).[50]

Another independent group of radical socialists is the Movement of the Socialist Left (Movimento de Esquerda Socialista: MES). The MES was organized by a group of radical socialists who had earlier detached themselves from the communist-dominated MDP/CDE. In

December 1974, the MES suffered a leadership split when a group of moderate socialist intellectuals called the Socialist Intervention Group (Grupo de Intervenção Socialista: GIS), left the party.

The two other radical socialist parties are the result of differences of opinion within the PS. The Unified Socialist Worker's Party (Partido Operário Unificado Socialista: POUS), one of these, was organized in September 1979 by Carmelinda Pereira and Aires Rodrigues, the two socialist deputies who were expelled from that party when they broke party discipline and voted against their party's budget for 1977, which they claimed had "abandoned the toiling masses." The second of these is the Left Union for Social Democracy (União de Esquerda para a Democracia Social: UEDS). The UEDS was organized in August 1979 by Lopes Cardoso, a dissident who had left the PS in January 1978. Cardoso and other radical socialists within the PS called the Association of Socialist Culture-Workers' Brotherhood accused the PS of abandoning the working class and accused Mário Soares of social democratic tendencies. After leaving the PS, Cardoso organized a political group called the Democratic and Socialist Left (Esquerda Socialista e Democrãtica), the precursor of the UEDS. In 1980 the UEDS joined the socialist-led electoral alliance FRS.

The only radical communist party is the Marxist-Leninist Communist Party of Portugal (Partido Comunista de Portugal, Marxista-Leninista: PCP, ML), a result of the general schism that emerged in the 1960s within the West European communist movement which pitted the older leadership against a new generation of radical communists. The radicals saw the established leadership as Stalinist and revisionist and, as these young radicals were beginning to identify with Maoism, sought to emphasize pure Marxism and Leninism.

The first manifestation of this split in the Portuguese context came with the organization of the Portuguese Marxist-Leninist Committee (Comité Marxista-Leninista Portuguesa: CM-LP). Splitting from the PCP in 1964, the CM-LP contained numerous factions claiming Marxist-Leninist purity. In 1968, one of these factions, led by Martins Rodrigues, left the CM-LP and later, in 1970, organized the PCP, M-L. The PCP, M-L itself contained two major factions which split the party into three groups when the party emerged from clandestinity in 1974. One faction became the Maoist, Peasants and Workers Alliance (Aliança Operária Componesa: AOC) in October 1974. A second faction became the Party of Popular Unity (Partido de Unidade Popular: PUP) in December 1974.[51] The third faction, the rump of the party, retained the PCP, M-L name.

Trotskyist tendencies are represented by the Revolutionary Party of the Workers (Partido Revolucionário dos Trabalhadores: PRT) and the International Communist League (Liga Comunista Internacionalista: LCI). These two parties were organized in the early 1970s by radical students and youths independent of other leftist parties then extant. The LCI was clandestinely organized in December 1973 by radical students and the PRT was formed in February 1975 by the coalescence of the Socialist Youth Alliance (Aliança Socialista de Juventude: ASJ), the Marxist Revolutionary Groups (Grupos Marxista Revolucionários: GMR), and militants from the radical newspaper Combate Socialista. In the autumn of 1980 the LCI and the PRT merged to form the Revolutionary Socialist Party (Partido Socialista Revolucionário: PSR).

Maoist tendencies are represented by the already mentioned AOC, the Reorganizing Movement of the Party of the Proletariat (Movimento Reorganizativo do Partido do Proletariado: MRPP) and the Popular Democratic Union (União Democrática Popular: UDP). The MRPP was organized in 1970 by members of a radical student organization called the Democratic Student Left (Esquerda Democrática Estudantil: EDE). In 1979 the MRPP changed its name to the Portuguese Workers' Communist Party (Partido Comunista de Trabalhadores Portugueses: PCTP). The UDP was formed in October 1974 by the coalescence of three Marxist-Leninist groupings: the Support Committee for the Reconstruction of the Marxist-Leninist Party (Comité de Apoio da Reconstrução do Partido Marxista-Leninista: CARP, M-L), the Marxist-Leninist Revolutionary Communist Committees (Comités Comunistas Revulucionários, Marxistas-Leninistas: CCR, M-L), and the Marxist-Leninist Revolutionary Union (União Revolucionária, Marxista-Leninista: UR, M-L). The UDP is the only extremist party of the right or left which has gained representation in parliament, having won one seat in the 1975, 1976, 1979, and 1980 elections.

As during the liberal era and the First Republic, the party system that has emerged since 1974 is quite fragmented and riven by elite rivalries. The situation is, however, different today because four parties--PCP, PS, PSD, and CDS--have fairly large bases of support, a claim that could not be made by any party previous to this time, except perhaps the PRP during the First Republic and the UN/ANP during the early years of the New State. Although factionalism has appeared within three of the major parties, elite rivalries tend to be concentrated at the left and right margins of the spectrum and tend to be a manifestation of the quest for ideological purity as well as personal interest and status. As before, these rivalries have little support beyond the elite level.

CONCLUSIONS: ELECTORAL SYSTEMS
AND PARTY SYSTEMS

The above discussion of the evolution of Portugal's party system is recapitulated graphically in Figure 5.1, which shows its development from a relatively narrow system of elite factions within the liberal fold to a full-blown multiparty system comprising the entire gamut of ideological possibilities.[52] What light does this development shed on the issue of whether constitutional or political factors account for the emergence of a multiparty system?

First, the figure clearly shows that as the party system has evolved, it has fanned out to encompass a wider variety of ideologies and, therefore, has become progressively fragmented. This fragmentation is not, however, the product of the type of electoral system in use in Portugal. Indeed, the above discussion has made clear that the electoral system itself has been a major political issue ever since the advent of liberalism in the early nineteenth century and changes in the method of choosing representation have generally followed changes in specific governments or regime types. Such changes had much to do with different conceptions among elite factions as to the degree to which the citizenry ought to be involved in electoral politics and calculations about how that involvement would impact upon their present and/or future political fortunes. The general trend has been movement from a system of restricted suffrage, indirect, limited vote, minority system to a universal suffrage, direct, proportional system. Moreover, until 1974, elections had little impact outside of the major towns, and governments were in the habit of calling elections to obtain parliamentary majorities, which was possible because of electoral fraud, corruption, and caciquismo. Thus, until recently, power emanated from the top down through a system of patron-client networks.

The fragmentation of Portugal's party system, at least until 1974, was, then, not a result of PR. It was, rather, caused by the fact that early parties were not institutions as such but were, by and large, elite factions that formed around important personalities, charismatic figures, major political office holders, and local notables. Politics functioned, therefore, on the basis of charisma, personal authority, and ambitions, not broad societal interest and ideology. Even the UN/ANP during the New State was, by and large, an elite faction, not a mass movement, composed of individuals personally loyal to Salazar.

Second, Figure 5.1 shows that the number of parties within the party system has markedly increased after certain decisive changes in regime type. Parties proliferated when Portugal became a constitutional monarchy

(1822-1834), a republic (1910), and a plural democracy (1974). The correlation between the fragmentation of the party system with sharp discontinuities in regime type suggests that "political" factors are thus determinative of Portugal's present multiparty system.

However, such a conclusion may be premature. Figure 5.1 also depicts graphically the fact that many of the parties which have appeared after dramatic changes in regime actually have connections with the past. While some parties have sprung up, de novo, out of nothing, many others, primarily the most significant ones, can be clearly linked to previous parties, movements, or ideological traditions. Indeed, the evolution of Portugal's party system, not unlike that observed for France by Berger,[53] has been one of accretion and erosion, not radical creation and elimination. The parties such as the PSD, CDS, and PPM on the right side of the present political spectrum are clearly the heirs of Portugal's monarchist/authoritarian and liberal traditions while those like the PS and the PCP on the left side are the direct descendants of the republican and socialist traditions which emerged in the middle and late nineteenth century. Thus, political factors are important, but not necessarily determinative. Multipartyism in Portugal seems to have as much to do with the elitism and personalism which has characterized much of modern Portuguese political history and continues today.

In conclusion, it can be said then that neither constitutional nor political factors are causative of Portugal's multiparty system. But, what of broad social forces? Is there any correlation between multipartyism in Portugal and the society's socio-economic cleavages? Do elite factions themselves reflect underlying social cleavages within civil society? The following chapter seeks to answer these questions.

NOTES

1. Gordon Smith, Politics in Western Europe: A Comparative Analysis (New York: Holmes & Meier, 1973), pp. 80-81.
2. See Seymour M. Lipset and Stein Rokkan, "Cleavage Structures, Party Systems, and Voter Alignments: An Introduction," in Party Systems and Voter Alignments: Cross-National Perspectives, ed. Seymore M. Lipset and Stein Rokkan (New York: The Free Press, 1967), pp. 1-64; Seymour M. Lipset, "Party Systems and the Representation of Social Groups," in Readings in Modern Political Analysis, ed. Robert A. Dahl and D. E. Neubauer (Englewood Cliffs, N.J.: Prentice-Hall, 1968), pp. 84-114; Richard Rose and Derek W. Urwin, "Social Cohesion, Political Parties and Strains in Regimes," Comparative Political Studies 2 (April 1969): 7-67; Erik Allardt and Stein Rokkan, Mass Politics (New York: The Free Press, 1970); Richard Rose, Electoral Behavior: A Comparative Handbook (New York:

110

MONARCHY	CONSTITUTIONAL MONARCHY	FIRST REPUBLIC	ARMY
1800 1836		1910	1926
MIGUELISTS		LUSITANIAN INTEGRALISM	
	CHARTISTS REGENERATORS	PORT. ROYALIST ACTION	
		MONARCHIST CAUSE	
		PORT. CATHOLIC CTR.	
	HISTORICALS PROGRESSIVES	LIBERAL UNION	
	SEPTEMBERISTS REFORMISTS	NATIONALIST PARTY	
	REPUBLICANISM PRP	REPUBLIC ACTION	
	UTOPIAN SOCIALISM	DEMOCRATS	
	SOCIALISM	RADICALS	
LIBERALS		PORT. MAXIMALIST FEDERATION	

- - - - - Denotes clandestine existence

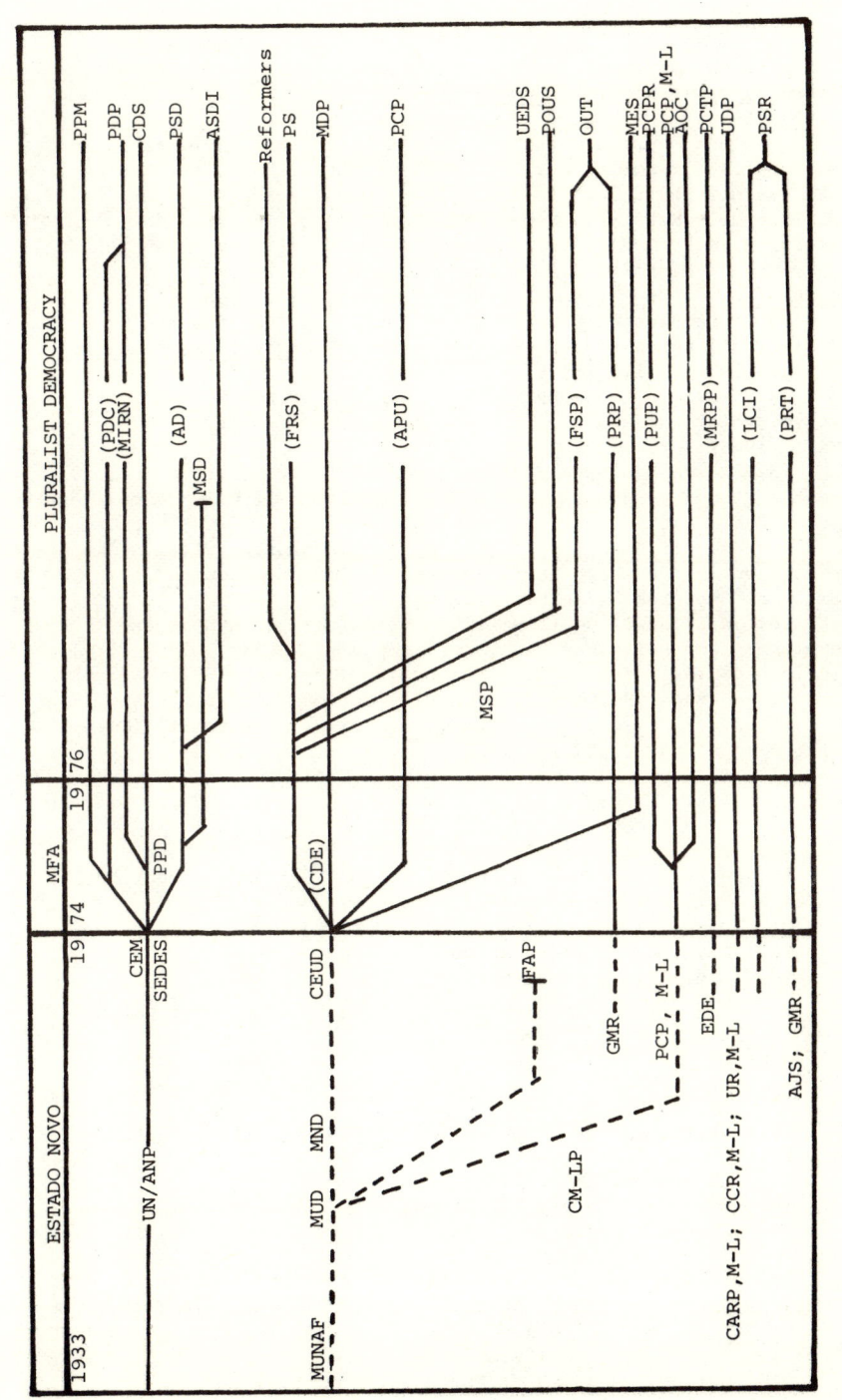

Figure 5.1 The evolution of the Portuguese party system

The Free Press, 1974); and Frank H. Aarebrot and Derek W. Urwin, "Politics of Cultural Dissent: Religion, Language, and Demonstrative Effects in Norway," Scandinavian Political Studies 2 (Spring 1979): 75-98.

3. See Maurice Duverger, Political Parties (New York: Methuen, 1954); Colin Leys, "Electoral Systems and Party Systems: The Duverger Doctrine," in Comparative Government: A Reader, ed. Jean Blondel (New York: Macmillan, 1969), pp. 138-141; and William H. Riker, "The Two-Party System and Duverger's Law: An Essay on the History of Political Science," American Political Science Review 76 (December 1982): 753-766. See also, W. Philips Shively, "The Elusive Psychological Factor: A Test for the Impact of Electoral Systems on Voters' Behavior," Comparative Politics 3 (October 1970): 115-125.

4. Gerhard Loewenberg, "The Remaking of the German Party System: Political and Socio-Economic Factors," Polity 1 (Fall, 1968): 89.

5. Gosta Esping-Anderson, "Social Class, Social Democracy, and the State: Party Policy and Party Decomposition in Denmark and Sweden," Comparative Politics 11 (October 1978): 42-48; and Sten Berglund and Ulf Linstrom, "The Scandinavian Party System(s) in Transition (?): A Macro-Level Analysis," European Journal of Political Research 7 (1979): 187-204.

6. William Claggett et al., "Political Leadership and the Development of Political Cleavages: Imperial Germany, 1871-1912," American Journal of Political Science 26 (November 1982): 643-663.

7. Suzanne Berger, "The Development of the Party System," in Patterns of Government, 3rd ed., Samuel H. Beer et al. (New York: Random House, 1973), p. 386.

8. Stanley G. Payne, A History of Spain and Portugal, Vol. 2 (Madison, Wis.: The University of Wisconsin Press, 1973), pp. 513-517.

9. Ibid., pp. 526-528.

10. H. V. Livermore, A New History of Portugal (Cambridge: Cambridge University Press, 1969), pp. 287-288.

11. Payne, A History of Spain and Portugal, Vol. 2, p. 532.

12. A. H. de Oliveira Marques, History of Portugal, Vol. 2 (New York: Columbia University Press, 1976), pp. 47-48.

13. Douglas L. Wheeler, Republican Portugal: A Political History, 1910-1926 (Madison, Wis.: The University of Wisconsin Press, 1978), pp. 32-34.

14. Ibid., p. 43.

15. Ibid., pp. 82-83.

16. Ibid., p. 85; and Payne, A History of Spain and Portugal, Vol. 2, p. 561.

17. Ibid., pp. 268-270.

18. Marques, History of Portugal, pp. 160-162.

19. Payne, A History of Spain and Portugal, Vol. 2, pp. 572-574.

20. Philippe C. Schmitter, "Portée et Signification des Elections dans le Portugal Autoritaire (1933-1974)," in Elections without Choice, ed. G. Hermet, R. Rose, and A. Rouquie (London: Macmillan, 1978), pp. 92-122.

21. Marques, History of Portugal, pp. 191-192.

22. Hermínio Martins, "Opposition in Portugal," Government and Opposition 4 (Spring 1969): 253. See also Hugh Kay, Salazar and Modern Portugal (New York: Hawthorn, 1970), Chap. 11.
23. Mário Soares, Portugal's Struggle for Liberty (London: Allen & Unwin, 1975), Chap. 4; and António de Figueiredo, Portugal: Fifty Years of Dictatorship (New York: Holmes & Meier, 1976), chap. 5.
24. Ibid.
25. Soares, Portugal's Struggle for Liberty, pp. 250-261.
26. Martins, "Opposition in Portugal," p. 254.
27. Soares, Portugal's Struggle for Liberty, pp. 31-35.
28. Reports of investigations of the murders carried out after April 25, 1974 can be found in Expresso, No. 260, October 22, 1977.
29. After the golpe the BR emerged from clandestinity and renamed itself the Popular Revolutionary Party (Partido Revolucionário Popular: PRP). The PRP was outlawed for its involvement in the unsuccessful golpe of November 25, 1975 attempted by extreme left-wing groups. Legalized later, the PRP unsuccessfully campaigned in 1976, calling for abstention from "bourgeois" elections.
30. Norman Blume, "SEDES: An Example of Opposition in a Conservative Authoritarian State," Government and Opposition 12 (Summer, 1977): 351-366.
31. The following discussion of these parties is drawn in part from Ben Pimlott, "Parties and Voters in the Portuguese Revolution: The Elections of 1975 and 1976," Parliamentary Affairs 30 (Winter 1977): 37-43; and Howard J. Wiarda, "Spain and Portugal," in Western European Party Systems, ed. Peter H. Merkl (New York: The Free Press, 1980), pp. 298-328.
32. Soares, Portugal's Struggle for Liberty.
33. See Tom Gallagher, "Portugal's Bid for Democracy: The Role of the Socialist Party," West European Politics 2 (May 1979): 198-217.
34. Ibid.
35. The statistical details of this election and subsequent ones will be presented in the next chapter.
36. Tom Gallagher, "The Growing Pains of Portuguese Democracy," The World Today 37 (February 1981): 102-109.
37. After leaving PS, the FSP contested the 1975 constituent assembly and 1976 parliamentary elections alone and received only 1.2 and 0.8 percent of the vote, respectively. In April 1978, the FSP coalesced with the Revolutionary Party of the Proletariat (Partido Revolucionário do Proletariado: PRP) to form the United Organization of Workers (Organização Unida de Trabalhadores: OUT).
38. The two PS deputies in question were Carmalinda Pereira and Aires Rodrigues. The POUS received only 0.2 percent of the vote in the interim parliamentary elections of 1979 and 1.4 percent in the regular parliamentary elections in 1980.
39. This split had to do with a controversy that developed during the first socialist government (July 1976-December 1977) over the way Barreto was handling the question of land reform. It was perceived by many socialists that the price Barreto, a latecomer to the party, demanded from the party was too high for his

support of and role in the second PS government. Consequently, he was dropped from the government but permitted to remain in the party. After the collapse of the PS-CDS government, Barreto and others, who were known as the Reformers (Reformadores), developed a close relationship with President Eanes. When the PS voted against Eanes' non-party government headed by Nobre de Costa, the Reformers bolted from the party and later allied themselves with AD.

40. Expresso, No. 442, April 17, 1981.
41. Ibid.
42. Ibid., No. 473, November 21, 1981.
43. The MSD subsequently dissipated as an organized group.
44. In October 1980, the ASDI joined with the PS and the UEDS to form the FRS electoral alliance.
45. Expresso, No. 520, October 16, 1982.
46. The PDC emerged after April 25, 1974 as the chief party of the ultraconservative right. In January 1975, in preparation for the constituent assembly elections, the PDC joined with the CDS to form an electoral coalition called the Union of the Christian Democratic Center (União do Centro Democrata Cristã: UCDC).
47. Expresso, No. 518, October 2, 1982.
48. In addition to Pimlott, "Parties and Voters in the Portuguese Revolution" and Wiarda, "Spain and Portugal," this discussion of the PCP draws from the following: Eusébio M. Mujal-León, "The PCP and the Portuguese Revolution, Problems of Communism 26 (January-February 1977): 21-41; Eusébio M. Mujal-León, "Portuguese and Spanish Communism in Comparative Perspective," in The Many Faces of Communism, ed. Morton A. Kaplan (New York: The Free Press, 1978), pp. 122-145; Philippe Schmitter, "Le Parti Communiste Portugais entre Le 'Pouvoir Social' et le 'Pouvoir Politique,'" Etudes Internationales (September 1975): 375-388; Kenneth Maxwell, "Portuguese Communism" in Euro-Communism: The Ideological and Political-Theoretical Foundation, ed. George Schwab (Westport, Conn.: Greenwood Press, 1981), pp. 269-303; and Manuel Villaverde Cabral, "The Portuguese Communist Party: The Weight of Fifty Years of History," in National Communism in Western Europe: A Third Way to Socialism, ed. Howard Machin (London/New York: Methuen, 1983), pp. 180-199.
49. This strategy was employed with special vigor after AD's tandem electoral victories in 1979 and 1980.
50. The OUT was led by Major Otelo Saraiva de Carvalho, the former charismatic commander of COPCON. Relieved of his command after being implicated in the attempted left-wing golpe of November 25, 1975, Otelo ran in the presidential election of June 1976 as a candidate of the extreme left. He made a second unsuccessful bid for the presidency in December 1979.
51. After contesting the 1975 constituent assembly elections, the PUP itself splintered into two groups: one called itself the Portuguese Marxist-Leninist Committee (Comité Marxista-Leninista Português: CM-LP) (not to be confused with an earlier party of the same name). The splinter group supported the Popular Democratic Union (União Democrática Popular: UDP). The rump of the

PUP renamed itself the Reconstituted Portuguese Communist Party (<u>Partido Comunista Português, Reconstruido</u>: PCP, R).

    52. Parties professing a fascist ideology are forbidden by the constitution.

    53. Berger, "The Development of the Party System."

6
Elections:
Socio-Economic Ecologies and Voting Behavior

In the previous chapter it was shown that there is no clear and precise connection between Portugal's multipartyism and the electoral system. While a certain correlation between the configuration of the party system and political factors was noted, the relationship was not a clear and precise one in which sharp political changes produced radically new parties. It was shown that Portugal's party system developed by an evolutionary process of accretion and erosion, the multiplicity of parties being until recently primarily little more than elite factions within broader political traditions.

What of socioeconomic cleavages? Does Portugal's multiparty system reflect in any way the country's class and regional differences? Have such variations been manifested in electoral support for the various parties? Assuming that such a connection is present, has voting around socioeconomic cleavages been stable over time or have there been significant oscillations in such behavior?

The question of the relationship between socioeconomic cleavages and electoral behavior has generated two positions in the theoretical literature on this issue within the West European research tradition. On the one hand, it has been argued that without a history of electoral experience, party identification and loyalty will be weak; consequently, electoral behavior will be unstable, prone to capricious fluctuations among parties and the "flash" party phenomenon.[1] On the other hand, it has been suggested that this argument about weak partisanship and electoral instability does not apply to West European electorates among whom the choice of party is made much more instrumentally; that is, by the voter's sense of socioeconomic differences and conflict and his or her place within that conflict. In these systems, it has been argued, stable voting patterns have appeared early, practically at the moment of their creation, and have changed very little over time. Voting behavior in such systems, then, is not a measure of the identification of the voter with a particular party but, rather, an expression of immediate voting choice.[2]

The purpose of this chapter is to examine the evolution of Portuguese voting behavior in order to determine, first, if there is any correlation between voting for the various parties on the spectrum and socioeconomic cleavages and, second, to see if the patterns observed are stable over time. The chapter will conclude with a discussion of these as well as the previous chapter's findings as they relate to the determinants of Portugal's party system and the behavior of the electorate.

SOCIETAL CLEAVAGES AND VOTING BEHAVIOR BEFORE 1974

It has been argued that there is a strong connection between Portuguese politics and socioeconomic cleavages that goes back to the eighteenth century, if not earlier. In this view, Portugal, like France, has been divided into two primary social blocs, one rural and the other urban. The urban bloc is bourgeois, secular, rationalist, outward and West European-looking, and nascently democratic and equalitarian. The rural bloc is two-class, traditional, "feudal," religious, inward-looking, hierarchical, and authoritarian. According to this view these two fundamental blocs have structured Portuguese politics into two corresponding political "families": the family of order and the family of change.[3]

While there is no doubt that the rise of liberalism and the instauration of the First Republic in the broadest sense represent the victory of the urban bloc and the advent of the New State the counter-victory of the rural bloc, this generalization does not explain narrower partisan electoral behavior. As was discussed in the previous chapter, partisan politics during the liberal era as well as the First Republic was not structured by conflict between urban and rural sectors but rivalry among elite factions situated within the major towns and cities, especially Lisbon and Porto. The support bases of the contending elites consisted, for the most part, of narrow urban classes such as artisans for the Septemberists and the petty bourgeoisie for the republicans. The advent of the First Republic did not structure political conflict around urban-rural differences nor did political parties have any more societal support than previously. By and large, partisan conflict in Portugal, until recently, has been restricted to cliques and elite factions with little or no involvement of significant numbers of ordinary individuals.

The franchise during the liberal era and First Republic was greatly restricted by literacy and tax-paying requirements. Moreover, throughout both periods electoral corruption was widespread, and in rural areas, caciques manipulated the politically relevant population; that is, the wafer-thin sector of the populace who could meet the tax-paying and literacy requirements. Political activity reflected personalism, charisma, and patron-client networks not underlying socioeconomic cleavages, in general, or the urban-rural "families" dichotomy, in particular. The effect of caciquismo on voting behavior can be seen in Figure 6.1, which presents the geographic distribution of the constituencies in which each party was victorious in the 1915 election for the Congress of the Republic. The map does not show any clear dichotomy between urban and rural zones, or any other pattern for that matter. The geographical distribution of constituencies where parties which opposed the PRP were victorious reflects not socioeconomic cleavages but, rather, the personal influence of local caciques.[4]

Although, as has been discussed, the New State involved the mobilization of Portugal's provinces, especially the Catholic north against cosmopolitan and secular Lisbon, politics during this period continued to be an elite activity. Even though the franchise was gradually expanded to include college educated women and female heads of households and the number of individuals who met the literacy and tax-paying requirement increased, as can be seen in Table 6.1, electoral turnout for the National Assembly remained low. Voter registration was not encouraged. Oppositionist activity too was quite elitist in nature, and, as was shown in the previous chapter, riven by factionalism and personalism.

By the late 1960s and early 1970s, however, the beginnings of a systematic connection between partisan political activity and broad social and economic forces was being manifested in Portuguese electoral behavior. In his analysis of the seventeen general elections held during the New State, especially those of 1969 and 1973, Schmitter observed correlations between the vote for the government's UN/ANP, rates of abstention, and non-voting and broad socio-economic categories. He found that votes for the UN/ANP tended to come from northern constituencies and was strongest among small farmers, practicing Catholics, and illiterates. He also found that correlations between abstentions and non-voting and socioeconomic variables tended to be higher among the bourgeoisie, industrial workers, non-practicing Catholics, and literates.[5] These connections can be seen in Figure 6.2, which shows the distribution of the vote for the semi-legal opposition (CDE and CEUD) in the 1969 National Assembly elections. Figure 6.2 clearly shows the opposition running well in Lisbon and its industrial suburbs, parts of the Alentejo, and along the northern littoral, the most urbanized region of the country.

120

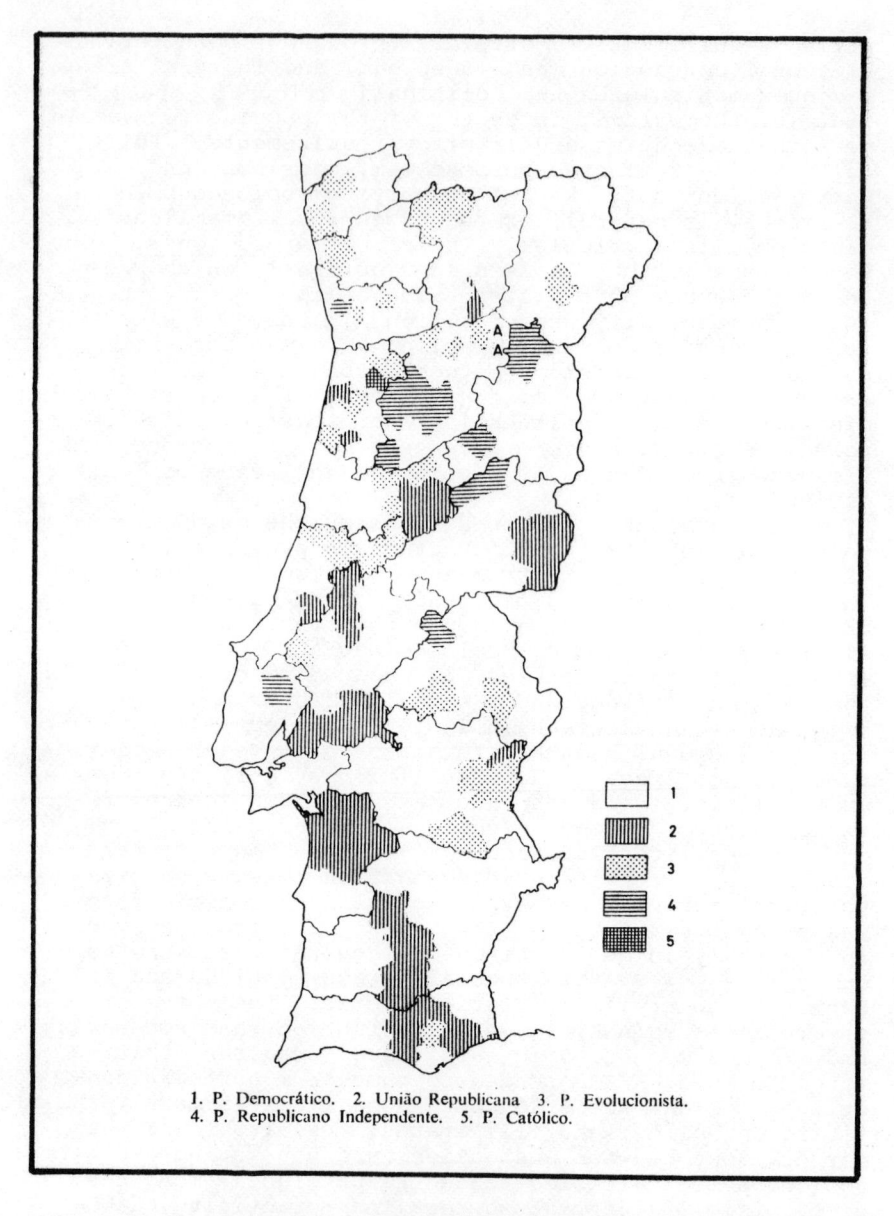

Figure 6.1   Distribution of the vote for the winning
             parties in the 1915 election, by concelho

Source: Jorge Gaspar and Nuno Vitorino, As Eleições de
         25 de Abril (Lisbon: Livros Horizonte, 1976),
         p. 24.

These patterns suggest that by the end of the New State, partisan political activity and the mobilization of voters was beginning to be structured by broad social and economic forces and prefigured future patterns.

TABLE 6.1
Turnout for National Assembly elections, 1934-1973

Year	Total Population	Number of Registered Voters	Number of Votes	% of Voters	% of Population
1934	7,148,046	478,121	337,792	79.0	5.3
1938	7,505,554	777,033	649,028	83.5	8.6
1942	7,830,026	772,578	668,578	86.6	8.5
1945	8,045,774	992,723	569,257	57.3	7.1
1949	8,333,400		948,695		11.4
1953	8,621,102	1,351,192	991,161	73.4	11.5
1957	8,908,766	1,427,427	1,030,891	72.2	11.6
1961	8,932,000	1,440,148	1,112.557	77.3	12.0
1965	9,234,400	1,609,485	1,211,577	75.3	13.1
1969	9,582,600	1,784,314	1,115,248	62.5	11.6
1973	8,564,200	1,965,717	1,320,952	67.2	15.4

Source: Philippe C. Schmitter, "Portée et Signification des Elections dans le Portugal Autoritaire (1933-1974)," in *Elections without Choice*, ed. G. Hermet et al. (London: Macmillan, 1978), p. 94.

SOCIAL CLEAVAGES AND VOTING AFTER 1974

The election of a constituent assembly on April 25, 1975 was the first election held under the conditions of universal suffrage in Portuguese history, and, perhaps, the country's first truly free election ever.[6] As can be seen in Figure 6.3, which shows the 1975 constituent assembly vote for the four major parties--PCP, PS, PPD/PSD, and CDS--there appears for the first time a clear connection between voting and broad socioeconomic ecologies. The vote for these parties is neatly arranged into northern and southern as well as urban and rural zones of support.

These two zones have different histories and socioeconomic characteristics which influence northerners to support parties of the center and right (primarily PSD and CDS) and southerners parties of the left (principally PCP but also PS). The north is more conservative, traditional, and Catholic. The Portuguese spoken

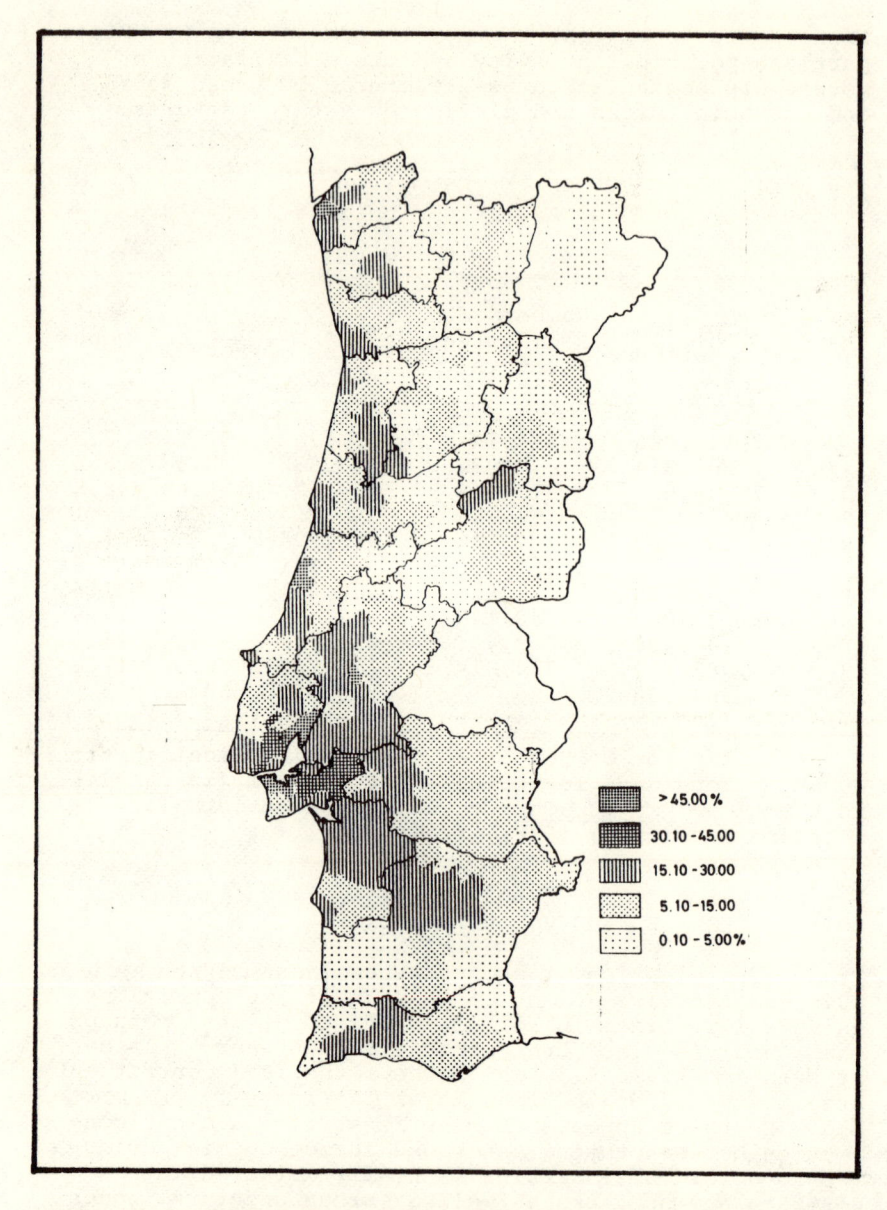

Figure 6.2   Distribution of the vote for the democratic opposition (CDE + CEUD) in the 1969 election, by concelho

Source: Jorge Gaspar and Nuno Vitorina, <u>As Eleições de 25 de Abril</u> (Lisbon: Livros Norizonte, 1976), p. 28.

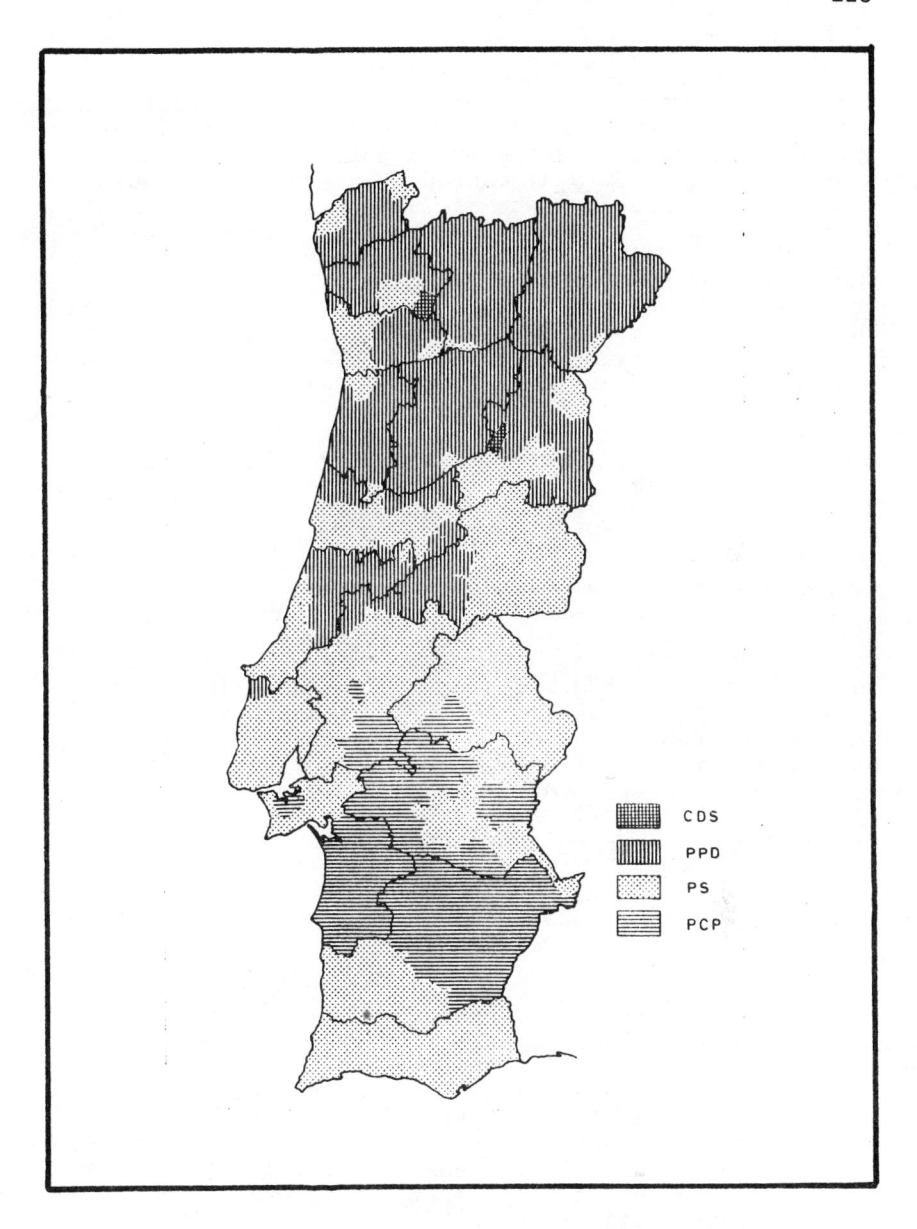

Figure 6.3   Distribution of the vote for the four major
             parties in 1975, by concelho

Source: Jorge Gaspar and Nuno Vitorino, As Eleições de
         25 de Abril (Lisbon: Livros Horizonte, 1976),
         p. 25.

in the north is close to Galician Spanish and, as was discussed in Chapter 2, is the region of the country where the nation was born. In the north the dominant form of agriculture is the small parcel of owned or rented land (<u>minifundia</u>) manned by a strong and independent class of peasants who eke out an existence on the region's mountainous terrain. Agriculture is labor intensive. Mechanization has not occurred because of the small size of the farms and rough terrain; therefore, entire families work the land as a unit. These factors have reinforced the traditional family structure and the church remains a viable social force. Even in the urban and industrial zones of the north, these patterns prevail. Factories and businesses are family affairs and employees often maintain a small farm on the side. Thus, urbanization and industrialization have not broken down the tight-knit and self-reliant families and individualism of the northerner to the extent that it has elsewhere in Portugal.[7]

The south, or Alentejo, in contrast, was until 1974 a region of large parcels of land (<u>latifundia</u>) and large factories where prevailed a two-class system consisting of landowners and a large class of landless peasants who worked for wages as day laborers. These peasants lived in towns and, if they were factory workers, large cities like Lisbon and Setúbal. Agriculture was much more mechanized than in the north and agricultural workers were much less traditional and conservative. Migration to the factories, which were large, often foreign-owned concerns, had the effect of breaking down the traditional family. The church in the south is comparatively weak.[8]

According to Hammond, these two contrasting socioeconomic ecologies influenced party support and electoral behavior by predisposing

> southern agricultural workers to opposition [to the New State] . . . and contributed to the development of a radical political consciousness, largely channeled by the Communist Party, while northern small holders were predisposed to apolitical but implicitly conservative views. These patterns carried over to some extent to urban industrial workers in north and south, since migrants to cities tended to come from the rural area nearest those cities.[9]

Furthermore, Hammond suggests that:

> Structural conditions in industry further contributed to making southern industrial workers more radical than northern industrial workers: though the north is proportionately slightly more industrialized than the south, its industry is more

dispersed, industrial enterprises are somewhat smaller, and many industrial workers are able to maintain small plots of land. The southern industrial workers are concentrated into larger plants and are geographically concentrated in the Lisbon-Setúbal belt.[10]

An urban-rural cleavage can also be seen in Figure 6.3 as exemplified by the vote for the PS. The socialist vote is strongest in urban areas, even in the north. Thus, in the north, the vote for PS is on average higher in the metropolitan areas of Porto and Coimbra and, in the south, it is high in the Algarve where there is considerable urbanization. The PS also ran well in what might be called the central zone of the country; that is, the midsection between north and south. This is due to the fact that the socioeconomic ecologies of the center share characteristics of both northern and southern zones. Thus, support for PS is high in Portalegre despite its geographic location in the Alentejo because it does not have all of the socioeconomic characteristics of the "deep" south. In similar manner, support for PS is high in Leiria, Santarém, and Castelo Branco because these districts, although situated to the north of the Tejo, do not share all northern socioeconomic characteristics. The only variation in the support for PS in the central region is the high turnout for PSD in the north of Leiria and Santarém. This is produced by the presence of the religious shrine of Fátima, which is situated in the extreme north of Santarém, literally in the center of this PSD anomaly. This area is, therefore, more strongly Catholic and conservative than would be otherwise expected and has a tradition of supporting conservative and Catholic parties that dates to the First Republic.[11]

The presence of clear linkages between party support and broad social forces does not mean, however, that caciquismo is no longer relevant. It has been argued that the vote for CDS, which is high in the north, especially in the interior districts of Bragança, Viseu, and Guarda, but somewhat randomly distributed within them, is probably produced by the action of caciques, particularly local notables and priests.[12]

The connection between party support and broad socioeconomic differences can also be seen by analyzing voting behavior according to labor force sector. Table 6.2, which presents the percentages of votes in various labor force categories who voted for each party, shows that tertiary workers tended to vote PCP and to a considerable degree PS. Self-employed agricultural or primary workers tended to vote CDS or PSD while those who were employed by others tended to vote for PS and PCP. The north-south cleavage can be seen in the voting of workers in the secondary sector. Secondary workers in

TABLE 6.2
Vote for CDS, PSD, PS, and PCP by labor sector, 1976

Sector	Percent			
	CDS	PSD	PS	PCD
Rural North				
Primary, self-employed	20	63	2	-3
Primary, employed	13	45	22	2
Secondary	18	45	25	3
Tertiary	-16	-20	92	21
Urban North				
Primary, self-employed	25	51	9	-3
Primary, employed	-5	9	40	16
Secondary	12	24	48	5
Tertiary	5	30	44	11
Rural South				
Primary, self-employed	4	20	45	-18
Primary, employed	2	2	32	55
Secondary	3	16	46	15
Tertiary	2	8	60	9
Urban North				
Primary	6	14	59	1
Secondary	-4	-3	30	59
Tertiary	9	20	51	7

Note: Figures are regression estimates of the percentage of voters in each labor-force category by party. Because of their small numbers in the urban south, reliable separate estimates for farmworkers and self-employed farmers were not possible.

Source: John L. Hammond, "Electoral Behavior and Political Militancy," in *Contemporary Portugal: The Revolution and Its Antecedents*, ed. Lawrence S. Graham and Harry M. Makler (Austin, Texas: University of Texas Press, 1979), p. 264.

the north tended to vote PSD and CDS along with rural proprietors. In the south, they tended to vote PS and in the south's urban areas, PCP. In both north and south secondary workers gave some support to PS.

The degree of urbanization and Catholicism were differently related to vote in the north and south. In the south, support for PSD and CDS tended to be higher in urban areas than rural while in the north the relationship was the reverse. In the north, support for PS and PCP was highest in the urban areas. Practicing Catholic voters overwhelmingly supported CDS and PSD. The relationship between Catholicism and right-of-center voting was strongest in northern rural areas and southern urban areas.

As was mentioned above, support for PS is strongest in urban areas and in the central zone between the north and south. In the 1975 election, PS was also able to capture support from a variety of social, economic, and regional groups. From Table 6.2 it can be seen that nationally the only consistent source of support for PS came from tertiary workers. In other sections PS support varied considerably more from north to south. In the south the socialists were supported by rural proprietors and, in the north, by rural employed workers. The party did well among secondary sector workers in the north but not as well among such workers in the south where they were attracted by PCP. The PS was rejected in the strongest Catholic areas of the north but was able to attract Catholic support in the urban areas of the south.

The correlations in Table 6.2 show that in general the parties of the center-right, PSD and CDS, were strongly supported in rural regions of low prosperity and strong Catholicism in the north while PCP was supported in the rural areas of the "deep" south by employed workers. The vote for the right was highest, thus, in the poorest, most traditional, most remote, backward areas of the country. Support for PS, more than any other party, cut across all classes, regions, and urban-rural dichotomies. For all intents and purposes, PS appeared in 1975 to be Portugal's first "catch-all" party capable of commanding a broad center of the political spectrum.

Thus, in Portugal's first free election under conditions of universal suffrage, the electorate voted in some clear and well-defined patterns of party support which correlate extremely well with broad social forces and regional dichotomies. The outcome of the 1975 election did not have the random and capricious configuration that would be expected by party identification theory, a randomness that did, however, exist during the liberal era and the First Republic. But perhaps the 1975 results were unique, a function of the events surrounding the establishment of a new political regime.

Have these patterns been maintained in subsequent elections or have fundamental realignments taken place? In other words, has a stable pattern of voting emerged? The answer to these questions is given in the following section.

ELECTORAL DYNAMICS SINCE 1974

The figures presented in Table 6.3 provide a statistical overview of the electoral trends in Portugal since 1974. The numbers in the table represent the proportion of the registered voters which supported each party in the first four parliamentary elections held since April 25, 1974.[14] Since all eligible individuals are registered in Portugal,[15] these figures also allow the estimation of the changing magnitude of non-voting in Portuguese elections.[16]

TABLE 6.3
Nonvoters and party vote as a proportion of the eligible electorate

Election	PCP	PS	PSD+CDS (AD)	Other	Non-voters
All Concelhos (N = 301)					
1975	.117	.349	.308	.143	.083
1976	.123	.292	.329	.088	.168
1979	.166	.243	.393	.072	.126
1980	.145	.240	.402	.068	.145
Northern Concelhos (N = 214)					
1975	.050	.312	.417	.136	.086
1976	.053	.278	.412	.085	.172
1979	.095	.257	.452	.069	.127
1980	.080	.243	.459	.067	.151
Southern Concelhos (N = 86)					
1975	.219	.406	.145	.153	.077
1976	.231	.313	.202	.093	.161
1979	.281	.220	.299	.077	.124
1980	.249	.234	.311	.069	.136

The "other" category in the table consists of all voters who did not support either PCP, PS or AD (PSD and CDS prior to 1975). Except for the PPM in 1975 and 1976 and the PDP in 1980, these marginal parties are of the extreme left. As the PPM accounted for only .006 percent of the vote in 1975 and .005 percent in 1976 and the PDC received a scant .004 percent in 1980, the "other" category is considered to be composed of supporters of the radical socialist, radical communist, Maoists, and Trotskyists on the extreme left of the political spectrum.

Separate figures are also reported for the northern and southern regions of the country, as well as for the nation as a whole. Regional figures are presented in order to determine if the dynamic of change is different within Portugal's contrasting north-south socioeconomic zones.

The most obvious trend that can be seen in Table 6.3 is the .109 decline in support for PS in the nation as a whole between 1975 and 1980 and the .094 increase in AD support during the same period. This trend compelled some scholars as well as knowledgeable Portuguese observers to conclude that during this period the "Italianization" of Portugal's party system had begun.[17] That is, to use Sartori's nomenclature, a situation of "polarized pluralism" was developing in which a large center-right bloc and a strong anti-system communist party confront one another while socialist voters, caught in between, flow to one or both of the extremes, in this case, primarily toward the center-right.[18] However, as will be shown below, this characterization greatly oversimplifies the actual dynamics of the changes that have occurred since the 1975 constituent assembly election because it pays too much attention to the losses by PS and the gains of the AD and PCP without considering the impact on these changes of defections from the extreme left, nonvoting, and new voters. Moreover, the results of the 1983 elections suggest that these changes were more apparent than real.

As was discussed above, the different socioeconomic ecologies between northern and southern Portugal are associated with different levels of support for the parties. Changes in such levels of support constitute an important aspect of the dynamic of Portugal's party system. An examination of the regional breakdowns in Table 6.3 shows that AD grew, both absolutely and proportionately, much more rapidly in the south than in the north. PS, on the other hand, lost the least in the north. Thus, in relative terms, both of these parties made their greatest gains, or smallest losses, in each other's regional strongholds. The pattern of change for the other parties and nonvoters, on the other hand, is similar across regions. These findings suggest that the Portuguese party system was more "nationalized" in 1980 than it was in 1975; that is, the variation in party support across geographical regions is much less in 1980 than in 1975.

This does not mean, however, that geographic bases of support are no longer relevant. Table 6.4 examines the geographical coherence of each party's support over time; that is, the degree to which areas of relative strength in 1975 persisted in 1980. This was accomplished by correlating each party's proportion of the registered voters in the election of 1975 with its proportion in 1980.[19] For all but the extreme left, the parties still show a substantial degree of geographical coherence.

TABLE 6.4
The correlation between the proportion of eligibles supporting the same party in 1975 and 1980

	PCP	PS	AD	Other	Non-voters
All Concelhos	.978	.784	.922	.438	.704
Northern Concelhos	.960	.857	.859	.350	.626
Southern Concelhos	.951	.742	.882	.473	.803

However, the geographical coherence of PS and nonvoters is substantially less than that of either PCP or AD. The correlations for PS imply that this party did not lose the same proportion of its 1975 supporters in every area as might be expected if its losses were simple reactions to nationwide, short-term forces engendered by unpopular policies or poor leadership. Rather, the correlations are indicative of a general weakening or unraveling of the party's 1975 mass electoral base. It may be that between 1975 and 1980 PS was collapsing from a broad but weakly rooted coalition in 1975, whose purpose it was to defeat efforts of PCP to establish a communist dictatorship, to a more narrowly but firmer-based party in 1980.

The dynamics of the changes which occurred between 1975 and 1980 can be determined by examining the origins and destinations of voters across the four elections. Table 6.5 portrays the correlations between the change in a party's proportion of registered voters between 1975 and 1980 (proportion in 1980 minus proportion in 1975) with the support bases of the various parties in 1975. These correlations indicate the 1975 political coloration of the areas in which the parties experienced their largest and smallest gains and losses. For a particular party, a positive correlation implies that it experienced its largest gains (or smallest declines) in areas of its greatest strength in 1975.

TABLE 6.5
The correlation between partisan change between 1980 and 1975 and the support level of each party in 1975

Change in Support Level	1975 Support Level for				
	PCP	PS	AD	Other	Non-voting
All Concelhos					
PCP	.203*	.366	-.374	.322	-.283
PS	-.561	-.779	.798	-.272	.387
AD	.529	.644	-.801	.580	-.211
Other	-.130	-.199	.436	-.929	-.116
Nonvoters	-.209	-.065	.142	.018	.116
Northern Concelhos					
PCP	.264	.432	-.435	.316	-.314
PS	-.451	-.751	.753	.345	.173
AD	.389	.574	-.734	.659	.035
Other	-.155	-.221	.513	-.941	-.169
Nonvoters	-.130	-.062	.086	.012	-.001
Southern Concelhos					
PCP	-.124	.148	-.101	.241	-.109
PS	.063	-.536	.028	.496	-.375
AD	-.106	-.118	.221	-.057	-.263
Other	.289	.287	-.122	-.894	-.378
Nonvoters	-.297	.242	.005	.202	.401

*Table entries are Pearson's rs.

The clearest pattern that emerges from the correlations in Table 6.5 is the difference between PCP and the remaining parties in terms of that party's ability to build on its existing base of support. Only PCP tended to register its largest gains in areas where it was already strong. For PS, AD, and the other parties, the greatest gains (or smallest losses) came in areas in which they did relatively poorly in 1975. Only the "party" of nonvoters resembles PCP in this regard; that is, growing where nonvoting was already prevalent. The correlations also show that PCP achieved its greatest gains in areas where PS and the other parties were the strongest in 1975. On the other hand, AD experienced its largest gains in areas where, in 1975, PCP, PS, and other parties were strong. The largest gains (or smallest losses) for PS occurred in only two areas: areas where AD and nonvoting were strong in 1975. The other parties lost the most in areas of strength for all parties except AD. Finally, the correlations indicate that the changes in nonvoting show little or no relationship to support bases in 1980.

The correlations in Table 6.5 provide the first clue about the flow of individuals among the parties between 1975 and 1980. Table 6.6, which displays the correlations between the change in each party's proportion of the registered voters between 1975 and 1980, continues this search. Negative correlations imply that areas in which one party experienced the most favorable change between 1975 and 1980 were areas where the other party experienced the least favorable change in their electoral fortunes. Positive correlations indicate that the relative fortunes of both parties tended to change in the same way over time. The data in Table 6.6 suggest that the same three pools of individuals—former PS voters, other party supporters, and previous nonvoters—may have fueled the expansion of the two parties which grew between 1975 and 1980; that is, AD and PCP. At the very least, these data suggest a more complex partisan dynamic than the simple movement of PS supporters to the extremes.

Unfortunately, several problems plague this analysis. First, one possible source of new voters for PCP and AD in 1980 is those individuals who came of age between 1975 and 1980. These individuals are excluded from the above analysis. Second, the correlations in Table 6.6 are zero-order correlations; that is, they do not show the change relationship between two parties while controlling for the changes in a third and, therefore, the correlations may be spurious. Finally, the negative correlations have been interpreted to mean that one party is gaining and the other party losing votes across areas. This is certainly one possibility. But it is not the only possibility because a negative correlation could arise between two parties even though both parties gained votes in every area (i.e., if one party's largest gains occurred only in areas where the other party's gains were the smallest). Hence, it would be difficult to argue in this case that one party's former supporters fueled the expansion of the other party.

To rectify these problems the 1980 registered voters were partitioned into subgroups on the basis of which party they supported in 1975 including nonvoters and into new voters.[20] This procedure gives the proportion of each of these groups which supported a particular party in 1980 or became nonvoters in 1980. To determine these proportions regression equations were estimated.[21]

TABLE 6.6
Correlations between the degree of partisan change for all parties, 1975-1980

	\multicolumn{5}{c}{1975-1980}
1975-1980	PCP	PS	AD	Other	Non-voters
\multicolumn{6}{c}{All Concelhos}
PCP	1.0*				
PS	-.405	1.0			
AD	.269	-.824	1.0		
Other	-.321	.191	-.573	1.0	
Nonvoters	-.236	.112	-.379	.053	1.0
\multicolumn{6}{c}{Northern Concelhos}
PCP	1.0				
PS	-.263	1.0			
AD	.206	-.796	1.0		
Other	-.297	.260	-.659	1.0	
Nonvoters	-.216	.038	-.383	.058	1.0
\multicolumn{6}{c}{Southern Concelhos}
PCP	1.0				
PS	-.455	1.0			
AD	.133	-.460	1.0		
Other	-.305	-.479	-.121	1.0	
Nonvoters	-.275	.070	-.416	-.074	1.0

*Table entries are Pearson's rs.

The results of these regression analyses are displayed in Table 6.7. Before discussing these results, it should be pointed out that while the analysis described above minimizes the problems noted in conjunction with Table 6.6, it is not a panacea. This procedure is based on the assumption that there are no contextual effects. However, some of the previous analyses suggest that the patterns of change differ by region.

Although separate regional analyses have been conducted, the presence of estimated proportions of less than zero and greater than one suggests that problems still remain. But, in the absence of survey data these aggregate estimates will have to suffice.

TABLE 6.7
Regression estimates of "change" proportions from 1975 to 1980

To 1980	From 1975					
	PCP	PS	AD	Other	Non-voters	New voters
All Concelhos						
PCP	1.07	.041	-.012	-.096	-.179	.168
PS	-.161	.677	.055	-.007	.054	.280
AD	.045	.137	.826	.530	.085	.347
Other	.027	.082	.042	.194	.011	.064
Nonvoters	.018	.064	.089	.141	1.03	.141
Northern Concelhos						
PCP	1.09	.045	.001	.088	.153	.120
PS	-.113	.761	.077	-.098	-.105	.244
AD	.018	.038	.761	.652	.371	.472
Other	.013	.087	.050	.163	.005	.055
Nonvoters	-.013	.068	.110	.195	.881	.109
Southern Concelhos						
PCP	1.01	.111	-.253	.350	-.532	.242
PS	-.157	.547	-.059	.172	.415	.289
AD	.167	.151	1.47	.208	-.523	.213
Other	.003	.087	-.019	.240	.066	.084
Nonvoters	-.025	.106	-.144	.034	1.57	.175

As AD experienced the largest growth between 1975 and 1980, the sources of this expansion are examined first. In both the north and south, AD was largely successful in retaining its former 1975 supporters. In fact, no supporters were more loyal than those southerners who supported AD in 1975. Even in the north, the AD was able to retain about three-fourths of its former supporters. In the north, AD was unable to attract to any appreciable degree previous PCP or PS supporters. It did, however, gain substantial support from former other party voters, 1975 nonvoters, and new voters. In fact, about .65 of former other party supporters, .47 of new voters, and .37 of former nonvoters cast ballots for the AD in 1980 in the north.

In the south, AD's gains came from a broader array of sources. In addition to other party supporters and new voters, AD was able to attract about .15 of former PCP and PS voters. AD's gains among other party voters was much smaller, however, in the south than in the north (.208 vs. .652). Finally AD was unable to mobilize southern 1975 nonvoters to its banner. The defections which AD experienced between 1975 and 1980 went primarily to nonvoting in 1980 (about .10) and to PS and the other parties (about .04 each), at least in the entire nation and in the north. AD voters did not generally defect to PCP.

Turning to the other major party which gained support between 1975 and 1980, it can be seen that with the exception of southern 1975 AD supporters, no other party's former supporters were as loyal as 1975 PCP voters. In both north and south a major source of PCP expansion was former supporters of the other leftist parties; that is, 1975 supporters of PS and the extreme left. This is particularly true in PCP's southern heartland. Here about .10 of former PS voters and about one-third of other party voters cast ballots for PCP in 1980. A second source of PCP's expansion between 1975 and 1980 was new voters. Again, the effect was larger in the south than in the north. Nearly a full quarter of new voters in the south supported PCP in 1980. Finally, in neither region was PCP able in 1980 to attract 1975 supporters of the center-right; that is, PSD and CDS voters. Interestingly, the only significant defections from PCP occurred in the south, the region of its most solid base of support. About .17 of its former supporters defected to AD. Beyond these defections, few PCP voters abandoned their party. This, of course, is what would be expected from PCP with its strong incapsulating type of party organization.

The only other party to increase between 1975 and 1980 was the "party" of nonvoters. The largest source of nonvoters in 1980 was nonvoters in 1975; i.e., 1975 nonvoters remained quite loyal to their "party," especially in the south. The increase in nonvoting in the north derives from several sources. The most interesting source of new nonvoters was 1975 other party supporters in the north. About .20 of these voters did not turn out in 1980. A substantial proportion (.06-.10) of northern 1975 AD and PS supporters also failed to cast ballots in 1980 as was the case for new voters. While an appreciable proportion of new voters and 1975 PS voters were nonvoters in 1980 in the south, very few

1980 nonvoters were other party supporters in 1975. That is to say, other party supporters were not as demobilized in the south as they were in the north. Defections from the "party" of nonvoters differ by region. In the north, only AD was able to mobilize a sizeable segment (.37) of former nonvoters. In the south, only PS was able to attract a large fraction (.42) of 1975 nonvoters in 1980.

The decline in PS support is, of course, largely attributable to the defection of former PS voters. In fact, in the south the flow of defectors reached hemorrhage proportions as only a little more than .50 of the 1975 PS supporters returned to the party in 1980. The losses for PS would have been even greater had it not been for the fact that the party was able to capture about .25 of the new voters. It was also able to make some minor inroads into AD's base of support in the north, drawing about .08 of these former AD voters. In the south the only sources of PS support besides new voters were 1975 nonvoters and supporters of the parties of the extreme left.

Defections from PS in both regions were spread nearly equally over all possibilities. In the north about .09 of the 1975 PS voters supported the parties of the extreme left; .07 were demobilized; and about .04 defected to both PCP and AD. In the south defections from PS were higher but were also spread across all possibilities: about .15 defected to AD; .11 were demobilized; .11 supported PCP; and .09 supported the parties of the extreme left.

For their part, the parties of the extreme left were able to hold less than a quarter of their original 1975 supporters. The only other source of support for these parties in 1980 was former PS voters and new voters. But neither of these sources provided a major boost for the parties of the extreme left: only .09 of former PS voters and between .04 and .08 of new voters supported these parties in 1980. Defections from the extreme left varied by region. In the north, as was mentioned above, the AD was the largest beneficiary. The only other significant destination for 1975 extreme left voters in the north was nonvoting. In the south, all parties, with the exception of nonvoters, received a proportion of defectors from the extreme left. The largest beneficiary in the south was PCP with the AD and PS sharing the remaining defectors about equally.

The first and most obvious observation to draw from this analysis of electoral dynamics between 1975 and 1980 is that the data simply do not show a simple process of polarization of the system fueled by the centrifugation of PS voters to the AD and PCP at the extremes. Indeed, the data show that a much more complex process accounts for the changes in electoral fortunes experienced by the various parties between 1975 and 1980. All parties gained roughly an equal number of voters as a result of the decline in support for PS. Moreover, AD's expansion came from several sources: in particular, nonvoters, new voters, and other parties in the north and, in the south, from all sources equally, save former nonvoters.

If the party system is not becoming Italianized, what is its future configuration likely to be? In the first place, the data show the system to have become less regionalized; that is, the broad north-south cleavage that emerged in the first two elections diminished considerably in the 1979 and 1980 elections. This was especially true for the AD and the PS. In the second place, the melting away of 1975 voters for the parties of the extreme left and their inability to recruit new supporters suggest a bleak future for these parties. In the third place, the substantial losses of PS should not be construed to mean that the socialists are being squeezed from the political spectrum and will disappear in the near future. The ability of the PS to retain about two-thirds of its former supporters and, more importantly, its ability to capture approximately one-third of the new voters suggest that this party will continue to be a major element of the party system for the foreseeable future.

The first sign that PS had not been eviscerated and was still a force with which to contend appeared in the 1982 local elections when the socialists received .333 of the vote, an increase of about .6 from the 1980 parliamentary elections. Conclusive evidence came in the fifth parliamentary election (held after this analysis was completed), occasioned by the unexpected collapse of the AD. In that election, which took place on April 25, 1983, PS won a plurality of the vote with .363 of the ballots. They were followed by PSD with .270, PCP with .182, and CDS with .240 of the vote. Abstentions were .210 of the electorate. These results, except for the somewhat higher proportion of nonvoting, were almost a mirror image of the 1975 and 1976 elections. Thus, as the above analysis suggests and these results show, the Portuguese party system is not become polarized. Rather, a quadripartite system is in place. The PS and PSD will continue to be larger than PCP or CDS. Although nonvoting was somewhat higher in the 1983 elections, it is not expected to continue to increase because the abstention rate among new voters is only about .15. Thus, nonvoting ought to vary around this level for the foreseeable future.

The dynamics of electoral change analyzed above also suggest something of the character of Portugal's quadripartite party system. The PCP maintained itself principally by retaining previous supporters but also by recruiting new voters, and by attracting supporters of the parties of the extreme left, especially in their southern stronghold. Due to the regional source of this support, new PCP voters may rather closely resemble older ones in their sociological characteristics, and this fact suggests a strategy of mobilizing the party's natural constituency. Hence, while there may be some expansion of the PCP, it will continue to retain its narrow group and regional base and, therefore, remain a party of ideology. On the other hand, PS and the PSD (and CDS within the AD) are apparently following a different strategy. These parties have tried to expand by broadening their appeals to a variety of sectors in the population. This has already been noted by Hammond[22] for PS with respect to their campaign strategy in 1975 and 1976. The sources of support for the AD suggest a similar approach and the decline in regional differences in PS and AD support in 1979 and 1980 observed above is also indicative of this strategy. However, the results of the 1983 elections suggest that of the two AD partners, the CDS, when running alone, like the PCP, is incapable of breaking out of its regional stronghold.

The above analyses based on disaggregated national level data show, and the outcome of the 1983 parliamentary elections confirms, that while there have been changes in the losses and gains of the various parties, these fluctuations in voter support have not been great and the basic pattern of electoral behavior observed in Portugal's first post-1974 election has been maintained over time. Thus, despite Portugal's lack of a history of competitive, free elections, voting behavior is quite stable and not prone to capricious fluctuations or the "flash" party phenomenon. It seems then that the party system has stabilized such that two regionally-based smaller parties, one on the left (PCP) and the other on the right (CDS), and two broadly-based centrist type parties, one left of center (PS) and the other right of center (PSD) will dominate Portuguese electoral politics for the foreseeable future.

CONCLUSIONS: PARTIES AS
DETERMINANTS OF ELECTORAL BEHAVIOR

This chapter and the one previous have sought explanations for the emergence of multipartyism in Portugal. The previous chapter focused on the presumed connection between the method of election and political factors and the configuration of Portugal's party system. In that chapter it was shown that there does not appear to be any simple causal connection between the electoral system and discontinuities in regime type and Portugal's present multiparty system. The fragmentation of the system was found to be much more the result of the fact that Portuguese politics has been and continues to be influenced by personalism and elitism, itself a result of Portugal's particular pattern of nationstate development. Portuguese parties have not been well institutionalized and, except possibly the PRP during the First Republic, have been little more than factions among the various contending elites that formed around important personalities, charismatic figures, major office holders, and local notables. Partisan politics has thus functioned, for the most part, on the basis of personal ambition, charisma, petty differences over specific policies, and the quest for ideological purity.

However, in the present chapter, a connection was shown to exist between broad social forces and the party system although it did not manifest itself completely until after the advent of universal suffrage in 1974. Since then, the Portuguese electorate has voted in clear and well-defined patterns of support for various parties which have a high degree of correlation with Portugal's different socioeconomic and regional ecologies. The above analysis of the party system between 1975 and 1980, as well as the results of the 1983 elections, clearly establish that the quadripartite party system which appeared at the moment of creation in 1975 has stabilized and will probably change very little in the future. Portuguese voters have not been capricious in their voting behavior, nor has the flash party phenomenon appeared.

These results seem to lend support to the theory that Portuguese voters, like other West European electorates, cast their ballots instrumentally such that voting behavior is not a measure of partisan identification and loyalty but, rather, an expression of immediate voting choice. However, the above analysis of voting trends since 1975, which shows that, to varying degrees, Portuguese political parties have blocks of loyal supporters who have stayed with their parties across elections, suggests support for the opposite theory that there is some measure of partisan identification among the Portuguese electorate. Added support for this theory is provided by results of the above analysis of the dynamic of electoral change between 1975 and 1980 which showed that fluctuation in the support for the various parties was not the result of large-scale shifts of voters among the parties but, rather, the ability of certain parties to maintain their base of support and attract new voters. How can these contradictory findings be rectified?

The answer to this paradox is probably related to the activities of the political parties and their leaders. It has been suggested that parties, which are, of course, central to the electoral process, not only orient their voters toward already existing socioeconomic cleavages but may, through these activities, bring such cleavages into existence by making them relevant for individual voters and mobilizing support around such differences. In this view, political parties determine voting behavior through their organizational activities.[23] Thus, a correlation between socioeconomic cleavages and voting behavior is found to exist not because voters themselves are consciously making means-ends, instrumental calculations, but, rather, because parties are actively mobilizing voters along cleavage lines.

This sort of interaction between socioeconomic ecologies, parties, and voters in Portugal as well as certain other political systems of Western Europe, contrast sharply with what is found in the United States and Great Britain, for example, where there is a high degree of partisan identification independent of socioeconomic cleavages among the electorate. This contrast is the result of the different order in which the participation crisis was resolved in these two types of systems. In the United States and Great Britain, the participation crisis was resolved sequentially sooner and resulted in the early institutionalization of a political infrastructure of parties and parliament. Such institutionalization has tended to override and submerge socioeconomic cleavages in these two countries. In Portugal, on the other hand, where the participation crisis is only now being resolved and the parties are organizing themselves and seeking loyal followers, made necessary by universal suffrage, elites have been orienting the electorate toward the socioeconomic cleavages within the society and have made such differences highly salient for individual voters. Hence, voting behavior appears to be shaped by a voter's independent assessment of the importance of such cleavages for their instrumental concerns when, in fact, they are actually responding to the mobilizing efforts of the parties. The slight decline in correlations between socioeconomic factors and electoral support for the parties observed in more recent elections is probably the result of the voter mobilization strategies of the parties, especially PS and PSD, both of which seek to become "catchall" parties. Whether such mobilization will eventually lead to partisan identification independent of socioeconomic cleavages as the party system institutionalizes remains to be seen and awaits further research.

Notes

1. See Philip E. Converse, "Of Time and Partisan Stability," Comparative Political Studies 2 (July 1969): 139-171; Jack Dennis and Donald J. McCrone, "Preadult Development of Political Party Identification in Western Democracies," Comparative Political Studies 3 (July 1970): 243-263; and Philip E. Converse and Georges Dupeux, "Politicization of the Electorate in France and the United

States," Public Opinion Quarterly 26 (1962): 1-23.

2. W. Philip Shively, "Party Identification, Party Choice, and Voting Stability: The Weimar Case," American Political Science Review 56 (December 1972): 1203-1225. Some research has even questioned the validity of using the concept of party identification in the West European context. See Helmut Norpoth, "Party Identification in West Germany: Tracing an Elusive Concept," Comparative Politics 11 (April 1979): 36-61; and Jacques Thomassen, "Party Identification as a Cross-National Concept: Its Meaning in the Netherlands," in Party Identification and Beyond, ed. Ian Budge et al. (New York: Wiley, 1976), pp. 63-79.

3. Howard J. Wiarda, "Electoral Competition and Participation in Portugal: Has Democracy Been Institutionalized?" in Competitive Elections in Developing Countries, ed. Myron Weiner and Ergun Ozbudun (forthcoming).

4. Jorge Gaspar and Nuno Vitorino, As Eleições Legislativas: Algumas Perspectivas Regionais (Lisbon: Livros Horizonte, 1978), p. 22; see also their As Eleições de 25 de Abril: Geografia e Imagen dos Partidos (Lisbon: Livros Horizonte, 1976).

5. Philippe C. Schmitter, "Porteé et Signification des Elections dans le Portugal Autoritaire (1933-34)," in Elections Without Choice, ed. G. Hermet et al. (London: Macmillan, 1978), pp. 111-119.

6. Douglas L. Wheeler, "Portuguese Elections and History," paper presented at the Conference on Modern Portugal, Yale University, 1975.

7. Wiarda, "Electoral Competition and Participation in Portugal," p. 32.

8. Ibid., p. 33.

9. John L. Hammond, "Electoral Behavior and Political Militancy," in Contemporary Portugal: The Revolution and Its Antecedents, ed. Lawrence S. Graham and Harry M. Makler (Austin, Texas: University of Texas Press, 1972), p. 259.

10. Ibid.

11. Gaspar and Vitorino, As Eleições Legislativas, p. 28.

12. Ibid.

13. The analysis which follows is based on a paper titled "The Dynamics of Electoral Change in Portugal Since 1974," presented by the author and his colleague, William Claggett, at the 1982 annual meeting of the American Political Science Association, Denver, Colorado, September 2-5, 1982.

14. A fifth general election was held on April 25, 1983 after the research for this analysis was concluded. The importance of the results of that election for this analysis of electoral dynamics will be discussed below.

15. According to the Electoral Registration Law (Lei do Recenseamento Eleitoral 69/78), voter registration is obligatory for all Portuguese citizens over the age of 18 who reside on the mainland or in the two autonomous regions of the Azores or Madeira. See Walter C. Opello, Jr., "Electoral Law and Candidate Selection" in Portugal at the Polls, ed. Howard J. Penniman (Washington, D.C.: American Enterprise Institute, forthcoming), for more details.

16. The figures in Table 6.3 result from the aggregation of concelho-level data. Four concelhos had to be omitted because

either their total raw vote for PCP, PS, and AD (or CDS plus PSD in 1975 and 1976) exceeded the concelho's total vote or the concelho's total vote surpassed the concelho's figure for registered voters in one or more elections. Since the figures for the "other" category were calculated by subtracting the total vote for PCP, PS, and AD from the total vote in the concelho and the figures for nonvoters were derived by subtracting a concelho's total vote from its registered population, the inclusion of these four units would have led to some erroneous results. The vote totals which were used in the calculations are from Atlas Eleitoral (Lisbon: Editorial Progresso Social e Demacracia, S.A.R.L., 1981).

17. See Tom Gallagher, "The 1979 Portuguese General Election," Luso-Brazilian Review 18 (Winter 1981): 253-262.

18. Giovanni Sartori, Parties and Party Systems: A Framework for Analysis (Cambridge: Cambridge University Press, 1976), esp. Chap. 6.

19. This analysis as well as the following analyses is based on the smallest units for which electoral data are readily available, the 305 concelhos into which the mainland and the archipelagoes of Madeira and the Azores are divided.

20. The "New" category was calculated by subtracting the total registered voters in a concelho in 1975 from the total registered voters in 1980. Hence it represents the net change in the registered population in a concelho between these elections. Besides measuring the coming of age of new voters it also reflects the death of older voters and the movement of population both within the country and abroad.

21. These equations were in the following form:

$$P80_i = a + b_1 X_1 + B_3 X_2 + b_3 X_3 + b_4 X_4 + B_5 NV$$

where

$P80_i$ = the proportion of the total registered voters in 1980 voting for the ith party

$X_i - X_4$ = the proportion of 1980 registered voters that voted for a particular party in 1975

NV = the proportion of 1980 registered voters that had been nonvoters in 1975

A separate equation was estimated for each party in 1980, including nonvoters; i.e., each party's 1980 proportion appeared as the dependent variable in one equation. The new voter term was omitted from these equations in order to produce identifiable equations. The constant term in these equations therefore provides an estimate of the proportion of new voters supporting the ith party. The estimates of the other proportions are derived through the appropriate manipulation of the estimated coefficients. On this statistical technique, see Eric A. Hanushek and John E. Jackson, Statistical Methods for Social Scientists (New York: Academic Press, 1977), pp. 101-106.

22. By Hammond, "Electoral Behavior and Political Militancy."

23. For more details on this position see Alan Zukerman and Mark Irving Lichbach, "Stability and Change in European Electorates," World Politics 24 (July 1977): 523-551, especially p. 535ff.

7
The 1976 Constitution: Cycles in Portuguese Constitution Making

According to Smith, constitutional government in Western Europe arose as the result of two different sets of historical forces. The first was the prolonged struggle to bring absolute monarchy under legal control; the second was to bring government under popular control.[1] The first gave rise to theories of constitutionalism and governments which stressed the concept of balance among the various policymaking institutions and were the result of the increasing power of the new urban bourgeoisie during the liberal era. The second set of historical forces gave rise to the demand for the complete representation of the entire people and as such can be seen as an effort to resolve the crisis of participation.

As the conflict between these two sets of historical forces can best be seen in executive-legislative relations, the focus of this chapter is on such relations within the Portuguese constitution-making experience. The purposes of this chapter are to show that the 1976 constitution is similar to those written in other West European countries after World War II and that revisions recently made to it fit a historical pattern also found among West European states.

CYCLES IN PORTUGUESE CONSTITUTIONAL
HISTORY

Portugal's regime change in 1974 from authoritarianism to pluralist democracy produced a new constitution. This document, which was approved by the constituent assembly on April 2, 1976, has been recently revised. Although it has been correctly observed that these revisions are "extremely political,"[2] the result of changes in the conjunction of political forces within Portugal since the period of exception, they can also be explained by the fact that they are historically opportune. That is, the revisions fit into the pattern of Portuguese constitutional history. Like France, the history of Portuguese constitution-making can be divided into cycles, each beginning with a liberalization and ending with a conservative reaction.[3] These cycles, not unlike those of France, have been the result of changing constellations of political elites within Portuguese society around conflicting theories of constitutionalism.[4]

One theory derives from Rousseau's thought, as elaborated in the Social Contract, and holds that in order to be truly democratic, a constitution must be based on the principle of popular sovereignty and must delegate decisionmaking power solely to a legislature. The second derives from the constitutional theories of Benjamin Constant, which hold that all three political institutions--legislative, executive, and judicial--spring equally from the popular will and therefore must be coordinated by some fourth institution granted the power to moderate the interaction among the other three.[5] At the heart of the difference between these two theories is the constitutional relationship between legislatures and executives. In the first, the legislature is made supreme, while in the second supremacy is given to the fourth branch. The West European pattern is one of oscillation between legislative supremacy and executive dominance, as competing political forces, utilizing these contrasting theories of constitutional engineering, have vied with one another for control of their respective societies.[6] Portuguese constitutional history is no different in this regard. It is the shift between legislative supremacy and executive dominance which defines constitutionally liberal and conservative reactions of Portugal's cycles of constitution-making.

The Rousseau doctrine was clearly reflected in the constitution of 1822 and marks the beginning of the first cycle. The legislature (cortes), which was composed of a single house elected every two years, was made supreme. Numerous important powers were granted to the cortes, most of which concerned the governance of the country and could be carried out without royal sanction (Art. 103). The cortes was empowered to elect its own officers and initiate legislation. Although the king's secretaries of state could propose legislation, it had to be examined and adopted by a committee of the cortes before it could be introduced (Art. 105). The government was thus directly responsible to the cortes and could be called to appear before it to explain policy. The king had only the "suspensive veto"; that is, he could not veto legislation but could only return to the cortes laws with which he did not agree.

As has already been discussed, the constitution of 1822 was shortlived. Its brief existence was a result of the fact that it was too liberal for the time. It alienated landowners, who saw the enfranchisement of literate males as a threat to their power as well as nobility and clergy, who were granted no special representation nor power. Moreover, it did not satisfy the king, who had been humiliated by having been stripped of almost all royal prerogatives. Suspended in 1823, Portugal was governed by King João's moderate absolutism until his death in 1826.

The end of the first cycle of constitution-making came in March 1826 with the granting of a new constitution called the Constitutional Charter. This document, which was a direct result of the settlement of the question of succession after João's death, was also an attempt to reconcile monarchists and Jacobin political forces. In reaction to the Rousseau doctrine embodied in the 1822 constitution, the makers of the charter turned to the constitutional theories of Benjamin Constant. The charter clearly shifted the locus of decisional power away from the legislature toward the executive and the king was granted the power to moderate the relationship between them. Executive dominance over the legislature was assured by drastically reducing the powers of the cortes, which was divided into two houses (House of Deputies and House of Peers); granting to the crown the power to appoint the presidents and vice-presidents of both houses (Art 21); giving the king an absolute veto over all legislation (Art. 58), as well as the power to name peers, dissolve the cortes, and appoint and dismiss governments (Art. 74).

As was discussed in Chapter 2, Miguel's nullification of the charter and claim to absolute power plunged Portugal into civil war. The defeat of the absolutists by liberal forces in 1834 began Portugal's second cycle of constitution-making. The constitution of 1838 was a result of the differences that emerged at the end of the civil war between radical and moderate Jacobins. The radicals wanted a return to the constitution of 1822, while the moderates wanted to restore the charter of 1826. The result of these differences of constitutional preference was the constitution of 1838. This document, which abolished the moderative power, simultaneously granted vast powers to both the legislative and executive branches. The cortes was made bicameral (Senate and House of Deputies) and given vast decisionmaking and taxing power (Art. 37). The king, who was granted executive power, could veto legislation, dissolve the cortes, and appoint government ministers and secretaries of state (Arts. 81-82).

Like the 1822 constitution, however, the 1838 document was shortlived. As the political balance between radical and moderate Jacobins began to shift in favor of the moderates, they succeeded in overthrowing the 1838 constitution and restoring the charter. The restoration of the charter in 1842 was a conservative reaction to the liberalism of the 1838 constitution and brought to an end the second cycle of Portuguese constitution-making.

The third cycle began sixty-eight years later with the republican revolution in 1910. The 1911 republican constitution was a liberal reaction to the charter and represented a return to the Rousseauistic emphasis on popular sovereignty and legislative supremacy. The legislature (<u>Congresso da República</u>) was granted vast decisional power and considerable responsibilty for directing the daily operation of the government (Art. 46). It was also empowered to elect the president of the republic and his ministers, who were obliged to appear before the congress to whom they were responsible. In addition, the president had no power to veto legislation nor dissolve the legislature.[8]

Salazar's 1933 constitution was a conservative reaction to the liberalism of the republican constitution and marks the end of the third cycle of Portuguese constitution-making. This document, which returned to the quadripartite organizational format of the charter, was designed by Salazar to remove decisional power away from the legislature so that the executive was completely independent and accountable only to the president of the republic.[9] Accordingly, the powers of the legislature, now called the National Assembly (Assembleia Nacional) were greatly reduced and the Corporative Chamber was granted only consultative power (Arts. 91-103). The executive was granted extensive control over the internal workings of both bodies. The executive dictated the legislative process by controlling the order of each day's business which was fixed by a list drawn up by the prime minister (Art. 101). Salazar greatly reduced the legislative purview of the National Assembly and in matters of overseas (colonial) policy bypassed the legislature altogether (Art. 93). Government ministers were empowered to take an active part in the work of the committees of the National Assembly (Art. 95). The power of individual deputies was curtailed and that of the government enhanced by granting to the latter the right to refuse to answer questions submitted by members of parliament on grounds of "national security" (Art. 96). The independence of deputies was further curtailed by making them liable for speeches made in parliament considered by the government to be defamatory, insulting, injurious to public morals, or provoking the public to engage in "criminal" activity or subversion (Art. 89).

Although the executive was made responsible to the president of the republic in the 1933 constitution (according to Article 81, the president constitutionally had the power to appoint the prime minister and exonerate him), there was a gradual abdication of power from successive presidents toward the prime minister; that is, Salazar. This was accomplished, in part, by amending the constitution and by the gradual personalization of political power; that is, by completely identifying the New State with Salazar. This usurpation of presidential power became so complete that it was Salazar who chose Portugal's presidents and not the other way around, as required by the constitution.[10] Thus, Salazar, as prime minister, gained absolute control over the legislature and the presidency and ruled Portugal almost single-handedly until 1968.

In sum, Portuguese constitutional history up to the end of the New State, not unlike French constitutional history, is marked by cyclical oscillations between executive dominance and legislative supremacy, depending upon the particular conjunction of political forces. These shifts in the center of gravity were responses by constitution makers who were trying to rectify the flaws they perceived in earlier constitutional regimes. In those documents where the parliament was made supreme (1822, 1911), institution builders tried to restrict executives because it was perceived that these constitutions prevented popular participation by granting only the slightest role to parliament in the formulation of government policy. In those documents where the king or executive were made supreme (charter, 1838, 1933), constitution builders, in reaction to previous documents, tried to moderate and curb what was seen as the excessive popular participation as exemplified by parliamentary obstructionism.

THE 1976 CONSTITUTION

The 1976 constitution, like those before it, was a reaction to things past. In many respects, the rationale behind the latest of Portuguese constitutions was similar to that which was applied to other constitutions written immediately after World War II in Western Europe, especially in West Germany, Italy, and France. These constitutions, and Portugal's present one, were the result of what Friedrich has termed "negative revolutions"; that is, they were the consequence not of a "positive enthusiasm for the future" but rather a negative distaste for the "dismal past."[11]

In the case of Portugal, this distaste for the past not only included the authoritarianism of the New State but the instability of the First Republic as well. Consequently, the original version of the 1976 constitution was simultaneously an attempt to overcome the shortcomings of parliamentary supremacy and executive dominance. Following the French example, the Portuguese created a hybrid system which incorporates elements from both parliamentary and presidential types. Dubbed "semi-presidential" by Duverger, such regimes grant ultimate representation and decisional responsibility to the parliament and simultaneously create a strong president immune from parliamentary pressure and empowered to ensure the harmonious working of the system.12

It would seem that because the 1976 constitution did not clearly elevate the legislature to supremacy, as would be expected after the executive dominance of the New State, it does not fit Portugal's cyclical pattern of constitution-making. Such a conclusion would be acceptable only if the 1976 constitution were considered in its original version. If the revisions that have been recently made to it are taken into account, then Portugal's latest constitution clearly fits the historical pattern. The recent revisions can be thus viewed as the denouement of the constitution-making process initiated in the aftermath of the golpe of April 25, 1974.

Moreover, it can be argued that if the constitution-makers had been left to their own devices, the original version of the 1976 constitution would have established parliamentary supremacy. According to Domingos, this tendency was temporarily prevented from fully manifesting itself because of the interference of the MFA in the constitution-making process.13 This interference came in the form of the two "pacts" signed between the MFA and the political parties during the period of exception which laid down the conditions for a return to civilian rule. The first of these pacts, as has been already mentioned, clearly made the armed forces the guarantors of pluralist democracy and institutionalized their role in an organ called the Council of the Revolution (Conselho da Revolução: CR), composed of the president of the republic, the chief of the general staff, the chiefs of staff of the army, navy, and air force, and fourteen officers from the three services (Art. 142). The CR was empowered to advise the president of the republic with respect to such matters as declaring war and making peace, deciding on the constitutionality of any law referred to it, and approving the president's choice and dismissal of prime ministers and their governments (Arts. 146, 281).14

The second MFA-parties pact was signed on February 26, 1976 after the convening of the constituent assembly. This pact was the result of the new "situation" after the success of the Group of Nine and the defeat of the far left on November 25, 1975, and compelled the parties within the constituent assembly to alter radically the method of choosing and the powers of the president of the republic. Before the imposition of the second pact, the constitutional drafts of the major parties proposed that the president be chosen by an electoral college appointed by the parliament, a provision which would have clearly established legislative supremacy. After the pact was signed, the method was changed to direct, popular election, and presidential powers were greatly enhanced.15 It was thus the action of forces outside the constituent assembly which frustrated the immediate creation of parliamentary supremacy.

Although the powers of the president were strengthened, the Portuguese constitution makers did not, however, go as far as the French and create a "quasi-monarchical" executive.[16] While the president was granted the power to appoint and relieve the prime minister and the government, dissolve and send messages to parliament, and call it into special session, he was not given the power to preside over the cabinet, introduce legislation, or appoint prime ministers without previously consulting parliament. Moreover, the president's power to veto legislation was restricted by the ability of parliament to override by a two-thirds majority. The president was also prevented from being elected for more than two five-year mandates and denied the power of referendum.

In place of the New State's National Assembly and Corporative Chamber, the 1976 constitution created a unicameral parliament called the Assembly of the Republic (Assembleia da República: AR). Deputies elected to the Assembly run on plurinominal lists in twenty-four electoral districts. Election is by universal suffrage and selection is by the d'Hondt method. The basic unit of organization within the AR is the parliamentary group composed of the members of each party represented. The AR has a system of standing committees organized to parallel the functions of the various government ministries.[17]

The AR was an attempt at compromise. It represents an intermediate position between the legislative supremacy of the First Republic's Congress and the subservience of the New State's National Assembly. The intent of the 1976 constitution-makers, mindful of Portugal's past experience with legislative bodies, was to create an institution which would satisfy the Rousseauistic impulse and give to the political parties a significant role in the policy process without simultaneously making it impossible for the government to formulate and implement a coherent program.

While parliament has been granted the power to bring down the government by rejecting its program which must be submitted for approval within ten days of the appointment of the prime minister (Art. 195), voting motions of censure, and rejecting motions of confidence (Arts. 196, 197), this power is circumscribed by the requirement that such actions can only be initiated by parliamentary groups with a "cooling off" period of forty-eight hours before debate begins. The constitution also mitigates this power by limiting debate on such issues to three days, which forces a vote; by allowing for the withdrawal of the motion after the debate; and by prohibiting a failed motion of censure from being reintroduced during the same session (Art. 197).

Although the AR has been given exclusive control over its own internal organization, finances, rules of order, and the legislative timetable (Arts. 178, 179), complete autonomy is curtailed by the requirement that these prerogatives be in strict accord with the constitution. Moreover, the government can influence the way parliament spends its time through its right to request that matters requiring urgent attention be given priority (Art 179). The rules of order of parliament have been drafted to reduce the possibility of legislative stalemate by imposing strict time limits on debate. This prevents the AR from stymieing government action by holding interminable discussions on government bills.

Even though committees are more powerful than they were in the National Assembly, they are circumscribed by limits on the time they can consider bills; and the constitution forbids committees to amend legislation out of recognition. Moreover, committee members are effectively under party control which further reduces the independence and autonomy of the committees.

Despite the fact that the power to declare national emergencies and states of siege, make treaties, and issue decree-laws were constitutionally apportioned to the president and the government, these measures have to be approved by parliament (Arts. 164, 165, 172). This gives parliament a certain amount of control over such matters and is designed to prevent government and presidential arbitrariness.

Although parliament was granted a broad range of areas in which it has legislative power, the government was also authorized to issue decree-laws in these areas of responsibility (Art. 164). To ensure that the AR would not abdicate its responsibility and the government would not usurp these powers, authorizations to legislate must clearly define subject matter, scope, and duration. Moreover, authorization to legislate in a particular area cannot be granted more than once and lapses when there is a change in government, the legislative session ends, or parliament is dissolved (Art. 168).

Even though the hybrid system created by the constitution-makers of 1976 was somewhat more parliamentary than presidential, the fact that the government derived from and was responsible to the president and parliament simultaneously (Art. 193) led to considerable conflict between the president and the prime minister and has been a major impulse toward the modification of the constitutional order in favor of parliamentary supremacy.

This conflict emerged almost immediately after the 1976 constitution went into effect and was precipitated by the collapse of the second constitutional government in June 1978. Following the fall of this government, the president of the republic, General Ramalho Eanes, began to exert his influence and moved to appoint a non-party government of independent technocrats under the prime ministership of Alfredo Nobre de Costa, a highly respected engineer and former manager of Portugal's national steel works. As the AR was not consulted, nor were any party members involved in the formation of this government, de Costa had no support in parliament. Outraged at this "unconstitutional" action by the president, the parliament promptly voted down de Costa's plan and budget in September, 1978. Undaunted, Eanes again attempted to appoint a government of technocrats but this time, in deference to parliament, sought party support for his prime minister. With the tacit approval of the PSD and the CDS, Eanes appointed as prime minister, Carlos Mota Pinto, a professor of law at Coimbra University. This government was approved but only survived until March 1979 when the PSD withdrew its support.

Faced with the collapse of two governments in succession, cognizant that the parliament was incapable of putting together a viable coalition government, and now painfully aware that an appointed government of independent technocrats was unacceptable to parliament, President Eanes dissolved parliament and held fresh elections. It was these elections that rearranged the balance of political forces within parliament and opened the door for revisions to the 1976 constitution that shifted the balance among governmental institutions within Portugal's hybrid system clearly in favor of parliament.

THE POLITICS OF CONSTITUTIONAL REVISION

As already discussed in Chapter 5, the 1979 elections brought to power a center-right coalition called the Democratic Alliance (AD). Among other things, one of the primary objectives of the coalition was the revision of the 1976 constitution. The then-leader of the PSD, Francisco Sá Carneiro, and moving force behind the organization of the AD, had even written an entirely new constitution which he hoped to have substituted for the 1976 document.[18]

The victory of the AD served to exacerbate the already considerable tension in the system between the president and the CR on the one hand, and the prime minister (Sá Carneiro, until he was killed in an air crash on December 3, 1980) and the AR on the other. President Eanes, to the dismay of the prime minister, began to travel extensively throughout Portugal and abroad defining domestic and foreign policy issues. He vetoed several government bills and had the CR declare unconstitutional a major bill on the AD's legislative agenda which would have opened up the economy to more

private initiative by clearly delineating the public
and private sectors. The AD government's program was
clearly distinct from that of previous socialist governments and contrary to the orientations of President
Eanes. The system more than ever was working at cross
purposes: the government, based on a majority in the AR,
was operating in parliamentary fashion, while the president, supported by the CR, was operating in a presidential fashion. The AD increasingly defined itself in
opposition to the system established by the 1976 constitution, while the president and the CR continued to
defend it and the "gains" of April 25, 1974.[19]

While the AD was the most ardent advocate of revision, all political parties sitting in the AR wanted
some changes in the 1976 document. Even the PCP, which
saw the AD's program for constitutional revision as a
betrayal of the "revolution," wanted to revise certain
of its minor articles. The two-thirds majority required
to make amendments gave to the PS a key role in the
revision process because without its support the AD
would not have sufficient votes to pass a revisions law.
To assure PS backing, the AD signed an agreement with
the socialists that limited the extent to which such
revisions would affect certain economic changes made
during the period of exception; i.e., key sectors of the
economy would remain nationalized. Thus, all the major
parties submitted drafts for constitutional revision.
These proposals were presented to the AR in the first
week of November 1981.[20]

As would be expected, the AD proposal envisioned
the most far-reaching changes to the constitution. It
called for major modifications in the articles dealing
with the organization of political power, and the economy, as well as the rights and liberties of the citizenry. In the opinion of some observers, the AD proposal went beyond the limits on revision established by
Article 290 of the original 1976 constitution and was,
in effect, an entirely new basic law.[21]

With respect to the relationship between the president and the AR, the AD called for a drastic reduction
in the powers of the former in favor of parliament. In
the AD proposal, the government was no longer to be
simultaneously responsible to the president and the
parliament but only to the latter. The president was
to be denied the power to appoint and exonerate prime
ministers, dissolve parliament, veto laws, and appoint
the chiefs of the three branches of the armed forces
as well as the chief of the general staff. Moreover,
control of the military was to be concentrated in the
hands of the government instead of being disbursed among
the president, the CR, and the AR.

At the opposite extreme was the PCP proposal which
called for the fewest changes. Indeed, the communists
sought only minor alterations while maintaining their

support for the distribution of power in the original version, especially that of the presidency, as well as for the CR.

In between these two extremes was the socialist proposal which called for major alterations in the powers of the president and the extinction of the CR. However, the PS sought no significant changes in those articles dealing with economic organization or the rights and liberties of the citizenry. Moreover, the military was not to be placed squarely under government control but was to be administered through a special organ set up for this purpose, the Superior Council of National Defense. This organ would be presided over by the president and would include the armed services chiefs as well as representatives from the government and parliament.

Both the AD and the PS proposed that two new organs be created to take over the powers that the 1976 constitution had assigned to the CR. The AD called for the creation of a Council of State--comprising the president (who would preside without vote), the president of the supreme court, the president of the supreme military court, the attorney general, the ombudsman, the presidents of the governments of the autonomous regions (the Azores and Madeira), five deputies chosen by parliament, and a Constitutional Tribunal composed of the president of the supreme court, two judges appointed by the president, two appointed by the AR, two elected by the supreme court, and two elected by the supreme administrative court. The PS called for the creation of a Council of the Republic composed of the president of the republic (who presides), the president of the supreme court, the ombudsman, the president of the national planning committee, presidents of the regional associations of the autonomous regions, the president of the AR, five citizens selected by parliament, and five chosen by the president, and a Constitutional Tribunal composed of five citizens of recognized merit selected by the president, five nominated by the AR, and five judges selected by the supreme court.[22]

This clear movement toward parliamentarianism sparked a reaction by the president. Reminiscent of de Gaulle, Eanes threatened to resign from the presidency if his powers were reduced. He summoned the leader of PS, Mário Soares, to Bélem, the presidential palace, in order to remind him of the accord they had signed before the 1979 elections in which Soares had agreed not to alter the semi-presidential nature of the constitution during the process of revision. Eanes considered the AD and PS proposals for revision to be aimed at creating a parliamentary as opposed to a semi-presidential system because the prime minister would no longer be simultaneously responsible before the president and parliament and therefore in violation of this pre-election accord. For his part, Soares maintained that the revisionists were only reducing presidential power, not fundamentally altering the semi-presidential nature of the system, and therefore were not contrary to the agreement. Eanes was successful, however, in convincing Soares that the PS proposal for revision went too far and needed to be modified to maintain the "dual responsibility" of the prime minister and the government before the president and parliament. In exchange, Eanes gave up the power to appoint military chiefs of the general staff.[23]

This new socialist "understanding" with Eanes resulted in a new accord between the PS and the AD concerning the powers of the president. In order to satisfy the "non-negotiable" demand by Eanes that semi-presidentialism be maintained and the AD's strong desire to move toward a truly parliamentary regime, the PS worked out a compromise with respect to the "dual responsibility" problem. Article 193 of the revised constitution would have three sections. The first section would establish the responsibility of the prime minister and his government to parliament; the second would specify that this responsibility was political in nature; and the third would establish that the prime minister was responsible to the president, but only institutionally. In practice this meant that while the prime minister was responsible to the president, the president did not have the power to dismiss a prime minister who enjoyed the confidence of the AR. The prime minister and government could be dismissed only when the functioning of democratic institutions was threatened and only after consultation with the Council of State.[24]

Although this compromise was not well received by Eanes, who saw it as a bit of legerdemain that obscured a fundamental loss of presidential power in dealing with governments in which the president had lost political confidence, there was not much that could be done to stop the revision process from continuing. The PS and the AD had cleverly maneuvered around Eanes' non-negotiable demand that the semi-presidential nature of the regime be maintained. The 1976 constitution, which Eanes had so vigorously defended, stated in Article 286 that the president's veto power did not extend to laws of constitutional revision. Thus, caught between the "sword and the wall" (<u>a espada e a parede</u>), as the Portuguese say, Eanes reluctantly promulgated the revised constitution on September 24, 1982, making it clear that if not compelled to do so by Article 286, he would not have done so.[25]

CONSTITUTIONAL REVISIONS

The new text of the constitution clearly defines a system that is much more semi-parliamentary than semi-presidential. The key change in this regard is Article 194, which makes it clear that the prime minister is responsible politically to parliament and not the president, to whom he is only "institutionally" responsible. Article 194 will effectively prevent the president from dismissing the prime minister and the government except when it is necessary to assure the regular functioning of democratic institutions and after consultation with the Council of State. Thus, the president can no longer dismiss governments which enjoy the confidence of parliament.

The powers of the president have also been limited. Relative to the autonomous regions, he no longer can suspend regional governments except when such suspension is initiated by the government and with the approval of the Council of State. Although the president retains the power to veto legislation, the exercise of this power has been restricted in such a way as to prevent the "pocket veto." Now, the president has only two options with respect to legislation passed by parliament: it must be either signed or vetoed. The president's veto can be overridden by an absolute majority rather than a two-thirds majority as was required by the previous text of the constitution. The president is now obliged to promulgate within eight days vetoed bills overridden by parliament.[26] The revised version of the constitution designates the president as the commander-in-chief of the armed forces, but grants to a new organ, the Superior Council of National Defense, the power to deal with defense questions and the organization of the armed forces. The president's power to dissolve parliament has also been restricted: he cannot dissolve the AR within six months after the general election nor in the last six months of his mandate or during a state of siege or emergency.

In addition to the withdrawal of power from the president, the powers already allocated to parliament have been accentuated and reinforced. States of siege and emergency can be declared only if authorized by the AR and are limited to fifteen days instead of thirty. Interim elections are now forbidden so that each election begins a new legislative period that continues for four years. The Permanent Commission of the Assembly[27] will now continue to function in the interim between a dissolution and the seating of a new legislature. Moreover, parliament has been empowered to elect, by a two-thirds majority, the members of the Constitutional Tribunal. Finally, the power of the AR has been somewhat enhanced with respect to the prime minister, since a single vote of censure, instead of two within thirty days as previously required, can bring down a government.

Furthermore, the revisions clearly establish civilian control over the military. All references to the "MFA" or "Povo/MFA" in the original version were dropped. According to Article 136, the president can appoint only military chiefs nominated by the government. Article 270 also restricts the political activity of individuals while they are serving on active duty. Article 202 grants to the prime minister managerial control over the armed forces. Finally, the CR was abolished and its powers disbursed between two new organs of government: the Council of State and the Constitutional Tribunal. The Council of State advises the president and is empowered to pronounce on government dismissals, parliamentary dissolution, states of siege or emergency, and declarations of war. The Constitutional Tribunal, composed of six judges and seven members elected by parliament, has the power to determine the constitutionality and legality of legislation.

Finally, very little of the 1976 programmatic content was changed except that the constitution no longer considers private property to be a residual aspect of the socialist economy. Article 62 now affirms the right of private ownership of property and Article 61 allows private initiative to be freely exercised.

In sum, then, Duverger's "new regime type" in the Portuguese context can better be described as "semi-parliamentary" rather than "semi-presidential," and in this regard resembles not the government of France but those of Finland and the Weimar Republic.[28] Although legislative supremacy has not been fully reestablished, there is no doubt that the pendulum has swung in the direction of parliamentary government.

CONCLUSIONS

If the 1976 constitution marks the beginning of Portugal's fourth cycle of constitution-making, it is important to ask: How long will it be before there is a reaction? In other words, will the constitution be a lasting one? Probably the most important requisite for the survivability of any constitution is the presence of consensus about the most important matters. Spiro has separated such consensus into two components: consensus about procedures and consensus about substance.[29] According to Spiro, procedural consensus is the most important of these for the survivability of a constitution and has to be built up gradually over time.

The most stable constitutions are those which are basically procedural in nature and such procedures are the ones used by the society both in and out of government in dealing with conflict and making decisions.30

The problem in the Portuguese case is that there has been little accumulation of democratic procedures for the resolution of conflict and decisionmaking. No Portuguese constitutional regime has succeeded in establishing itself firmly enough to be immune from the danger of attempts to overthrow it. Resolution of conflict has been all too often achieved in nondemocratic ways. Moreover, Portuguese constitutions have been in the main more a reflection not of procedural consensus but, rather, of temporary substantive agreements among various elite factions and, therefore, highly transitory. Thus, Portugal, to use Lowenstein's words, has not been able to create a "real" or "living" constitution so that "the competitive struggle for political power is actually conducted within the frame offered by the constitution. . . ."31 Portuguese constitutions have too often been manipulated by various political elites as substantive issues have come and gone with little involvement of the great mass of the citizenry in such issues.32 The sequence and timing of the resolution of Portugal's participation crisis has not encouraged the building up of democratic procedures among elite factions and within the broad mass of the citizenry.

Is the 1976 constitution, as revised, any different? By virtue of the fact that it was revised as soon as possible (the original version prohibited revision for five years after promulgation) to reflect the changes which have occurred in the constellation of political forces since it was originally written, the answer must be, no. Moreover, as this is being written, calls for further revisions are being raised.33 Thus, whether the present constitution survives will depend entirely upon the political elite and the extent to which it can become over time the framework which actually structures the competitive struggle for power rather than being manipulated within that struggle.

Notes

1. Gordon Smith, Politics in Western Europe (New York: Holmes and Meier, 1973), pp. 124-125.
2. Thomas C. Bruneau, "Politics in Portugal, 1976-1981, and Revision of the Constitution," paper presented at the SSRC Conference on Contemporary Change in Southern Europe, Madrid, November 25-28, 1981, p. 1.
3. Dorothy Pickles, The Fifth French Republic (New York: Praeger, 1960), pp. 9-12.

4. William Safran, The French Polity (New York: David McKay, 1977), p. 52.
5. On Constant's life and work see John Cruickshank, Benjamin Constant (New York: Twayne, 1974).
6. Smith, Politics in Western Europe, p. 135.
7. A. H. de Oliveira Marques, History of Portugal, Vol. 2 (New York: Columbia University Press, 1976), p. 44.
8. Ibid., Vol. 1, pp. 160-162.
9. Jorge Campinos, O Presidencialismo do Estado Novo (Lisbon: Perspectivas & Realidades, 1978).
10. Ibid., pp. 141-230.
11. Carl J. Friedrich, "The Political Theory of the New Democratic Constitutions," in Comparative Politics: A Reader, ed. Harry Eckstein and David Apter (New York: The Free Press, 1963), p. 141.
12. Maurice Duverger, "A New Political System Model: Semi-Presidential Government," European Journal of Political Research 8 (1980): 165-187.
13. Emídio da Veiga Domingos, Portugal Político: Análise das Instituições (Lisbon: Edições Rolim, 1980).
14. Determinations as to the constitutionality of legislation was made with the assistance of a Constitutional Committee composed of one member of the CR, four judges, one citizen of recognized merit appointed by the president, one appointed by the AR, and two citizens chosen by the CR.
15. Domingos, Portugal Político, p. 94.
16. Safran, The French Polity, p. 55.
17. Details on the structures and processes within the AR can be found in Walter C. Opello, Jr., "The New Parliament in Portugal," Legislative Studies Quarterly 3 (May 1978): 309-334.
18. Francisco Sá Carneiro, "Uma Constituição para os anos 80," in Sistema de Governo e Sistema Partidário, ed. Pedro Santana Lopes and José Durão Barroso (Lisbon: Livraria Bertrand, 1980), pp. 179-224.
19. Bruneau, "Politics in Portugal, 1976-1981 . . . ," pp. 15-16.
20. The proposal can be found in Revisão Constitucional (Lisbon: Assembleia da República, July 15, 1981).
21. Rito Canedo, "Os Projectos de Revisão Constitucional: O Poder Político e as Forças Armadas," Expresso (Lisbon) No. 471, November 7, 1981.
22. Ibid.
23. Expresso, No. 482, January 23, 1982.
24. Ibid., No. 498, May 15, 1982.
25. Ibid., No. 523, November 6, 1982.
26. The two-thirds majority has been retained, however, for certain matters: states of emergency, delimitation of public and private sectors, military affairs, etc.
27. The Permanent Commission is presided over by the president of the AR and is composed of its vice-presidents and deputies chosen by each of the parties sitting in parliament.
28. Duverger, "A New Political System Model . . . ," pp. 173-177.

29. Herbert J. Spiro, <u>Government by Constitution</u> (New York: Random House, 1959), p. 367.
30. Ibid., p. 395.
31. Karl Loewenstein, "Reflections on the Value of Constitutions in Our Revolutionary Age," in <u>Comparative Politics</u>, ed. Eckstein and Apter, p. 150.
32. An opinion poll published in <u>Expresso</u>, No. 538, February 19, 1983, revealed that two-thirds of those surveyed paid little or no attention to the constitutional revision process.
33. CDS plans to introduce into parliament a bill which would, if passed, revise four-fifths of the portion of the constitution dealing with economic matters. See <u>Expresso</u>, No. 565, August 27, 1983.

8
The Policy Process: Making the Administrative State Responsive to Democracy

It is widely recognized that the power to make public policy in West European political systems has shifted away from parliament toward administrative agencies.[1] This shift is, in part, the product of the new tasks these systems have undertaken since World War II in the management and development of their economies and societies. It is also the result of a change in the fundamental conception of the proper role of the state in economic and social life. As Berger has written with respect to France, "[p]roblems once regarded as political, in the sense of involving choices between competing sets of values, have come to be considered and treated as administrative and technical."[2] Thus, in Western Europe generally, the content of politics has shifted away from devisive ideological issues toward issues in which technical expertise and bureaucratic speculation are more salient than fundamental value conflict.

In Portugal, however, since the instauration of a democratic regime on April 25, 1974, the trend has been in the opposite direction. Problems regarded during the New State as administrative and technical are now considered to be political, and Portugal's new governing elite has attempted to shift the focus of policymaking from within the administrative apparatus of the state toward external political structures. This was done by creating the democratic political infrastructure of parties and parliament as well as by attempting to make the public bureaucracy more efficient and responsive to the democratic policymaking process.

This attempt to reform the administrative system in order to make it more compatible with the new political infrastructure and policy process of democracy took several directions. First, a movement to reform Portuguese bureaucracy, which had appeared briefly during the late 1960s, was revitalized.[3] Second, a national training center for high level administrative personnel, called the National Institute of Administration (<u>Instituto Nacional de Administração</u>: INA) was created.

Modelled on the French École Nationale d'Administration, INA's objectives are to educate better the civil service in modern administrative and managerial techniques, carry out basic research on administrative problems, and provide technical support to various agencies of the state as needed.[4] Third, purges (saneamentos) were carried out against those high level civil servants most closely identified with the New State and its administrative, technocratic style of policymaking: the Directors-general (Directores-gerais: DGs).

These individuals were the prime targets of Portugal's new political elite because of the central role they had come to play in the governance of Portugal during the authoritarian period. As was shown in Chapter 3 the New State, despite Salazar's early attempts to create an organic-statist regime, evolved into a demobilized, administrative polity in which the making and implementing of public policy were essentially bureaucratic enterprises. At the apex of this administrative polity was Salazar who ruled through the hierarchically arranged, but compartmentalized, state apparatus. Immediately below Salazar were various ministers, civilian and military, personally loyal to him. Although these ministers formed a cabinet (Conselho dos Ministros), Salazar preferred to deal with his ministers on an individual basis or in small groups. It was not until Caetano took over the prime ministership that the cabinet became a more collegial decisionmaking body. Surprisingly, however, the New State was marked by a considerable amount of ministerial turnover. Therefore, stability and continuity of public policy gradually devolved on the permanent civil servants directly below the ministers: the DGs. Operating from strategic positions just below the apex of each ministerial hierarchy, DGs, all of whom had lifetime appointments (cargos vitalícios), came to control the programs and resources of the New State and, in effect, became the regime's policymakers.[5]

Although April 25, 1974, brought many external changes in the number of ministries, it did not bring any significant change in their internal organization and operation.[6] Directors-general continued to be key personnel in the policymaking process. Therefore, to begin to make the administrative apparatus more responsive to democratic leadership, Portugal's new political elite sought to install individuals in these positions whom they thought would be more open to the new democratic policy process. What have been the results of the saneamentos effected after the golpe? Have there been significant changes in personnel or was Portugal's administrative elite able to resist attempts at change? Has there been any significant change in the social background of this elite? Are its political attitudes more compatible with democratic policymaking?[7]

The purpose of this chapter is to provide some answers to these questions by ascertaining the social origins of Portugal's administrative elite and by assessing the relative importance of background characteristics on political attitudes for individuals appointed to their posts before and after April 25, 1974. The major presumption of the chapter is that an administrator's political attitudes are important determinants of behavior and must be compatible with and responsive to democratic styles of decisionmaking if the administrative apparatus in Portugal is ever to be reformed.

ASSESSING THE ADMINISTRATIVE ELITE[8]

It can reasonably be assumed that the administrative apparatus will not be responsive to democratic policymaking if Portugal's administrative elite is composed of traditional bureaucrats; that is, individuals who display a monistic conception of the public interest, believe that political issues can best be solved by applying objective technical, legal, and administrative standards, reject and distrust political parties and parliament, and prefer the depoliticized environment of dictatorship. Indeed, such an administrative elite may threaten the very existence of democracy in Portugal by sabotaging and blocking the action of democratically elected governments. If, on the other hand, Portugal's administrative elite is composed of "political" bureaucrats; that is, individuals who demonstrate a pluralistic conception of the public interest, recognize the necessity for bargaining and compromise and prefer political programs to administrative procedures, then it can reasonably be assumed that the administrative apparatus will be responsive to democratic policymaking.[9] The presence of such an administrative elite in Portugal would greatly enhance the chances that the Portuguese citizenry will have a significant role in the policy process. There should be differences between those DGs appointed before April 25, 1974 and those appointed since that date, if the purges have had any appreciable effect on the social origins and political attitudes of Portugal's administrative elite. Data on social origins and political attitudes were gathered using a survey instrument based on a closed questionnaire developed at the University of Michigan to study political attitudes of administrative and political elites in West Europe and the United States.[10] A somewhat abbreviated version of this instrument, translated into Portuguese, was sent in 1980 to all 120 DGs in eleven of Portugal's thirteen ministries.[11] Sixty-eight DGs completed and returned the questionnaire to give a return rate of 56 percent.[12]

As in the Michigan study, certain responses were combined into the following political attitude indices: first, questions that tapped various aspects of tolerance or hostility toward politics were combined into a tolerance for politics index.[13] Directors-general who scored high on this index were more tolerant of the institutions and political activity of liberal democracy, while those who scored low were less tolerant of such institutions and politics. Second, questions that tapped the extent to which program objectives and political ideals were considered important to a DG in the policy process were combined into an index of programmatic commitment.[14] Directors-general who scored high on this index believed that a government's program is more important for policymaking than the government's strength, while DGs who scored low believed that the strength and power of a government are more important than its specific policy objectives or ideology. Third, questions that tapped the degree to which Portuguese DGs supported political equality and popular participation in government were combined into an elitism index.[16] Directors-general who scored high on this index were not positively oriented to political equality and popular involvement, while those who scored low were more supportive of such democratic behavior. Fourth, questions that tapped the extent to which DGs accepted group conflict were combined into a tolerance for political conflict index.[16] Directors-general who scored high on this index were those who saw conflict as uselessly exacerbating problems, while those who scored low were those who viewed conflict as useful for problem solving. Scores on all four indices could range from a minimum of 10 to a maximum of 90.

As in the Michigan survey, information on the following social background characteristics was collected: (1) age, (2) year of entrance into the civil service, (3) tenure in present post, (4) class, (5) place of birth, (6) parent or relative in the civil service, (7) educational attainment, and (8) sex. Values on these characteristics were combined into categories as follows: five categories were used for the age, tenure in present post, educational attainment, and year of entrance into the civil service characteristics. For age, the categories were (1) 25-34, (2) 35-44, (3) 45-54, (4) 55-64, (5) 65 and over. Categories for year of entrance into the civil service were (1) 1930-39, (2) 1940-49, (3) 1950-59, (4) 1960-69, and (5) 1970-79. The categories for time in present post were (1) 0-2 years, (2) 3-5 years, (3) 6-10 years, (4) 11-20 years, and (5) 21-30 years. The five categories for educational attainment were (1) primary school, (2) second lyceum year or equivalent, (3) fifth lyceum year or equivalent, (4) seventh lyceum year or equivalent, and (5) university. Three categories were used for the class, place of birth, and parents or relatives in the civil service characteristics. For class origin, the categories were (1) upper--higher managerial and professional occupations, (2) middle--all other non-manual occupations, and (3) lower--all manual occupations. For place of birth, the categories were (1) Lisbon, (2) Porto, and (3) provinces--anywhere outside of Lisbon and Porto. The categories for the parents or relatives in the civil service were (1) yes, regular civil service, (2) yes, but only the post office and schools, and (3) no. The categories for sex were, of course, (1) male and (2) female.

SOCIAL ORIGINS

Before discussing the results of the analysis of political attitudes, it is necessary to present the background data for the sample. These data will give an indication of the extent of the purge carried out by Portugal's new political elite and the degree to which patterns of administrative elite recruitment and selection for the rank of director-general have been affected.

The frequency distribution for each background characteristic is displayed in Table 8.1. The table shows Portugal's administrative elite to be mainly young (55 percent between 25 and 44), relatively recently appointed (65 percent since 1960), universally college educated, primarily from middle-class and upper-class families (76 percent), principally of provincial origin (65 percent), overwhelmingly male (93 percent), and from regular civil service families about one-half of the time (52 percent). When compared to the data on senior civil servants in Western Europe provided by the Michigan group, Portuguese DGs are found to be similar in terms of sex, educational attainment, class, and family connections to the civil service. Portuguese DGs are decidedly younger and more recently recruited than their West European counterparts.[17]

As can be observed in Table 8.1, 38 percent of Portugal's DGs were appointed to their posts since April 25, 1974 (categories 1 and 2), and 62 percent were appointed before that event. While it is debatable whether a 38 percent change in personnel represents a purge, there is little doubt that it is significant. Its significance can be seen when compared with Italy, for example, where there were considerably more carry-overs in high-level personnel subsequent to the collapse of the fascist regime after a comparable period of time.[18] Thus, the purge in Portugal in the aftermath of the April 25 *golpe* does seem to have made a substantial impact on personnel although the numbers of high-level civil servants appointed during the New State remain high.

TABLE 8.1
Backgrounds and careers of a sample of Portuguese directors-general (N = 68)

Characteristics and Categories	Number*	Percent
Age		
25-34	15	23
35-44	22	32
45-54	17	25
55-64	12	18
65+	2	3
Years entered civil service		
1930-39	2	3
1940-49	10	15
1950-59	11	17
1960-69	25	37
1970-79	19	28
Tenure in present post		
0-2 years	7	12
3-5 years	16	26
6-10 years	7	12
11-20 years	16	27
21-30 years	14	23
Class		
Upper	17	28
Middle	30	48
Lower	15	24
Birthplace		
Lisbon	20	30
Porto	3	5
Provinces	42	65
Relatives in civil service		
Yes, regular civil service	28	42
Yes, post office, schools only	7	10
No	32	48
Education (highest level)		
University	68	100
Sex		
Male	63	93
Female	5	7

*Numbers in the categories for some characteristics do not add up to 68 because of missing data.

But does this level of change mean that the purges have also had an appreciable effect on other background characteristics? Do DGs appointed after 1974 come from different social classes? Do they come from Portugal's two major cities, Lisbon and Porto, or the provinces? Are they more or less likely to have family ties to the civil service? Are there more women among the post-1974 appointees? In order to answer these questions, the sample was broken down into two groups: those appointed before 1974 and those after. The frequencies for each category of the various background characteristics were calculated and compared for these two groups, except for education, which was the same for all respondents.

The frequencies for age, which can be seen in Table 8.2, show clearly that DGs appointed since 1974 are decidedly younger, 68 percent being between 25 and 44, and those appointed before are considerably older, 43.5 percent being 45 years of age or older. Thus, the relative youthfulness of Portugal's DGs stems from the fact that a fairly large proportion of appointees since 1974 have been younger individuals. The data on class background show no appreciable differences between DGs appointed before 1974 and those appointed after; that is, about the same proportion of both groups come from the upper, middle, and lower classes. It is interesting to note that the largest percentage of both groups comes from middle class backgrounds. The frequencies for place of birth show a clear tendency for DGs appointed before 1974 to originate in the provinces while those appointed after are about as likely to come from Lisbon or the provinces, with a slight edge to the latter. This suggests a certain tendency away from the provincial domination of the highest reaches of the bureaucracy so evident among the pre-1974 appointees. Frequencies for relatives in the civil service show no significant differences between the two groups. Surprisingly, the frequencies for sex show that all five of the women in the sample were appointed before April 25.[19]

It can be concluded from these findings that the purge of the high-level civil service carried out by Portugal's new political elite had its most significant impact on the age of DGs and their place of origin. These data suggest that there has been not only a fairly important purge of individuals associated with the old regime but also some change in recruitment patterns and appointment preferences. The most important of these changes is in the discernible shift from a clear preference for individuals from the provinces because of the light it sheds on the social origins of the New State and the fundamental social cleavage which brought it to power in the late 1920s. Political life during the First Republic was marked by clashes between the interests and style of Lisbon and those of the provinces, especially the traditional, Catholic, small landowners

TABLE 8.2
Frequencies for background characteristics by when appointed to post of director-general

Characteristics*	Before 1974 N	Before 1974 %	After 1974 N	After 1974 %
Age				
25-34	6	14.0	9	36.0
35-44	14	32.6	8	32.0
45-54	13	30.2	8	16.0
55-64	8	18.6	4	16.0
65+	2	4.7	0	0.0
Class				
Upper	11	25.6	6	24.0
Middle	20	46.5	10	40.0
Lower	9	20.9	7	28.0
Birthplace				
Lisbon	10	23.3	10	40.0
Porto	2	4.7	1	4.0
Provinces	30	69.8	12	48.0
Relatives in civil service				
Yes, regular civil service	18	41.9	10	40.0
Yes, post office, schools only	4	9.3	3	12.0
No	21	48.8	11	44.0
Sex				
Male	38	88.4	25	100.0
Female	5	11.6	0	0.0

*Total numbers for each characteristic vary because of missing data.

of the north. The New State was a result of the mobilization of this periphery against the center, especially Lisbon.[20] The victory of the periphery can be seen in the predominance of DGs from the provinces among those appointed before 1974. The relatively substantial purge of many DGs associated with the New State as well as the greater tendency for DGs appointed since 1974 to come from Lisbon might be suggestive of the reassertion of the center over the periphery.

POLITICAL ATTITUDES

Now that age and place of birth have been determined to be important variables in the recent recruitment of Portugal's administrative elite, what of their political attitudes? Do the political attitudes of DGs appointed after April 25, 1974, differ significantly from those appointed before? Table 8.3 shows the mean scores for the four political attitude indices for the two groups of DGs. It is apparent from the table that DGs appointed after 1974 show more tolerance for politics, programmatic commitment, and less elitism than their colleagues appointed during the New State. Surprisingly, however, the mean scores for tolerance for conflict show the post-1974 DGs to be less tolerant of conflict in general than those appointed before. Except for tolerance of conflict, then, the mean scores show a clear change in attitudes between DGs appointed before 1974 and those appointed afterwards towards a greater tolerance for and responsiveness to democratic policymaking. The greater intolerance for conflict among post-1974 DGs may be a reaction to the higher levels of conflict that have characterized Portuguese political life since 1974.

TABLE 8.3
Mean scores for the tolerance for politics, programmatic commitment, elitism, and tolerance for conflict indices by when appointed to post of director-general

Index	Pre-1974	Post-1974
Tolerance for politics	32.6	38.2
Programmatic commitment	34.3	40.0
Elitism	34.0	30.6
Tolerance for conflict	44.0	49.8

How do Portugal's DGs compare with high-level administrators from West European countries in terms of their political attitudes? Making some comparisons with scores from other countries for which comparable data are available will help answer the general question raised above about the overall level of support for democracy by Portugal's administrative elite.[21]

As can be seen in Table 8.4 Portugal's DGs, irrespective of whether they were appointed before or after 1974, score well below senior civil servants in Britain, Germany, and Sweden in terms of tolerance for politics. On average, only their Italian counterparts are less tolerant. Interestingly, however, Portugal's DGs, irrespective of when they were appointed, are the least elitist among high-level civil servants for the three countries for which comparative data are available.

TABLE 8.4
Mean scores on tolerance for politics and elitism indices for Portugal, Britain, Italy, Germany, and Sweden

Index	Pre-1974	Post-1974	Britain	Germany	Italy	Sweden
Tolerance for politics	32.6	38.2	62	59	26	58
Elitism	34.0	30.6	40	39	50	*

*Elitism score not available for Sweden.

Although no comparative data are available for the programmatic commitment and tolerance for conflict indices, some idea of the relative position of Portugal's senior civil servants can be achieved by comparing their scores with the mid-point of each of these scales. As both range from 10 to 90, the mid-point is 50. The mean score on the programmatic commitment index for DGs appointed before 1974 is 34.3 and 40.0 for those appointed since that date. Thus, irrespective of when appointed, the scores for Portuguese DGs are well below the mid-point. The mean score on the tolerance for conflict index for the pre-1974 group is 44.6 and 49.8 for the post-1974 appointees. On this index the scores for Portuguese DGs are only slightly below the mid-point of 50.

Unfortunately, these comparisons with other West

European countries and index mid-points do not give an unequivocal answer to the degree of support for democratic policymaking manifested by Portugal's senior civil servants as a whole. While there have been changes in the political attitudes from pre- to post-1974 appointees, Portuguese DGs appear to be comparatively intolerant of politics (but not the most intolerant) and demonstrate low levels of programmatic commitment as would be expected given the long tradition of administrative policymaking in Portugal. However, Portuguese DGs do seem to be comparatively the least elitist and relatively tolerant of conflict, which would not be expected given this tradition.

CONCLUSIONS

The foregoing discussion of the social origins and political attitudes of Portugal's administrative elite has noted, first, that Portuguese DGs, when compared to high-level civil servants from other West European democracies, differ significantly in terms of age and length of time in the civil service, being on average younger and more recently appointed to their posts than their West European counterparts. This youthfulness is a result of the purge carried out after 1974 which saw the replacement of well over one-third of Portugal's DGs.

Second, in addition to the lowering of the average age of Portugal's DGs, the analysis has noted that the post-1974 purge resulted in a discernible tendency in the recruitment of proportionately fewer individuals of provincial origins, indicating, perhaps, the reassertion of Portugal's center, that is Lisbon, over its periphery.

Third, the analysis showed some change in attitude from less to more tolerance and programmatic commitment and from more to less elitism for DGs appointed after 1974. The analysis also showed, however, that the post-1974 appointees were somewhat less tolerant of conflict than the pre-1974 group. Thus, it can be concluded that the purge has not affected the age and origins of Portugal's DGs as a whole but on three of the four indices has brought about some changes in political attitudes. These changes, except for the general intolerance of conflict, are favorable to democratic policymaking.

Fourth, the comparisons made with their counterparts in those West European countries for which data are available showed Portuguese DGs to be on the whole less tolerant of politics, less programmatically committed, and somewhat less tolerant of conflict, but less elitist.

These findings, while not uniformly favorable,

allow the conclusion that some measure of change in background characteristics and orientations toward democratic policymaking has been achieved by the post-1974 purge. This trend, if continued, would enhance the survival chances of Portugal's new democratic regime. Although they are not at present so disposed, Portuguese DGs could come to be as positively oriented toward democratic policymaking as their colleagues in the established democracies of Western Europe.

NOTES

1. On the deline of parliament and political parties as initiators of public policy see Alfred Grosser, "The Evolution of European Parliaments," in A New Europe, ed. Stephen R. Graubard (Boston: Beacon Press, 1967); Karl Dietrich Bracher, "Problems of Parliamentary Democracy in Europe," in ibid.; Gerhard Loewenberg (ed.), Modern Parliaments: Change or Decline? (Chicago and New York: Aldine/Atherton, 1971); and Otto Kirchheimer, "The Waning of Opposition in Parliamentary Regimes," Social Research 24 (Summer 1957): 127-156.

2. Suzanne Berger, "The Changing Politics of Policy Making," in Patterns of Government, 3rd ed., ed. Samuel H. Beer (New York: Random House, 1973), p. 419.

3. In 1968 a Secretariat for Administrative Reform was established; his function was to "readjust" the administrative machinery of the state. See Secretariat for Administrative Reform, Principles and Directives of the Administrative Reform in Portugal (Lisbon, 1968).

4. Rui Machete, "O Papel do Instituto Nacional de Administração na Formação dos Funcionários Superiores," Prospectivas, Nos. 10, 11, and 12 (April-December 1982): 11-18.

5. Lawrence S. Graham, "Bureaucratic Politics and the Problem of Reform in the State Apparatus," in In Search of Modern Portugal: The Revolution and Its Consequences, ed. Lawrence S. Graham and Douglas L. Wheeler (Madison, Wis.: University of Wisconsin Press, 1983), pp. 224-227.

6. Fernando Diogo da Silva, "Uma Administração Envelhecida," Revista da Administração Pública 2 (October-December, 1979):621-650.

7. For analyses of the social origins of other Portuguese elites see Paul H. Lewis, "Salazar's Ministerial Elite, 1932-1968," Journal of Politics 40 (August 1978): 622-647; and Harry M. Makler, "The Portuguese Industrial Elite and Its Corporative Relations: A Study of Compartmentalization in an Authoritarian Regime," in Contemporary Portugal: The Revolution and Its Antecedents, ed. Lawrence S. Graham and Harry Makler (Austin and London: University of Texas Press, 1979), pp. 123-165.

8. The data that follow first appeared in Walter C. Opello, Jr., "Portugal's Administrative Elite: Social Origins and Political Attitudes," West European Politics 6 (January 1983): 63-74.

9. This dichotomous typology of bureaucrats is from Robert D. Putnam, "The Political Attitudes of Senior Civil Servants in Britain, Germany, and Italy," in The Mandarins of Western Europe, ed. Mattei Dogan (New York and London: Halstead Press, 1975), pp. 89-91.

10. See the articles in the Mandarins of Western Europe reporting the results of this research.

11. The questionnaire was sent (May-June, 1980) to the Ministries of Internal Administration, Justice, Finance and Planning, Education and Culture, Labor, Social Affairs, Agriculture and Fishing, Communications and Transportation, Commerce and Tourism, Industry and Economy, and Housing and Public Works. The Ministries of Foreign Affairs and Defense were not sent questionnaires because the personnel in these services are not strictly part of the regular civil service.

12. It should be noted that the degree of bias in the sample is unknown because proportions of all DGs in the various independent variable categories were unavailable.

13. The following six questions from Putnam, "The Political Attitudes of Senior Civil Servants," p. 101, were combined to create the tolerance for politics index: (1) Fundamentally, it is not the political parties and the Assembly of the Republic but, on the contrary, public administration which guarantees satisfactory public policy in this country; (2) Often, those who enter politics think more of their own well-being and of their party than of the well-being of the citizens; (3) The interference of politicians in the affairs which are appropriately the function of public administration is a disturbing characteristic of contemporary political life; (4) In contemporary social and economic affairs it is essential that technical considerations have more weight than political factors; (5) The general well-being of the country is put in grave danger by the continual clash of groups with private interests; and (6) Although political parties play an important role in a democracy, frequently, they uselessly exacerbate political conflicts. To compute the tolerance for politics index, each DG was given one point for an "agree" response to a question, three points for an "agree with reservations," seven points for a "disagree with reservations" and nine points for a "disagree." The tolerance for politics index for each DG is the average score on the six questions multiplied by 10.

14. The following three questions from Putnam, "The Political Attitudes of Senior Civil Servants," p. 105, were combined to form the programmatic commitment index: (1) The force and efficiency of a government are more important than its specific program; (2) Generally, in political controversies, extreme positions should be avoided because the true answer lies somewhere in the middle, and (3) Politics is the art of the possible and, therefore, the leaders of the country ought to worry more about that which can be done in the short run than about ambitious long-range plans. As with the tolerance for politics index, the programmatic commitment index was computed by giving one for an "agree" response to a question, three points for an "agree with reservations," seven points for a "disagree with reservations," and nine points for a "disagree." The programmatic commitment for each DG is the average

score on the three questions multiplied by 10.

15. The following six questions from Putnam, "The Political Attitudes of Senior Civil Servants," p. 108, were combined to construct the elitism index: (1) Some people are more qualified to lead this country because of their traditions and family background; (2) It does not make sense to speak of control of the acts of government by ordinary citizens; (3) It will always be necessary to have a small group of strong and competent individuals who know how to take charge of the situation; (4) The people should be allowed to vote even if they do not know what they want; (5) Few people know what their true interests are in the long term; and (6) All citizens should have the same opportunity to influence government policy. The elitism index was computed by giving nine points for an "agree" response, seven points for an "agree with reservations," three points for a "disagree with reservations," and one point for a "disagree" for questions one, two, three, and five. Scoring was reversed for questions four and six, which were phrased so that to agree is to be antielitist. The index is each respondent's average score on the six questions multiplied by 10.

16. The tolerance for political conflict index was composed of the following four questions from Samuel Eldersveld et al., "Elite Perceptions of the Political Process in the Netherlands, Looked at in Comparative Perspective," in The Mandarins of Western Europe, ed. Mattei Dogan (New York and London: Halstead Press, 1975), p. 147: (1) Abstract principles of justice rarely resolve social problems; (2) When a group or individual gains a victory, it generally indicates that another group or individual loses; (3) Only by social conflict can progress be achieved in modern society; and (4) To compromise with political adversaries is dangerous because it normally leads to the betrayal of one's own group. The tolerance for conflict index was computed by giving nine points for an "agree" response, seven points for an "agree with reservations," three points for a "disagree with reservations," and one point for a "disagree" for questions one and four. Scoring was reversed for questions two and three, which were phrased so that to agree is to be intolerant. The index is each respondent's average score on the four questions multiplied by 10.

17. Comparative data are from Putnam, "The Political Attitudes of Senior Civil Servants."

18. Robert D. Putnam, "The Political Attitudes of Senior Civil Servants in Western Europe: A Preliminary Report," British Journal of Political Science 3 (1973): 278-281.

19. It should be noted that none of these differences were found to be statistically significant. This is probably due to the small size of the sample.

20. Philippe C. Schmitter, "The Regime d'Exception That Became the Rule: Forty-eight Years of Authoritarian Domination in Portugal," in Contemporary Portugal: The Revolution and Its Antecedents, ed. Lawrence S. Graham and Harry Makler (Austin and London: University of Texas Press, 1979), p. 12.

21. Comparative data are from Putnam, "The Political Attitudes of Senior Civil Servants."

9
Local Government: Political Culture and Structure

Perhaps the most important debate in the literature on political culture theory concerns the relationship between political culture and political structure.[1] That is to say, is it the political culture of a polity which determines the configuration of its political structure or is the political culture merely a reflection of such structure. Critics of political culture theory have pointed out that most studies of political culture have tended to examine political culture in isolation and assumed that political structures are congruent with and determined by the political culture in which they are embedded.[2] Almond, the father of political culture theory, has argued, however, that this characterization of the causal direction of the relationship between culture and structure is incorrect, that "political culture [has been] treated as both an independent and a dependent variable, as causing structure and as being caused by it."[3] Almond's defense to the contrary notwithstanding, there is little doubt that in the great majority of political culture studies, "the political structure side of the relationship receives much more cursory attention."[4] Even in a recent essay on this debate, Almond is primarily concerned with distinguishing "ideological political culture," "operational political culture," and the "real political culture" and whether culture imposes "significant constraints on effective behavioral or structural change. . . ."[5]

Local government in Portugal is an excellent laboratory for an investigation of the direction of causality between political culture and structure because it constitutes a "crucial experiment"[6] in regime change which makes possible the determination of cultural as well as structural change. The first order of business will be to examine the political structure side of the relationship. It is imperative that political structure be given more than cursory attention; therefore, the extent of structural change will be accurately determined. The second will be to examine the political culture side of the relationship. In this examination, the content of local Portuguese political culture, unlike earlier studies,[7] will not be inferred from the ideology of Portugal's new elite nor from the formal-legal arrangements of local governmental structures but, rather, will be measured independently using a survey instrument. In like manner, structural change will also not be inferred from the ideology of Portugal's new democratic elite. The author seeks to apply what Almond has called a "relaxed version" of political culture;[8] that is, one which views the relationship between political culture and structure as essentially an interactive one. In this view, political culture is conceived as complementary to but not a substitute for other explanations. Although structure and culture will be seen as establishing mutual limits for one another, political culture will be viewed largely as a response to a particular type of regime with a specific organizational format.[9]

LOCAL POLITICAL STRUCTURE: CONTINUITY AND CHANGE[10]

During the New State, local government in Portugal was organized into a three-tiered, hierarchical system of geographical units. The smallest of these was the parish (<u>freguesia</u>) which was administered by a board (<u>junta de freguesia</u>). The boards consisted of three members (<u>vogais</u>); a president, a secretary, and a treasurer and were required to hold regular meetings to carry out their responsibilities. At this level there was also a justice of the peace (<u>regador</u>) who represented the police. A number of parishes formed a county (<u>concelho</u>) which was governed by a mayor (<u>presidente da câmara</u>), who was appointed by the central government, and a municipal council (<u>câmara municipal</u>). The counties were combined into eighteen districts (<u>distritos</u>) on the mainland and four on the adjacent islands of Madeira and the Azores.[11]

Although the formal powers of the parishes were extensive (e.g., to tax, expropriate land, pass local ordinances and the like), they were in fact restricted to serving as administrative agents of the national government in four areas: (1) registering voters (<u>recenseamento</u>); (2) administering various legal papers (<u>atestados</u>); (3) certifying and providing welfare for the poor; and (4) establishing medical posts.[12] Moreover, each parish was financially dependent upon the municipal council, which itself was financially dependent upon the central government. Under the law, 25 percent of the total income received by the municipality (most of which was in the form of a central government subsidy) was to be spent on public works projects within the parishes. Of the money given to the parishes, 10 percent was to be distributed equally to all. Although the remaining 90 percent was to go to those parishes most in need, no single parish was to receive, over time, a sum greater than that of the others.[13]

The policymaking process at the local level was highly centralized and the decisional flow was from the top down. Most communication took the form of directives and administrative decrees which preempted local initiative and which the municipalities and parishes were obliged to carry out and enforce. Moreover, as has already been made clear in previous chapters, the New State vigorously discouraged political activity even within the structure of the system. The only political association that was allowed to organize was the UN/ANP, which was organizationally very weak at the local level and functioned only at election time to approve lists of candidates. Furthermore, there was an almost complete lack of economic, social, or religious associations which could have acted as aggregators and articulators of individual or group interests. Thus, local level political life during the authoritarian period was

> characterized by minimal and trivial politics . . . . [c]onstraints on local-level political activity in the Portuguese state emanated from the governmental administrative process and the manner in which decrees were enforced at the local level. Although the junta was ideally a "political" body and the regador an "administrative" position, they were both, in effect, administrative agencies. Power and decisionmaking within the parish were inconsequential, while the administrative bureaucracy was of utmost importance. . . .[14]

In order to make local government more democratic, elected legislative and executive components have been grafted onto previously existing structures.[15] Thus the parish is still the primary unit of local government but it now has a unicameral assembly (assembleia da freguesia) which is elected directly by the people living in the parish and serves for three years.[16] While the executive of the parish is still the parish board, the president, treasurer, and secretary are elected by the assembly from its own membership.[17] The president of the board is still the key official in the parish and as such coordinates the board's activities, convokes its meetings, and represents the parish before governmental units at higher levels.

The second level of local government is still the municipalities (municípios), which conform to the boundaries of the pre-1974 counties. However, there are now three elective organs of municipal government: (1) the municipal assembly (assembleia municipal) composed of the presidents of the county's parish boards as well as an equal number (plus one) of members elected directly;[18] (2) the municipal chamber (câmara municipal), the executive branch of the municipality composed of a mayor and a number of aldermen (vereadores) elected directly;[19] and (3) the county council (conselho), a consultative body composed of representatives from the county's economic, social, cultural, and professional organizations. The mayor is no longer appointed but is automatically the person who receives the most votes among those running for the chamber. The mayor is the only salaried elected official and, like the presidents of the parish boards, he is the key governmental official at the county level. As such, he convokes meetings of the chamber (usually every two weeks), executes directives, and supervises municipal employees.

As in the pre-1974 period, both levels of local government--the municipalities and parishes--have been granted extensive powers. Both theoretically can impose taxes, pass local ordinances, expropriate lands, grant licenses and set the number and salaries of municipal employees. In addition to these powers, in an effort to decentralize local government and involve the citizenry more directly in the decisionmaking process, the municipal chamber and the parish boards are now required to submit to their respective assemblies for approval a yearly plan of activities and budget. The chamber and parish boards must also submit to the assemblies yearly reports on the management and accounts of the municipality and parishes.

It would appear from this formalistic description of Portugal's new governmental structures at the local level that the citizenry of the counties are well integrated into the decisionmaking process and effective participation has been achieved. After all, local authorities have been granted power over a wide range of governmental activity; there is now direct election of local assemblies; the executives of the parishes and the municipalities are theoretically responsible to these local assemblies and have been granted control over local administration; and both the parishes and municipalities have the power to finance activities in their own locales.[20]

However, despite these changes, the reality is altogether different. Most of these powers are still preempted by the national state and the actual structure and policy formation of local government is little different from that of the previous regime. The municipalities and the parishes are actually little involved in local policymaking because of administrative and financial constraints on their ability to make independent decisions on local priorities that are similar to those constraints which existed during the New State. The parish boards and the municipal chambers are still,

for the most part, administrative arms of the state and
as such are required by the administrative code (Código
Administrativo) to attend to a wide range of local services. Thus, the plans of activities and budgets for
the municipal chambers are not really policy documents
setting forth concrete goals and priorities. Instead,
they resemble "shopping lists" of unprioritized projects
and needs within each municipality's public works
responsibilities. Moreover, the yearly reports of activities are simply detailed accountings of the administrative, technical, and financial activities of the
chambers.[21]

As for the parish boards, their function is still
primarily that of administrative conduit between the
parishes and the municipalities. Their activity plans
simply list parish public works needs in unprioritized
fashion. While there may be efforts by the presidents
of the various parish boards to influence the decisions
of their chamber to expedite requests, the general approach, as during the New State, is to avoid making
choices and to spread a municipality's meager resources
as evenly as possible among its parishes.

The chambers still function much like administrative committees doing little more than routinely considering building permits, granting licenses for markets
and fairs, and approving the disbursement of petty sums
of money to pay personnel and purchase equipment.[22]

Moreover, as before, the state must ultimately
approve all activities of the municipal chambers and may
veto any decisions considered illegal under the administrative code. Like the French system upon which it is
modeled, local government and the national state are
linked together by the administrative tutelage (tutela
administrativa) exercised by the civil governor of the
district. The governor, who is appointed by the Ministry of Internal Administration, has overall responsibility for the proper functioning of local government in
the district. Governors see to it that local governments carry out national laws and can conduct inquiries
and investigations into their activities. The governor
has the power to dissolve local authorities if it has
been demonstrated that they have behaved illegally,
failed to fulfill their administrative tasks, or refused
to carry out decisions made at higher levels.[23]

This means that despite the fact that they are
elected, mayors as well as presidents of parish boards
are still the administrative representatives of the
national state at the local level. As agents of the
state they are ultimately responsible to the civil
governor and not to their respective municipal and parish assemblies. Moreover, the presidents of the parish
boards still spend between 80 and 90 percent of their
time doing routine legal chores (atestados) and mayors
spend the bulk of their time carrying out administrative

duties connected with the management of the country.
  The second constraint on the ability of the municipality and parishes to make independent decisions on local priorities for themselves is financial. As during the New State, local governments have two sources of revenue. One source is "ordinary" revenue derived from direct taxes on agricultural and industrial production and businesses within the municipalities as well as taxes on building permits; markets and fairs; public advertising; hunting, dog, and bicycle licenses; and small fines. The other source is "extraordinary" revenue granted by the central government for specific projects such as the electrification of a village or building a school.[24]
  Table 9.1 shows the revenue, by source, of a typical rural municipality. It can be readily seen that about 30 percent of the municipalities' total revenue comes in the form of extraordinary grants-in-aid from the national state for specific public works projects. This financial dependence is compounded by the fact that 11,776,000 escudos of ordinary revenue, or about 40 percent, is still composed of grants-in-aid from the state, about one-half of which is earmarked for road maintenance and municipal employees' salaries. The remaining 5,300,000 escudos is a free grant to be used as the mayor and chamber see fit. This means that a total of 25,538,306 escudos or about 65 percent of the municipality's income is in the form of subsidies from the state. Without these grants-in-aid the chamber would not even have sufficient revenues from ordinary sources to pay the wages of its employees and meet its debt service obligations.

TABLE 9.1
Revenues of Porto de Mós, by source, 1977
(in millions of escudos)

Source	Amount	Percent of Ordinary	Percent of Total
Ordinary			
Locally derived	13,958,276	54	
State grants	11,776,000	46	
Ordinary subtotal	25,734,276	100	66
Extraordinary	13,762,306		34
Total revenue	39,496,682		100

Source: Municipal de Porto de Mós, "Relatório de Actividades e Contas de Gerência de 1977," p. 9. (Mimeographed.)

Thus, the administrative and financial dependence on the central government means that whatever independence and policymaking power municipalities have theoretically gained since April 25, 1974, much of it has, as before, been nullified in practice. These constraints limit municipalities to making decisions only on routine administrative matters and the maintenance and improvement of municipal services. While some projects and parishes may receive more attention than others because of a perceived need from a public works point of view, the municipalities are still not free to make political choices and decisions on local priorities. Such decisions are essentially made for the municipalities at the highest reaches of the state's administrative appratus where all projects, even the most petty, must be approved and financed.

What of personnel? Have there been any significant changes in the types of individuals holding key local offices--mayors and presidents of parish boards--and changes in their political attitudes and behavior? Research has shown that choosing mayors by election has not resulted in the selection of individuals who are markedly different from those who would have been appointed during the New State. As before, mayors are very likely to be "local notables," that is, relatively well-educated individuals from the local middle class.[25]

Moreover, the constraints imposed by the state have had a strong effect on the attitudes and behaviors of local elected officials. First, there is a tendency for elected officials to see themselves primarily as administrators and local governance as a question of efficient management, teamwork, and impartiality. Nonpartisan attitudes and behavior are fairly widespread. Very few elected officials conceive of themselves as representing a particular party and set of interests. Generally, party labels have much less meaning than they do at the national level and divergencies among the elected officials are nonideological and concerned almost exclusively with differing views on administrative matters.

Second, the submerging of individual and partisan interests suggests that local officials tend to view the municipality as a harmonious unit encompassing a uniform local interest which is constantly being exploited by the national state. Not unlike the French perception of their communes as fortresses, the municipality is perceived by the Portuguese as a fort (<u>forteleza</u>), besieged by the administrative apparatus of the state, and the mayor and his "team" of aldermen are its defenders.[26] The mayor is clearly viewed in paternalistic terms as the head (<u>patrão</u>) of a large family whose primary responsibility is to defend the county and use his influence to "bring home the bacon" from the central government.

Finally, local officials tend to express

considerable frustration with the administrative and financial constraints imposed by the central government which prevent them from representing their constituents and playing a more direct role in the local policy formation process. Because of this frustration and the fact that only mayors receive salary for their work, few elected officials have strong political ambitions.

In summary, it can be said that, despite attempts to make local government democratic by grafting on representative bodies and electing local officials, the actual working of local government structures of the municipalities and parishes has changed very little since April 25, 1974. Local political structures are still very much an integral part of the national administrative apparatus and local elected officials are essentially bureaucrats. Policymaking still takes place in the highest reaches of Portugal's administrative system.

LOCAL POLITICAL CULTURE

Now that it has been shown that the organization of local political structures and the policy process have not changed significantly since April 25, 1974, attention can be devoted to the analysis of local political culture. As conceived here, political culture is the pattern of individual attitudes and orientations among the members of a political system.[27] Such individual orientation can be broken down into two basic components: (1) orientations toward the political system and (2) orientations toward the self as political actor. Orientations toward the political system include knowledge of the political system (cognition); feelings of attachment to the political system (affectation); and judgements about the political system (evaluation). Orientations toward the self as political actor can be broken down into one's sense of how one should participate in politics (obligations) and one's feeling of political influence (competence).[28]

One of the primary tools for measuring political culture is attitudinal surveys.[29] The data which follow are based on such a survey. The personal interviews averaged 30 minutes in length and were designed to elicit a citizen's orientations to the local political system and the self as actor in that system.[30] The interviews were performed by a team of interviewers recruited from a local secondary school (liceu) at the research site and trained by the author. Respondents were selected from voter registration lists in such a way that every individual of voting age living within the county had an equal chance of being chosen. Within each of the county's thirteen parishes a sample was selected proportionate to the voters registered in that parish. By this process, 309 individuals were selected. Only 193 of these, however, were actually interviewed because many people were absent from home or had emigrated since the registration lists had been prepared. A much smaller number were too ill or refused to be interviewed.[31]

The first orientation examined is knowledge of the local political system. This orientation has two aspects: (1) awareness of local political affairs and (2) knowledge about how local government works. An index of levels of awareness was compiled from responses to the following three questions: Do you understand the political problems of the county? Are you interested in news about local politics? Do you talk about local politics with your family? The data, as portrayed in Table 9.2, suggest that the level of awareness of local politics among the citizenry is rather low. Only 30.6 percent of the respondents said that they understand the county's political problems; only 30.1 percent have more than an occasional interest in local political news; and only 21.2 percent said that they talked about local politics with their families.

TABLE 9.2
Citizen level of political awareness
(N = 193)

Level	Number of Respondents	Percent
Low	111	57.5
Medium	33	17.1
High	49	25.4

An index of political knowledge about the workings of local government was compiled from responses to the following two questions: Who makes the decisions in your parish and in the county? Do you know the names of any of the county's officials? The data given in Table 9.3 suggest that the level of political knowledge about the operation of local government among the county is medium. Of those respondents who had an opinion, 50.3 percent named either the president of their parish board, the president of the municipal chamber, or the board or chamber itself. Only 3.1 percent thought some other political entity such as one of the political parties or some other governmental body such as the municipal or parish assemblies made political decisions. A large number of the respondents (69.9 percent) could not name a local official. Of those respondents who could, 90 percent mentioned either the mayor or the president of their parish board.

TABLE 9.3
Citizen level of political knowledge
(N = 193)

Level	Number of Respondents	Percent
Low	66	34.2
Medium	81	42.0
High	46	23.8

The picture that emerges from the data presented on political knowledge suggests that the citizens of the county are oriented toward the "downward" side of the local political system; that is, the administrative apparatus. The respondents seemed to be reasonably knowledgeable as to who or what entity makes local political decisions. They were less knowledgeable, however, about who the individuals were making those decisions. On the other hand, the data suggest that the respondents have little awareness or interest in the "upward" side of the local political system; that is, its political policymaking structures. Only about one-third of the respondents claimed to understand the county's political problems, had an interest in local political news, or talked about politics at home. The great bulk of the citizenry of the county appears not to be oriented toward input structures and is generally disinterested in and ignorant of the county's political problems.

With respect to feelings of attachment to the local political system, the respondents were asked: When you give your point of view to an official of the parish board or the municipal chamber, do you feel that your opinion is taken into consideration? Here it is assumed that the affectation people have toward local government is influenced by the treatment they receive at the hands of functionaries. It can be fairly safely assumed that if fair and considerate treatment is expected, citizens will be favorably disposed toward the local political system.

Table 9.4 shows that these expectations are quite high among the respondents. Nearly one-half (46.6 percent) of the respondents expected to be treated fairly by local officials, while 32.7 percent did not or expected such treatment some of the time. These findings suggest that not only are the citizens of the county oriented toward the administrative side of the local political system but they are favorably inclined toward those structures as well. These positive feelings toward local government are also reflected in the citizenry's evaluations of the local political system.

TABLE 9.4
Citizen expectation of fair treatment
(N = 193)

Expectation	Number of Respondents	Percent
Yes	90	46.6
Sometimes	27	14.0
No	36	18.7
Don't know	40	20.7

To determine the respondents' judgements about the local political system, an index was compiled from two questions: Do you think that the activities of the parish boards and the municipal chamber tend to make conditions better in the county? Do you think that the people would be better off without the parish boards and municipal chamber? Table 9.5 reveals that local government receives a high evaluation by the citizens of the county. Well over one-half (65.3 percent) of the respondents had a high evaluation of the activities of local government and a huge majority (89.7 percent) had a medium to high evaluation.

TABLE 9.5
Citizen level of evaluation of local political system (N = 193)

Level	Number of Respondents	Percent
Low	19	9.8
Medium	47	24.4
High	127	65.3

These results indicate that not only are the citizens of the county oriented toward the administrative aspect of the local political system, but they also have very positive evaluations of the impact and effect of these bureaucratic structures on life conditions within the county. In fact, these orientations are so favorable that only a small minority of citizens (9.8 percent) rate local government low and believe that conditions within the county would improve if local government would disappear. These findings suggest that not only are the citizens of the county oriented to administrative structures, they are as well strongly allegiant to them.

But what of political structures? How does the citizenry of the county evaluate the parish and municipal assemblies? To find out, the respondents were asked: What do you think of the activities of your parish assembly or the municipal assembly? Table 9.6 shows that very nearly one-half of the respondents had no opinion about the activities of the local elected assemblies. Of those who expressed an opinion, only 26.9 percent viewed the assemblies in a favorable light, while 23.4 percent perceived them as not or only sometimes valuable. These findings are quite consistent with previous ones which show the citizenry of the county to be oriented toward and favorably disposed to administrative structures and not oriented toward and generally disinterested in and ignorant of the county's new political policymaking structures.

TABLE 9.6
Citizen evaluation of local assemblies
(N = 193)

Opinion	Number of Respondents	Percent
Valuable	32	26.9
Sometimes valuable	20	10.4
Not valuable	25	13.0
Don't know	96	49.7

Further evidence for this conclusion is provided by the respondents' answers to the following questions designed to measure the saliency of political policymaking structures: Do you have contact with any political group or organization? With which political party do you identify? The index compiled from these two questions is presented in Table 9.7. It shows that the salience level of input structures is generally low. This finding reinforces the earlier findings that political structures have only a vague silhouette for the citizens of the county at least as far as local government is concerned.

TABLE 9.7
Level of salience of input structures
(N = 193)

Level	Number of Respondents	Percent
Low	87	45.1
Medium	76	39.4
High	30	15.5

It can be concluded from the above results that Portugal's new political policymaking structures are not the recipients of feelings of attachment nor do they receive high evaluations for their performance. This is in sharp contrast to the strong attachments and positive evaluations of the administrative aspect of the local political system.

Now that orientations toward the political system have been explored, it is time to discuss the way the respondents view themselves as political actors and their feelings of competence as such actors. To find out how the respondents conceive of themselves as political actors, they were asked: What role should people like yourself play in local political affairs? The results displayed in Table 9.8 indicate that nearly 60 percent of the respondents either have a passive conception of their role or have no conception of the self as political actor. Typical responses of those classified as passives were: to be content with what one has; to cooperate; to work harder; to be humble; and to cooperate with the authorities. For those classified as actives, typical responses were: to speak to the parish board and municipal chamber; to discuss the issues and problems; and to look at the alternatives. Only three respondents mentioned participating in the parish or municipal assemblies; attending party meetings; or voting in one's own interest. The data suggest then that few citizens in the county conceive of themselves as active participants in politics.

TABLE 9.8
Citizen political role perception
(N = 193)

Role	Number of Respondents	Percent
Active	81	42.0
Passive	59	30.5
Don't know	53	27.5

A competency index was compiled from the following four questions: What would you do if your parish board or the municipal chamber were debating a regulation or project that you considered unjust? If such a situation were to occur in the future, would you try to do something to change it? If you tried to influence your board or the municipal chamber, do you think your efforts would be successful? How would you proceed if you wanted to get something done by your parish board or the municipal chamber? The data in Table 9.9 show a certain tendency toward a high level of competence among the respondents which is quite surprising in light of the earlier finding that they do not perceive of themselves as active political actors. How can this contradiction be reconciled?

TABLE 9.9
Citizen level of competence as political actors (N = 193)

Level	Number of Respondents	Percent
Low	59	30.6
Medium	43	22.3
High	91	47.1

The answer lies in the distinction that can be made between political and administrative competence.[32] It appears that the respondents do not perceive of themselves as able to influence local government by organizing groups or threatening to withdraw their support. Rather, they perceive of themselves as having influence over local government which they can exercise by individually attending meetings of their parish board or the municipal chamber and by appealing to a set of rules of proper and moral administrative conduct. As has been shown, a large proportion of the respondents expect fair treatment, at least some of the time, from local officials; believe that their point of view is given consideration; and seem willing to protest what they consider to be an unjust project or regulation.

This sense of administrative competence does not derive from the respondents' active attempts to influence but rather from their beliefs that local government officials should be controlled by rules of moral conduct that curb the arbitrary exercise of power. This orientation toward a moral code as protection against arbitrariness by local officials can be seen in the replies given by the respondents to the following question: In your opinion, what are the most important qualities for a local elected official to have? As can be observed in Table 9.10, only a little less than one-third (27.5 percent) of the respondents had no idea about the qualities they expected in elected officials. Of the 72.5 percent who did express an opinion, nearly one-half (32.6 percent) said that they expected local elected officials to be above all, honest. This attribute was followed in terms of frequency of mention by such qualities as hardworking, impartial, good men, just, and so forth.

TABLE 9.10
Qualities of local elected officials

Quality	Number of Respondents	Percent
Honest	63	32.6
Hardworking	22	11.4
Impartial	11	5.7
Good	9	4.7
Just	8	4.1
Serious	6	3.1
Sincere	5	2.1
Attentive	4	1.6
Active	2	1.6
Competent	3	1.6
Good politician	3	1.6
Knowledgeable	2	1.0
Don't know	54	27.9

Additional evidence of this orientation toward a set of rules of moral conduct can be seen in the responses to the following question: What would you do if you knew that an elected official of the county had accepted bribes? The data portrayed in Table 9.11 show that the great majority of the respondents would denounce and protest such behavior. This suggests that the respondents not only expect local officials to abide by a code of moral conduct but also expect them to behave according to a set of proper administrative procedures. It also suggests that ordinary citizens share the conception of elected officials as administrators and the running of local government as essentially a question of good management, impartiality, and conscientiousness.

TABLE 9.11
Citizen attitudes toward bribes
(N = 193)

Attitude	Number of Respondents	Percent
Don't know	26	13.5
Do nothing	42	21.7
Protest, denounce	125	64.8

The data gleaned by the survey suggest that the political culture of Portugal's counties is still a "subject" one. That is, the administrative aspect of the local political system is generally more salient than the political policymaking aspect and orientations toward the self as active political actors are quite low. The respondents seemed to be well aware of the various local specialized administrative political structures; they were affectively oriented toward them; and they generally evaluated the activities of local government favorably. Although the respondents did demonstrate a measure of administrative competence, they did not conceive of themselves as active and competent political actors capable of influencing the local decisionmaking process through participation and involvement in local policymaking structures.[33]

CONCLUSIONS

It has been shown that the real underlying structural links and the policy process within Portugal's new democratic system at the local level are primarily administrative and technocratic and not very much different from those of the old regime. It has also been demonstrated that Portugal's local political culture has not changed significantly since April 25, 1974. It appears that local Portuguese political culture is a set of subject and passive attitudinal and behavioral responses to the overwhelming power and control exercised by the administrative apparatus of the state. Moreover, the deliberate efforts by previous elites, especially during the New State period, to demobilize and depoliticize the citizenry and increase the efficiency and rationality of the administrative apparatus has brought about a fusion of bureaucratic and political roles and structures in the minds of the citizenry. Politics and politicians are seen by the local population in essentially bureaucratic terms and local elected officials tend to think of their roles administratively and the running of local government as an exercise in good management. Thus, there does not appear to be a clear-cut distinction in the public consciousness between the role of bureaucrat and that of politician.

This means that the local decisionmaking process operates largely without the benefit of autonomous "political brokers." Despite the fact that local officials are now elected and must gain "approval" for their "policies" from elected assemblies, there still are no institutionalized structures and roles for clarifying, delineating, accommodating, and channeling the demands and supports of the local citizenry in ways consistent with the democratic process. The absence of such structures and roles means that the local citizenry are still cut off from any meaningful voice in policy decisions.

These structural and role problems are compounded by the local political culture. The adaptive, subject orientations and behavioral patterns which have emerged in response to the overinstitutionalized apparatus of the state persist. The high frequencies of orientations toward the administrative infrastructure of the local political system and the passive conception of the self as political actor only serve to reinforce administrative structures and roles and inhibit the development of separate political structures and roles. The local citizenry do not yet have a set of appropriate orientations and attitudes toward the role of politician and toward autonomous policymaking structures.

This subject political culture is, in turn, reinforced by the extant local political system because the actual policymaking structures and roles are yet fundamentally congruent with the orientations and behavior patterns of the local citizenry. Their political cognitions are accurate, affective, and evaluations are quite favorable, at the local level at least. This means that the few citizens who hold orientations toward the policymaking aspects of the local political system and a political activist self-conception will have great difficulty becoming competent, self-confident, experienced political actors.

This analysis of local political structure and culture shows that not only does a prior set of attitudes and orientations persist but many structural elements and roles persist as well, despite efforts by Portugal's new democratic elite to transform them. In terms of political culture theory and the question of the direction of causality, it can be concluded then that culture and political structure are both independent and dependent variables; that is, structure causes culture and is caused by it. It is clear that both structure and culture impose significant constraints on effective change in old patterns of policymaking, behaviors, attitudes, and cognitions. While political culture is not easily transformed, such is also the case with political structures. It cannot be assumed that the advent to power of a new political elite automatically means that significant transformations of political structures and the policy process have occurred. Analyses must be done to determine the extent to which new elites actually succeed in changing political structures and the extent to which these changes actually modify the political process in the direction desired by the new elite. Older structures and policy process as well as political culture together act as powerful constraints on the attempts by elites to bring about desired change.

Thus, Portugal's overinstitutionalized administrative state, as before, acts as a major "confining condition" on the post-1974 democratic elite as they seek to move the system away from authoritarianism toward democracy. The persistence of a subject political culture also acts as a "confining condition" and interacts with and thus reinforces, and is itself reinforced by political structure. In contrast to the national level, then, the extent to which the policy process at the local level has become democratized is open to serious question. The significance of this finding as well as the findings of earlier chapters for the future survivability of Portugal's fledgling democracy are the subject of the concluding chapter, to which the book now turns.

Notes

1. Brian Barry, Sociologists, Economists and Democracy (London: Collier-Macmillan, 1970), p. 53.
2. Carole Pateman, "Political Culture, Political Structure and Political Change," British Journal of Political Science 1 (July 1971): 292.
3. Gabriel A. Almond, "The Intellectual History of the Civic Culture Concept," in The Civic Culture Revisited, ed. Gabriel A. Almond and Sidney Verba (Boston and Toronto: Little, Brown, 1980), p. 29.

4. Arend Lijphart, "The Structure of Inference," in The Civic Culture Revisited, ed. Almond and Verba, p. 38.

5. Gabriel A. Almond, "Communism and Political Culture Theory," Comparative Politics 15 (January 1983): 128.

6. Barry, Sociologists, Economists and Democracy, p. 51.

7. See Chapter 1.

8. Almond, "Communism and Political Culture Theory," p. 127.

9. Kenneth Jowitt, "An Organizational Approach to the Study of Political Culture in Marxist-Leninist Systems," American Political Science Review 58 (September 1974): 1171-1191.

10. The data utilized in this chapter have been previously published in Walter C. Opello, Jr., "Local Government and Political Culture in a Portuguese Rural County," Comparative Politics 13 (April 1981): 271-289; and Walter C. Opello, Jr., "The Continuing Impact of the Old Regime on Portuguese Political Culture," in In Search of Modern Portugal, ed. Lawrence S. Graham and Douglas L. Wheeler (Madison, Wis.: University of Wisconsin Press, 1983), pp. 199-222. The data were gathered in a mountainous county (concelho) of 20,290 inhabitants within the district of Leiria. Although the bulk of the population of the county consists of poor farmers and rural workers who cultivate apples, the region's primary agricultural produce, there is some light industry, especially ceramics and textiles. For the most part, the inhabitants reside in small population concentrations (povoações) scattered throughout the county. There are, however, two fairly large villages. One is Porto de Mós, from which the county takes its name; it is the seat of local government. The other is Mire de Aire, which is the focus of the county's industry and enjoys close proximity to a set of spectacular caverns, a major tourist attraction. Although the county has experienced some emigration, the population is fairly well balanced between the sexes, there being 97 men for every 100 women.

11. Joyce Firstenberg Riegelhaupt, "Peasants and Politics in Salazar's Portugal: The Corporate State and Village 'Nonpolitics,'" in Contemporary Portugal: The Revolution and Its Antecedents, ed. Lawrence S. Graham and Harry M. Makler (Austin, Texas: University of Texas Press, 1979), pp. 163-173. See also José Cutileiro, A Portuguese Rural Society (Oxford: Clarendon Press, 1971).

12. Norman Blume, "Neighborhood Administration in Lisbon: The Juntas de Freguesia," National Civic Review 64 (May 1975): 250.

13. Riegelhaupt, "Peasants and Politics in Salazar's Portugal," p. 171.

14. Ibid., p. 172.

15. The 1976 constitution authorizes two basic units of local government subordinate to the parliament, cabinet, and prime minister: (1) the autonomous regions of the Azores and Madeira and (2) the territorial politico-administrative subdivisions on the mainland: the parish (freguesia), municipality (município) and the district (distrito). Although the constitution has retained the New State's tripartite subdivision of the country, it calls for the substitution of administrative regions for the districts. For more details on the organization of local government see Walter C. Opello, "The Second Portuguese Republic: Politico-Administrative Decentralization since April 25, 1974," Iberian Studies 7

(Autumn 1978): 43-48.

16. Porto de Mós has thirteen parishes ranging in size from Alcaria, the smallest with about 300 citizens, to Mire de Aire, the largest with about 3,000. The size of their parish assemblies depends upon the voting-age population of the parish. The smallest, those with less than 1,000 registered voters, have nine members. The number increases with population size, reaching twenty-seven members in parishes with more than 20,000 registered voters. In parishes of greater than 30,000, representation is increased by one seat for every 5,000 registered voters. In parishes of less than 301 registered voters, the assembly is replaced by a "town meeting." All registered voters in the parish are entitled to attend and take part.

17. Parishes with less than 5,000 registered voters have two members; in those between 5,000 and 10,000 registered voters, there are two additional members; and in those of greater than 20,000, there are four additional.

18. The size of the municipal assemblies depends upon the number of parishes found within the municipality. The municipal assembly of Porto de Mós had twenty-seven members, thirteen of whom were the presidents of the parish boards and fourteen of whom were elected directly.

19. The number of aldermen varies with the number of registered voters in the municipality. Municipalities of more than 100,000 registered voters have ten; those between 50,000 and 100,000 have eight; those between 10,000 and 50,000 have six; and those of less than 10,000 have four. Porto de Mós has six aldermen.

20. These characteristics of effective decentralization and citizen involvement in local policy formation are from Gordon Smith, Politics in Western Europe (New York: Holmes and Meier, 1973), pp. 256-257.

21. See, for example, Câmara Municipal de Porto de Mós, Plano de Actividades e Orcamento para 1977 and Relatório de Actividades e Contas de Gerência de 1977 (Porto de Mós, Portugal: Mimeo, 1977, 1978).

22. See, for example, Câmara Municipal do Concelho de Porto de Mós, Actas das Reuniões da Câmara Municipal, Livro de Actas, Nos. 63-67.

23. To insure that the governor does not act arbitrarily, the dissolution of any local unit requires the approval of the district assembly (assembleia distrital), which is composed of the mayors of the district's counties and two members of each municipal assembly found in the district.

24. This dependency has not been significantly alleviated despite the fact that a new local finance law was passed in 1978 instituting a system of revenue sharing which returns about 18 percent of all taxes collected by the central government to the municipalities according to a taxes paid formula.

25. Lawrence S. Graham, "The Portuguese State: The View from Below," paper presented at the Colloquium on the Formation of Contemporary Portugal, Calouste Gulbenkian Foundation, Lisbon, December 2-5, 1981, pp. 10-12.

26. Mark Kesselman, The Ambiguous Consensus: A Study of Local Government in France (New York: Knopf, 1967).

27. On this conceptualization of political culture, see Gabriel A. Almond and Sidney Verba, The Civic Culture (Princeton, N.J.: Princeton University Press, 1963); and Lucian Pye and Sidney Verba (eds.), Political Culture and Political Development (Princeton, N.J.: Princeton University Press, 1965).

28. It should be noted that the strictly "non-political" orientations of the individual to social relations and civic cooperation are not included in this study.

29. See, for example, Almond and Verba, The Civic Culture; Donald J. Devine, The Political Culture of the United States (Boston: Little, Brown, 1972): and Bradley M. Richardson, The Political Culture of Japan (Berkeley/Los Angeles, Calif.: University of California Press, 1974). Some work on political culture has been done by using in-depth interviewing and emotive techniques. See, for example, Edward C. Banfield, The Moral Basis of a Backward Society (New York: The Free Press, 1958); Richard H. Solomon, Mao's Revolution and the Chinese Political Culture (Berkeley/Los Angeles, Calif.: University of California Press, 1971); and David D. Laitin, Politics, Language, and Thought: The Somali Experience (Chicago: University of Chicago Press, 1977).

30. The questionnaire was based on that of Almond and Verba, The Civic Culture.

31. Although no test-retest procedures nor reliability coefficients were employed, there is no reason to expect that the questionnaire would be inconsistent over time. The validity of the items was ensured, first, by asking colleagues if they thought the items measured what they were intended to measure and, second, by asking Portuguese colleagues if the items had been rendered into the Portuguese in a form understandable to the ordinary citizen. For an example of this approach to reliability and validity see Fred N. Kerlinger, Behavioral Research: A Conceptual Approach (New York: Holt, Rinehart and Winston, 1979), pp. 132-141.

32. The politically competent citizen is one who plans an influential role in the decisionmaking process and participates through the use of implied or stated threats or some type of deprivation if demands are not complied with. On the other hand, the administratively competent citizen is the individual who does not participate in the decisionmaking process but is aware of rights and duties under the rules to which he appeals, rather than demands, to guard against arbitrary action of government officials. See Almond and Verba, The Civic Culture, pp. 214-216.

33. See Almond and Verba, The Civic Culture, pp. 17-21 for the characteristics of a "subject" political culture.

10
Conclusion: Whither Portugal?

It has been suggested that political instability and the failure of liberal democratic regimes in Portugal have been caused by four tensions within Portuguese society: personalism, political and ideological factionalism, conflicting patterns of land ownership in different regions, and the conflict between Lisbon and the provinces.[1]

While there is no doubt that these tensions are connected to Portugal's instability, they are symptoms of that instability rather than its cause. The basic theme of this book has been that the particular sequence and timing of the resolution of the five crises of political development have had, and continue to have, an inimical effect on the political life of Portugal. The early and complete resolution of the identity and penetration crises, especially the latter, and the later appearance and failure to resolve the participation and distribution crises, especially the former, have created a condition of severe imbalance between Portugal's administrative and political infrastructures. Symtomatic of this condition of asymmetry are, on the one hand, a highly centralized bureaucratic state and, on the other, a party system fragmented by personalism and ideological factionalism. Tension between Lisbon and the provinces is a result of the overinstitutionalization of the state's administrative apparatus. Personalism and factionalism are the result of the underinstitutionalization of the political infrastructure.

In Portugal, not unlike France, the particular pattern of political development has clogged the landscape with previously successful administrative structures which have refused to give way such that there exists a scarcity of institutionalized means for linking the citizenry to the government and for accommodating, channeling, and containing participation.[2] Previous successes at institutionalizing the administrative state have contained serious breakthroughs to and the routinization of new democratic policymaking processes and political behavior. The failure to develop any political institutions which link the citizenry to various regimes means that the elite-mass gap has not been adequately bridged with political mediating structures. Thus, there has not been any institutional insulation, as it were, which would have protected the Portuguese people against personalism, charismatic appeals, populism, Sebastianism and ideological factionalism.

Portugal's asymmetrical polity is not the result of an inherent corporatist political culture nor Portuguese national character. The comparisons made above show clearly that what has been the case for Portugal is substantially the same for certain other West European countries having a similar pattern of political development. With respect to the crises and sequences of nationstate development, it was shown that the pattern of crisis resolution found in Portugal is not dissimilar from that of France and Italy. Indeed, France is the country of Western Europe with which Portugal appears to have the most in common. The Portuguese data suggest, contrary to the expectations of the SSRC framers, that an early resolution of identity, legitimacy, and penetration not only does not facilitate the resolution of participation and distribution but actually makes the resolution of these two crises more difficult, if not impossible, especially if penetration has been dealt with successfully. This makes the institutionalization of a political infrastructure capable of resolving the participation crisis a monumental task. The analysis of the sequence of crisis resolution does, however, support the SSRC's contention that a gradual but coincident resolution of the five crises would produce much less stress than the tandem pattern found in Portugal. There is no doubt that the Portuguese pattern in which the penetration crisis preceded that of participation and distribution has rendered the resolution of the latter more stressful. The Portuguese data also support the contention that the accumulation of crises, even if only two, makes crisis resolution more difficult and stressful than otherwise would be the case.

The extent to which Portugal's particular pattern of development has created institutional conditions which have confined breakthrough attempts by new elites is apparent in the analysis of regime change. Salazar, and later Caetano, were unable to transform the New State into an organic-statist polity in conformity to their shared corporatist ideology. Resistance from various sectors of Portuguese society, the vicissitudes of history, and the overinstitutionalized administrative apparatus acted as constraints and prevented the creation of a viable corporatist infrastructure capable of resolving the participation crisis. Throughout the New State period, the principal link between government and the citizenry was administrative not political.

A conscious policy of depoliticization was pursued and bureaucratic politics was de rigueur. When wars of national liberation broke out in the African colonies, there simply did not exist any political infrastructure which could have been used to rally support for the regime and its policy of remaining in Africa. As the regime was completely incapable of innovating, it fell back on old established institutions and procedures, tightened its control, and further isolated itself from the citizenry.

The experience of Portugal with authoritarianism suggests clearly that previous assumptions about the power and durability of authoritarian regimes are illusory. The political disconnection between the regime and its citizenry, considered to be such a regime's ultimate source of strength, is, like other regime types, its Achilles heel. Thus, the structural weakness and self-defeating tendencies of authoritarian regimes do not lie within the regime's monolithic structure but without, in its relationship to the broader society. The Portuguese case suggests that authoritarian regimes are not much different from other regime types in this regard. All regimes--authoritarian, totalitarian, democratic--must resolve the participation crisis by creating a political infrastructure of some kind that provides some sense of involvement among the citizenry in the decisionmaking process and could be used to rally the populace in support of the government and its policies. The failure of Salazar and Caetano to resolve the participation crisis with their corporatist infrastructure left the regime highly vulnerable to challenges from within and the regime ultimately broke down under pressure from the military, principally over a professional grievance, which escalated to a demand for a new regime and the subsequent instability and confusion of the period of exception.

The Portuguese experience of regime change between 1974 and 1976 does not necessarily require a reevaluation of the conventional assumptions about the meaning of the concept of revolution. Rather, it suggests the extent to which the term "revolution" has become vulgarized by participant and analyst alike. The term is no longer applied only to a deeprooted convulsive change in a society in which there are major alterations to its social, economic, and political structures brought about by a broad-based revolutionary movement, but to almost any rapid regime change with little regard to the source of the change or its internal dynamic. To describe the _golpe_ of April 25, 1974, and the events of the period of exception as revolutionary is to confuse rhetoric with the dynamic of what was actually taking place.

Regime change in Portugal has never been the result of the mobilization of broad sectors of society in a revolutionary movement, and it was not on April 25, 1974. The collapse of the New State was the result of a military conspiracy which initially had much less than revolutionary goals in mind. Moreover, events during the period of exception did not see the clash of broadly based revolutionary vs. counter-revolutionary forces but, rather, the maneuverings of various elite factions, frequently led by charismatic personalities, which were seeking to gain control of the "situation" and to impose their particular conception of what should be Portugal's new regime on society. Furthermore, the spontaneous mass-based outbursts that occurred were much less "spontaneous" and much more instrumental in their aims than has been assumed. As in the past, much of this activity was gradually frustrated and contained by Portugal's overinstitutionalized administrative state apparatus and the well-developed tendency to follow old routinized patterns during unstable times.

The analysis of the evolution of Portugal's present multiparty system does not support Duverger's hypothesis concerning electoral systems and party systems. Indeed, the discussion showed that the electoral system itself was a major source of political conflict and generally followed changes in governments or regimes. These changes had much to do with political competition among certain elite factions as they sought electoral leverage and advantage over others. The trend has been from a restricted, indirect suffrage to a direct, universal one, and from a partial to a true proportional system after 1974. The present proportional system is far from institutionalized.

Although the analysis of the evolution of Portuguese political parties, which showed a marked increase in the number of parties following certain major changes in regime type, suggests that political factors are important determinants of the configuration of party systems, such a conclusion is probably premature in the Portuguese case. Most of Portugal's present parties, despite the fact that they have only recently been allowed to organize themselves openly, have deep roots which connect them to previously organized parties and ideological traditions. The process of party system development in Portugal, not unlike that of France and other West European systems, has been one of accretion and erosion not radical creation or elimination. Thus, political factors are important but not necessarily determinative.

The multiparty system seems to be most connected with personalism and ideological factionalism both of which, as was suggested above, were consequences of Portugal's failure to resolve the participation crisis earlier and the consequent lack of an institutionalized political infrastructure. Except possibly in the case of the PRP during the First Republic and perhaps

Portugal's four major parties today, no Portuguese party has achieved any degree of institutionalization and grassroots support. Parties have been, at least until the present, little more than elite factions; and politics has functioned principally on the basis of personal ambition, charisma, petty policy differences, and the quest for ideological purity.

Correlations were shown to exist, however, between support for the various parties and broad social forces. Although it did not manifest itself fully until after 1974 and the advent of universal suffrage, the connection between social forces and the party system has appeared in well-defined patterns of support for various parties. These correlations, which were observed in Portugal's first free election after 1974, have been quite stable over time. They are not, however, the result of instrumental voting or the presence of strong partisan identification among the Portuguese electorate. The close association between socioeconomic ecologies and voting behavior exists in Portugal because of the activities of the political parties and political elites which have been, in their quest for loyal followers, orienting the Portuguese electorate toward such societal differences and making them salient for individual voters. The importance of socioeconomic ecologies in Portuguese voting behavior is a result of the timing of the resolution of Portugal's participation crisis. Unlike systems in which this crisis was resolved early and there exists an institutionalized party system capable of commanding the loyalty of voters independent of socioeconomic factors, Portugal's political parties are only now organizing themselves and seeking followers, something that was not required before the advent of universal suffrage. Such mobilization has taken place with reference to Portugal's contrasting socioeconomic differences, which gives the appearance of instrumental voting. The salience of such differences for Portuguese electoral behavior is, thus, dependent upon the activities of the parties.

Portuguese constitutions and the cycles in Portuguese constitution making are similar to those of other West European countries, especially France. Like France, the history of Portuguese constitution making has followed a cyclical pattern of oscillation between conflicting theories of constitutionalism which prescribed a system of either executive domination or legislative supremacy. Recent revisions to the 1976 constitution can be explained as the completion of one such cycle. Like constitutions written in other parts of Western Europe in the aftermath of World War II, Portugal's 1976 constitution is a result of a negative dislike for a dismal past, the chaos and political instability of the First Republic, and the authoritarianism of the New State. This history produced a hybrid, semi-presidential system which sought to avoid the pitfalls of either a pure parliamentary or executive dominated state. More presidential than parliamentary in its original version, revisions made in 1981 swung the pendulum toward parliament, thus completing Portugal's fourth cycle of constitution making and creating a system which resembles not the Frengh Fifth Republic but, rather, the Fourth Republic and the Weimar Republic.

The problem of Portuguese constitutionalism is, of course, the fact that no constitutional regime has succeeded in institutionalizing itself sufficiently to make it immune from tampering. Portuguese constitutions have resulted from temporary substantive agreements among various elites and have never provided an institutionalized framework within which the political struggle is conducted. As the conjunction of political forces in the society has changed, so have constitutions. Again, like personalism and ideological factionalism, such a history of constitution making is the result of the particular sequence and timing of Portugal's political development. Absolutism and the overinstitutionalized administrative state have made the task of creating and institutionalizing a democratic constitution extremely difficult. It remains to be seen whether the present constitution will achieve such institutionalization.

During the New State the policymaking process was guided by bureaucratic and technical considerations, and the regime's linkage with the broader civil society was primarily administrative not political. Since 1974 the focus of policymaking has shifted away from the bureaucracy toward political structures such as parties, parliament, and local elected assemblies. Consequently, attempts have been made at reforming the administrative system to make it more compatible with democratic policymaking. Within the administrative structure, Portugal's new political elite attempted to purge the system of high level administrators, the directors-general, who were perceived to be loyal to the bureaucratic policymaking of the New State and place in their stead individuals who would be more responsive to a more politicized and democratic policy formation process. These purges did bring about some changes in both background characteristics and attitudes of Portugal's administrative elite. Proportionately fewer of these individuals are now of provincial origins which indicates, perhaps, the reassertion after 1974 of the urban sector, principally Lisbon. These purges have also resulted in some changes in attitudes from less to more tolerance for politics and program commitment and from more to less elitism, all favorable to democratic policymaking.

The successes in effecting changes in the background and political attitudes of the administrative elite have not been, however, realized at the local level. Beyond the center, despite changes in structures, the underlying links between the broader civil society and the national government are still primarily administrative and technocratic. Concomitantly, there has been very little change in local political culture, which remains, as before, a subject one. These findings support the hypothesis that both culture and structure impose serious constraints on effective attitudinal or structural change. It is not that culture determines structure or structure culture but, rather, that structure and culture interact in subtle and complex ways to reinforce one another, thereby making alterations in established structures and attitudes extremely difficult.

Now that the findings of the various chapters of the book and the theoretical contribution of the Portuguese case have been summarized, all that remains to be presented are some speculations about the future of Portugal's fledgling democracy. Is Portugal's present democratic regime to go the way of its own First Republic? Is the fact that the constitution now resembles more that of the Weimar Republic than that of the French Fifth Republic an ominous sign? Or does the regime change which took place on April 25, 1974, constitute a significant breakthrough from the confining conditions of the past?

A stable democratic future depends upon the ability of Portugal's new political elite to eliminate the asymmetry in the polity by reducing the power and authority of the administrative infrastructure and increasing that of the political infrastructure. A politically mature democracy requires the development of an infrastructure of parties, elections and parliament capable of linking the broader civil society to the government and accommodating, channeling, and controlling participation. The state's overinstitutionalized administrative apparatus must be reformed and decentralized and public confidence and support for the parties, parliament, and local elected assemblies must be built up. In other words, the participation crisis must be resolved in ways consistent with democracy.[3]

There are some positive signs. There have been several transfers of power from government to opposition (PS to AD to PS-PSD) without mishap. There have been ten elections for national and local offices with high turnout rates. These elections have produced stable voting patterns. Four major parties control roughly 90 percent of the seats in parliament. To varying degrees these parties are well-organized and have bureaucratic structures reaching down to the grassroots. No major political group, such as the monarchist or communists, has been excluded from participation. The military has returned to the barracks and has been placed under civilian control. Parliament has become the arena where public policy is debated and approved. It is also the place where grievances are aired. The administrative elite is now more receptive to democratic policymaking. Efforts at administrative reform and decentralization have been made. At the local level, elected assemblies and municipal councils are in place and functioning.

It would seem from this list of positives that breakthrough has finally been achieved. Such a conclusion would be hasty, however, as there are some negatives which may eventually be the new democratic regime's undoing. Resolution of the crisis of participation has been made more difficult by the simultaneous appearance of the crisis of distribution. The clear shift toward distributional type policies has put a severe strain on the country's economic and financial capabilities. While four parties control 90 percent of the seats in parliament no one of them controls a majority. Moreover, one of these four, the PCP, is avowedly an antisystem party. As voting appears to have stabilized, there is little likelihood that any one of these parties will receive a clear majority in the next several elections. This means government by potentially unstable coalitions for the foreseeable future. The problem of creating a democratic infrastructure is compounded by the fact that the citizenry is not yet sufficiently oriented toward new democratic structures nor seems to care about the constitutional framework. There does not yet appear to be a clear cut distinction between political and administrative roles and structures in the public consciousness. Many citizens still harbor passive conceptualizations of the self as political actor and are oriented toward administrative structures. At the local level, the overinstitutionalized administrative state has changed very little and continues to contain and frustrate democratic policymaking. Attempts at decentralization have not, as yet, markedly changed the highly centralized nature of the decisional system. The various crises, both economic and political, have made many Portuguese cynical about politics and politicians. For many others the mood is one of despair. Many Portuguese do not believe that Portugal because of the flawed national character of her people, can be governed by democratic means.

In the final analysis, the future of Portuguese democracy depends upon the ability of Portugal's new political elite to successfully fill the institutional void between themselves and the ordinary citizen in ways consistent with democratic policymaking. Personalistic politics, private interests, and ideological nitpicking must be eschewed in favor of institution-building. Not to do so will leave the participation crisis unresolved and place Portugal's nascent democracy without an institutionalized way of rallying the support of the citizenry. Not to do so will make the resolution of the distributional crisis very difficult, if not impossible. Finally, not to do so will place the system not at the mercy of a broad revolutionary movement, but at that of the military, which may, once again, feel compelled to intervene in politics in order to save the nation.

Notes

   1. Douglas L. Wheeler, "The Revolution in Perspective: Revolution and Counterrevolution in Modern Portuguese History," in In Search of Modern Portugal: The Revolution and Its Consequences, ed. Lawrence S. Graham and Douglas L. Wheeler (Madison, Wis.: University of Wisconsin Press, 1983), p. 342.
   2. Henry W. Ehrmann, Politics in France, 3rd ed. (Boston: Little, Brown, 1976), pp. 336-337.
   3. The consequences for democracy of the asymmetry between political and administrative infrastructures as found in Portugal is discussed by Fred W. Riggs, Administration in Developing Countries: The Theory of Prismatic Society (Boston: Houghton-Mifflin 1964). See also Fred W. Riggs, "Bureaucrats and Political Development," in Bureaucracy and Political Development, ed. Joseph LaPalombara (Princeton, N.J.: Princeton University Press, 1963); Fred W. Riggs, "The Structure of Governmental and Administrative Reform," in Political and Administrative Development, ed. Ralf Braibanti (Durham, N.C.: Duke University Press, 1969), pp. 200-324; and Fred W. Riggs, "Bureaucratic Politics in Comparative Perspective," Journal of Comparative Administration 1 (May 1969): 5-38.

Acronyms

AD	Democratic Alliance (Aliança Democrática).
ANP	National Popular Action (Acção Nacional Popular).
AOC	Peasants and Worker's Alliance (Aliança Operária Camponesa).
APU	United People's Action (Acção Povo Unido).
AR	Assembly of the Republic (Assembleia da República).
ASD	Social Democratic Action (Acção Social Democrata).
ASDI	Independent Social Democratic Association (Associação Social Democrata Independente).
ASJ	Socialist Youth Alliance (Aliança Socialista de Juventude).
ASP	Portuguese Socialist Action (Acção Socialista Portuguesa).
BR	Revolutionary Brigades (Brigadas Revolucionárias).
CADC	Academic Center for Christian Democracy (Centro Académico de Democracia Cristã).
CARP,M-L	Support Committee for the Reconstruction of the Marxist-Leninist Party (Comité de Apoio da Reconstrução do Partido Marxista-Leninista).
CCR,M-L	Marxist-Leninist Communist Revolutionary Committees (Comités Comunistas Revolucionários Marxistas-Leninistas).
CDE	Democratic Electoral Committee (Comissão Democrática Eleitoral).
CDS	Party of the Social Democratic Center (Partido do Centro Democrático Social).

CGTP	General Confederation of Portuguese Workers (Confederação Geral de Trabalhadores Portugueses).
CEM	Monarchy Electoral Committee (Comissão Eleitoral Monárquica).
CEMGFA	Chief of the General Staff of the Armed Forces (Chefe do Estado-Maior General das Forças Armadas).
CM-LP	Portuguese Marxist-Leninist Committee (Comité Marxista-Leninista Portuguesa).
CEUD	Electoral Committee for Democratic Unity (Comissão Eleitoral para a Unidade Democrática).
COPCON	Continental Operations Command (Comando Operacional do Continente).
CR	Council of the Revolution (Conselho da Revolução).
DG	Director-General (Director-Geral).
DGS	General Directorate of Security (Direcção-Geral de Segurança).
EDE	Democratic Student Left (Esquerda Democrática Estudantil).
FAP	Front of Popular Action (Frente de Acção Popular).
FPLP	Patriotic Front for the Liberation of Portugal (Frente Patriótico para a Libertação de Portugal).
FRS	Republican and Socialist Front (Frente Republicana e Socialista).
FSP	Popular Socialist Front (Frente Socialista Popular).
FUR	United Revolutionary Front (Frente Unida Revolucionária).
GIS	Socialist Intervention Group (Grupo de Intervenção Socialista).
GMR	Marxist Revolutionary Groups (Grupos Marxistas Revolucionários).
ICS	Social Sciences Institute (Instituto de Ciências Sociais).
IMF	International Monetary Fund.
INA	National Institute of Administration (Instituto Nacional de Administração).
JAP	Board of Patriotic Action (Junta da Acção Patriótica).

JSN	Board of National Salvation (Junta de Salvação Nacional).
LCI	International Communist League (Liga Comunista Internacionalista).
MDP	Portuguese Democratic Movement (Movimento Democrático Português).
MES	Movement of the Socialist Left (Movimento de Esquerda Socialista).
MFA	Armed Forces Movement (Movimento das Forças Armadas).
MIRN	Independent Movement of National Reconstruction (Movimento Independente da Reconstrução Nacional).
MND	National Democratic Movement (Movimento Nacional Democrático).
MRPP	Reorganizing Movement of the Party of the Proletariat (Movimento Reorganizativo do Partido de Proletariado).
MSD	Social Democratic Movement (Movimento Social Democrata).
MSP	Popular Socialist Movement (Movimento Socialista Popular).
MUD	Movement of Democratic Unity (Movimento de Unidade Democrática).
MUNAF	Movement of Antifascist National Unity (Movimento de Unidade Nacional Antifascista).
OUT	United Organization of Workers (Organização Unida de Trabalhadores).
PC	Centrist Party (Partido Centrista).
PCP	Portuguese Communist Party (Partido Comunista Português).
PCP,M-L	Marxist-Leninist Communist Party of Portugal (Partido Comunista de Portugal Marxista-Leninista).
PCP,R	Reconstructed Portuguese Communist Party (Partido Comunista Português, Reconstruido).
PCSD	Christian Social Democratic Party (Partido Cristão Social Democrático).
PCTP	Portuguese Workers Communist Party (Partido Comunista de Trabalhadores Portugueses).
PDC	Party of Christian Democracy (Partido de Democracia Cristã).
PDP	Party of the Portuguese Right (Partido da Direita Portuguesa).

PIDE	International Police for the Defense of the State (<u>Polícia Internacional e Defensa do Estado</u>).
PL	Liberal Party (<u>Partido Liberal</u>).
PN	Nationalist Party (<u>Partido Nacionalista</u>).
POUS	United Socialist Worker's Party (<u>Partido Operário Unificado Socialista</u>).
PPD	Popular Democratic Party (<u>Partido Popular Democrática</u>).
PPM	Popular Monarchist Party (<u>Partido Popular Monárquico</u>).
PR	Reformist Party (<u>Partido Reformista</u>).
PRE	Republican Evolutionist Party (<u>Partido República Evolucionista</u>).
PRP	Revolutionary Party of the Proletariat (<u>Partido Revolucionário Proletariado</u>).
PRP	Portuguese Republican Party (<u>Partido Republicano Português</u>).
PRT	Revolutionary Party of the Workers (<u>Partido Revolucionário dos Trabalhadores</u>).
PS	Portuguese Socialist Party (<u>Partido Socialista Português</u>).
PSD	Social Democratic Party (<u>Partido Social Democrata</u>).
PSDI	Independent Social Democratic Party (<u>Partido Social Democrático Independente</u>).
PSR	Revolutionary Socialist Party (<u>Partido Socialista Revolucionário</u>).
PUP	Party of Popular Unity (<u>Partido de Unidade Popular</u>).
SEDES	Society for Economic and Social Development (<u>Sociadade para o Desenvolvimento Económico e Social</u>).
SSRC	Social Science Research Council.
SUV	Soldiers United Will Win (<u>Soldados Unidos Vencerão</u>).
UN	National Union (<u>União Nacional</u>).
UCDC	Union of the Christian Democratic Center (<u>União do Centro Democrático Cristão</u>).
UDP	Popular Democratic Union (<u>União Democrática Popular</u>).
UEDS	Union of the Left for Social Democracy (<u>União de Esquerda para a Democracia Social</u>).

UNR	Republican National Union (<u>União Nacional Republicana</u>).
UR	Republican Union (<u>União Republicana</u>).
UR,M-L	Marxist-Leninist Revolutionary Union (<u>União Revolucionária Marxista-Leninista</u>).
USD	Social Democratic Union (<u>União Social Democrática</u>).

Bibliography

Aarebrot, Frank H., and Derek N. Urwin. "Politics of Cultural Dissent: Religion, Language, and Demonstrative Effects in Norway." *Scandinavian Political Studies* 2 (Spring 1979): 75-98.
Allardt, Erik, and Stein Rokkan, eds. *Mass Politics*. New York: The Free Press, 1970.
Allardt, Erik, and Yrjo Littunen, eds. *Cleavages, Ideologies and Party Systems*. Helsinki: Westermark, 1964.
Almond, Gabriel A. "Communism and Political Culture Theory." *Comparative Politics* 15 (January 1983): 127-138.
Almond, Gabriel A., and G. Bingham Powell, Jr. *Comparative Politics: A Developmental Approach*. Boston: Little, Brown, 1966.
Almond, Gabriel A., and Sidney Verba. *The Civic Culture*. Princeton, N.J.: Princeton University Press, 1965.
_____, eds. *The Civic Culture Revisited*. Boston and Toronto: Little, Brown, 1980.
Apter, David E. *Introduction to Political Analysis*. Cambridge, Mass.: Winthrop Publishers, 1977.
_____. *The Politics of Modernization*. Chicago: University of Chicago Press, 1965.
Atlas Eleitoral. Lisbon: Editorial Progresso Social e Democracia, S.A.R.L., 1981.
Banfield, Edward C. *The Moral Basis of a Backward Society*. New York: The Free Press, 1958.
Barry, Brian. *Sociologists, Economists and Democracy*. London: Macmillan, 1970.
Beer, Samuel H., et al. *Patterns of Government*. 3rd ed. New York: Random House, 1973.
Berglund, Sten, and Ulf Linstrom. "The Scandinavian Party System(s) in Transition (?): A Macro-Level Analysis." *European Journal of Political Research* 7 (1979): 187-204.
Binder, Leonard, et al. *Crises and Sequences in Political Development*. Princeton, N.J.: Princeton University Press, 1971.

Blondel, Jean, ed. *Comparative Government: A Reader*. New York: Macmillan, 1969.
Blume, Norman. "Neighborhood Administration in Lisbon: The Juntas de Freguesia." *National Civic Review* 64 (May 1975): 249-253, 262.
_____. "SEDES: An Example of Opposition in a Conservative Authoritarian State." *Government and Opposition* 12 (Summer 1977): 351-366.
Bragança-Cunha, V. de. *Revolutionary Portugal (1910-1926)*. London: James Clarke, 1937.
Braibanti, Ralf, ed. *Political and Administrative Development*. Durham, N.C.: Duke University Press, 1969.
Brown, Bernard E., ed. *Eurocommunism and Eurosocialism: The Left Confronts Modernity*. New York and London: Cyro Press, 1979.
Bruce, Neil. *Portugal The Last Empire*. New York and Toronto: Wiley, 1975.
Bruneau, Thomas C. "Politics in Portugal, 1976-1981, and Revisions of the Constitution." Paper presented at the SSRC Conference on Contemporary Change in Southern Europe, Madrid, November 25-28, 1981.
Budge, Ian, et al., eds. *Party Identification and Beyond*. New York: Wiley, 1976.
Caetano, Marcello. *História Breve das Constituições Portuguesas*. Lisbon: Editorial Verbo, 1971.
Câmara Municipal de Porto de Mós. *Plano de Actividades e Orcamento para 1977*. Porto de Mós, Portugal: Mimeographed, 1977.
_____. *Relatório de Actividades e Contas de Gerência de 1977*. Porto de Mós, Portugal: Mimeographed, 1978.
Câmara Municipal do Concelho de Porto de Mós. Actas das Reuniões da Câmara Municipal. *Livro de Actas*. Nos. 63-67.
Campbell, Angus, and Henry Valen. "Party Identification in Norway and the United States." *Public Opinion Quarterly* 25 (1961): 501-525.
Campinos, Jorge. *O Presidencialismo do Estado Novo*. Lisbon: Perspectivas & Realidades, 1978.
Canedo, Rito. "Os Projectos de Revisão Constitucional: O Poder Político e as Forças Armadas." *Expresso* No. 471, November 7, 1981.
Carvalho, J. Vaz de. "As Constituições Portuguesas." *Economia e Sociologia*: Nova Leitura das Eleições-- 1975.
Chilcote, Ronald. *Portuguese Africa*. Englewood Cliffs, N.J.: Prentice-Hall, 1967.
Claggett, William, et al. "Political Leadership and the Development of Political Cleavages: Imperial Germany 1871-1912." *American Journal of Political Science* 26 (November 1982): 643-663.

Converse, Philip E. "Of Time and Partisan Stability." *Comparative Political Studies* 2 (July 1969): 137-171.
Converse, Philip E., and Georges Dupeux. "Politicization of the Electorate in France and the United States." *Public Opinion Quarterly* 26 (1962): 1-23.
Cruickshank, John. *Benjamin Constant*. New York: Twayne, 1974.
Cutileiro, José. *A Portuguese Rural Society*. Oxford: Clarendon Press, 1971.
Dahl, Robert A., and D. E. Neubauer, eds. *Readings in Modern Political Analysis*. Englewood Cliffs, N.J.: Prentice-Hall, 1968.
Dennis, Jack, and Donald J. McCrone. "Preadult Development of Political Party Identification in Western Democracies." *Comparative Political Studies* 3 (July 1970): 243-263.
Devine, Donald J. *The Political Culture of the United States*. Boston: Little, Brown, 1972.
Di Palma, Giuseppi. *Surviving Without Governing: The Italian Parties in Parliament*. Berkeley, Calif.: University of California Press, 1977.
Dogan, Mattei, ed. *The Mandarins of Western Europe*. New York and London: Halstead Press, 1975.
Domingos, Emídio da Veiga. *Portugal Político: Análise das Instituições*. Lisbon: Edições Rolim, 1980.
Duverger, Maurice. "A New Political System Model: Semi-Presidential Government." *European Journal of Political Research* 8 (1980): 165-187.
_____. *Political Parties*. New York: Methuen, 1954.
Easton, David. *A Systems Analysis of Political Life*. New York: John Wiley, 1965.
Eckstein, Harry, and David Apter, eds. *Comparative Politics: A Reader*. New York: The Free Press, 1963.
Ehrmann, Henry W. *Politics in France*. 3rd ed. Boston: Little, Brown, 1976.
Eisenstadt, S. N. *The Political System of Empire*. New York: Free Press, 1963.
Elkins, David J., and E. B. Simeon. "A Cause in Search of Its Effect, or What Does Political Culture Explain?" *Comparative Politics* 11 (January 1979): 127-145.
Ellul, Jacques. *Autopsy of Revolution*. New York: Alfred A. Knopf, 1971.
Esping-Anderson, Gosta. "Social Class, Social Democracy, and the State: Party Policy and Party Decomposition in Denmark and Sweden." *Comparative Politics* 11 (October 1978): 42-48.
Expresso. No. 260, October 22, 1977; No. 442, April 17, 1981; No. 482, January 23, 1982; No. 498, May 15, 1982; No. 520, November 21, 1981; No. 523, November 6, 1982; No. 538, February 19, 1983; No. 565, August 27, 1983.

Faye, Jean Pierre, ed. *Portugal: The Revolution in the Labyrinth*. London: Spokesman Books, 1976.

Fernandes, Carlos Roma. *Portugal a Europa e o Terceiro Mundo*. Lisbon: Editorial Pórtico, 1980.

Fields, Rona. *The Portuguese Revolution and the Armed Forces Movement*. New York: Praeger, 1976.

Figueiredo, António de. *Portugal: Fifty Years of Dictatorship*. New York: Holmes & Meier, 1976.

Fry, Earl H., and Gregory A. Raymond. *The Other Western Europe: A Political Analysis of the Smaller Democracies*. Santa Barbara, Calif. and Oxford: ABC-CLio, 1982.

Gallagher, Tom. "Controlled Repression in Salazar's Portugal." *Journal of Contemporary History* 14 (July 1979): 385-402.

_____. "The Growing Pains of Portuguese Democracy." *The World Today* 37 (February 1981): 102-109.

_____. "The 1979 Portuguese General Election." *Luso-Brazilian Review* 18 (Winter 1981): 253-262.

_____. *Portugal: A Twentieth-Century Interpretation*. Manchester: Manchester University Press, 1983.

_____. "Portugal's Bid for Democracy: The Role of the Socialist Party." *West European Politics* 2 (May 1979): 198-217.

Gaspar, Jorge, and Nuno Vitorino. *As Eleições Legislativas: Algumas Perspectivas Regionais*. Lisbon: Livros Horizonte, 1978.

Graham, Lawrence S. *Portugal: The Decline and Collapse of an Authoritarian Order*. Beverly Hills, Calif.: Sage Publications, 1975.

_____. "The Portuguese State: The View from Below." Paper presented at the Colloquium on the Formation of Contemporary Portugal, Calouste Gulbenkian Foundation, Lisbon, December 2-5, 1981.

Graham, Lawrence S., and Douglas L. Wheeler, eds. *In Search of Modern Portugal: The Revolution and Its Consequences*. Madison, Wis.: University of Wisconsin Press, 1983.

Graham, Lawrence S., and Harry M. Makler, eds. *Contemporary Portugal: The Revolution and Its Antecedents*. Austin, Texas: University of Texas Press, 1979.

Graubard, Stephen R. ed. *A New Europe*. Boston: Beacon Press, 1967.

Greenstein, Fred I., and Nelson W. Polsby, eds. *Handbook of Political Science*. Vol. 3: *Macropolitical Theory*. Reading, Mass.: Addison-Wesley, 1975.

Grew, Raymond, ed. *Crises of Political Development in Europe and the United States*. Princeton, N.J.: Princeton University Press, 1978.

Hagopian, Mark N. *The Phenomenon of Revolution*. New York: Dodd, Mead, 1974.

Hammergren, Linn A. "Corporatism in Latin American Politics: A Reexamination of the 'Unique' Tradition," *Comparative Politics* 9 (July 1977): 443-461.

Hanushek, Eric A., and John E. Jackson. *Statistical Methods for Social Scientists*. New York: Academic Press, 1977.
Harsgor, Michael. *Portugal in Revolution*. The Washington Papers, Vol. 3. Beverly Hills, Calif.: Sage Publications, 1976.
Harvey, Robert. *Portugal: Birth of a Democracy*. New York: St. Martin's Press, 1978.
Hermet, G., et al., eds. *Elections Without Choice*. London: Macmillan, 1978.
Holt, Robert T., and John E. Turner. "Crises and Sequences in Collective Theory Development." *American Political Science Review* 69 (September 1975): 979-994.
Huntington, Samuel P. *Political Order in Changing Societies*. New Haven, Conn.: Yale University Press, 1968.
Inglehart, Ronald. "Changing Paradigms in Comparative Political Behavior." Paper for the 1982 Annual Meeting of the American Political Science Association, Denver, Colorado, September 2-5, 1982.
Jowitt, Kenneth. "An Organizational Approach to the Study of Political Culture in Marxist-Leninist Systems." *American Political Science Review* 58 (September 1974): 1171-1191.
Kaplan, Morton A., ed. *The Many Faces of Communism*. New York: The Free Press, 1978.
Kay, Hugh. *Salazar and Modern Portugal*. New York: Hawthorn Books, 1970.
Kerlinger, Fred N. *Behavioral Research: A Conceptual Approach*. New York: Holt, Rinehart and Winston, 1979.
Kirchheimer, Otto. "Confining Conditions and Revolutionary Breakthroughs." *American Political Science Review* 59 (December 1965): 964-974.
_____. "The Waning of Opposition in Parliamentary Regimes." *Social Research* 24 (Summer 1975): 127-156.
Kramer, Jane. "A Reporter at Large: The Portuguese Revolution." *The New Yorker*, December 15, 1975. pp. 92-131.
Laitin, David D. *Politics, Language, and Thought: The Somali Experience*. Chicago: University of Chicago Press, 1977.
Landes, David S., ed. *Western Europe: The Trials of Partnership: Critical Choices for Americans*, Vol. 3. Lexington, Mass.: Lexington Books, 1977.
La Palombara, Joseph, ed. *Bureaucracy and Political Development*. Princeton, N.J.: Princeton University Press, 1963.
Lehmbruch, G., and Philippe C. Schmitter, eds. *Patterns in Corporatist Policy Making*. London and Beverly Hills, Calif.: Sage Publications, 1982.

Lewis, Paul H. "Salazar's Ministerial Elite, 1932-1968." Journal of Politics, 40 (August 1978): 622-647.
Linz, Juan J., and Alfred Stepan, eds. The Breakdown of Democratic Regimes. Baltimore and London: The Johns Hopkins University Press, 1978.
Lipset, Seymour M., and Stein Rokkan, eds. Party Systems and Voter Alignments: Cross-National Perspectives. New York: The Free Press, 1967.
Livermore, H. V. A New History of Portugal. Cambridge: Cambridge University Press, 1969.
Loewenberg, Gerhard. "The Remaking of the German Party System: Political and Socio-Economic Factors." Polity 1 (Fall 1968): 86-113.
_____, ed. Modern Parliaments: Change or Decline? Chicago and New York: Aldine/Atherton, 1971.
Lopes, Santana, and José Durão Barroso. Sistema de Governo e Sistema Partidário. Lisbon: Livraria Bertrand, 1980.
Machete, Rui. "O Papel do Instituto Nacional de Administração na Formação dos Funcionários Superiores." Prospectivas, Nos. 10, 11 and 12 (April-December 1982): 11-18.
Machin, Howard, ed. National Communism in Western Europe: A Third Way to Socialism. London and New York: Methuen, 1983.
Mailer, Phil. Portugal: The Impossible Revolution. New York: Free Life Editions, 1977.
Marcum, John A. The Angolan Revolution, Vol. 1. Cambridge, Mass.: M.I.T. Press, 1969.
Marques, A. H. de Oliveira, History of Portugal, 2 vols. New York: Columbia University Press, 1972.
Martins, Hermínio. "Opposition in Portugal." Government and Opposition 4 (Spring 1969): 250-263.
Maxwell, Kenneth. "Portugal: The Hidden Revolution. New York Review of Books, April 17, 1975, pp. 29-35.
_____. "The Thorns of the Portuguese Revolution." Foreign Affairs 54 (January 1976): 250-270.
Merkl, Peter H., ed. Western European Party Systems. New York: The Free Press, 1980.
Morstein-Marx, Fritz. The Administrative State: An Introduction to Bureaucarcy. Chicago: University of Chicago Press, 1957.
Mujal-León, Eusébio M. "The PCP and the Portuguese Revolution." Problems of Communism 26 (January-February 1977): 21-41.
Nevins, Lawrence. "The Portuguese Revolution." Worldview, July-August 1975, pp. 40-47.
Newitt, Malyn. Portugal in Africa: The Last Hundred Years. London: Longman, 1981.
Norpoth, Helmut. "Party Identification in West Germany: Tracing an Elusive Concept. Comparative Politics 11 (April 1979): 36-61.

Opello, Walter C., Jr. "Electoral Law and Candidate Selection." In *Portugal at the Polls*. Edited by Howard J. Penniman. Washington, D.C.: American Enterprise Institute, forthcoming.
―――――. "Local Government and Political Culture in a Portuguese Rural County." *Comparative Politics* 13 (April 1981): 271-289.
―――――. "The New Parliament in Portugal." *Legislative Studies Quarterly* 3 (May 1978): 309-334.
―――――. "Portugal's Administrative Elite: Social Origins and Political Attitudes." *West European Politics* 6 (January 1983): 63-74.
―――――. "The Second Portuguese Republic: Politico-Administrative Decentralization Since April 25, 1974." *Iberian Studies* 7 (Autumn 1978): 43-48.
Opello, Walter C. Jr., and William Claggett. "The Dynamics of Electoral Change in Portugal since 1974." Paper presented at the Annual Meeting of the American Political Science Association, Denver, Colorado, September 2-5, 1982.
Pateman, Carole. "Political Culture, Political Structure and Political Change." *British Journal of Political Science* 1 (July 1971): 291-305.
Payne, Stanley G. *A History of Spain and Portugal*, 2 vols. Madison, Wis.: University of Wisconsin Press, 1973.
Pickles, Dorothy. *The Fifth French Republic*. New York: Praeger, 1960.
Pike, Frederick B., and Thomas Stritch, eds. *The New Corporatism*. South Bend, Ind.: University of Notre Dame Press, 1974.
Pimlott, Ben. "Parties and Voters in the Portuguese Revolution: The Elections of 1975 and 1976." *Parliamentary Affairs* 30 (Winter 1977): 37-43.
―――――. "Socialism in Portugal: Was It a Revolution?" *Government and Opposition* 12 (Summer 1977): 332-366.
―――――. "Were the Soldiers Revolutionary? The Armed Forces Movement in Portugal, 1973-1976." *Iberian Studies* 7 (Spring 1978): 13-21.
Porch, Douglas. *The Portuguese Armed Forces and the Revolution*. London: Croom Helm, 1977.
Putnam, Robert D. "The Political Attitudes of Senior Civil Servants in Western Europe: A Preliminary Report." *British Journal of Political Science* 3 (1973): 257-290.
Revisão Constitucional. Lisbon: Assembleia da Republica, July 15, 1981.
"A Revolution Tamed: Survey of Portugal." *The Economist* 263 (May 28, 1977): 3-30.
Richardson, Bradley M. *The Political Culture of Japan*. Berkeley and Los Angeles, Calif.: University of California Press, 1974.

Reigelhaupt, Joyce Firstenberg. "Festas and Padres: The Organization of Religious Action in a Portuguese Parish." *American Anthropologist* 75 (1973): 835-852.

_____. "Saloio Woman: An Analysis of Informal and Formal Political and Economic Roles of Portuguese Women." *Anthropological Quarterly* 40 (July 1967): 109-126.

Riggs, Fred W. *Administration in Developing Countries: The Theory of Prismatic Society*. Boston: Houghton-Mifflin, 1964.

_____. *Administrative Reform and Political Responsiveness: A Theory of Dynamic Balancing*. Beverly Hills, Calif.: Sage Publications, 1970.

_____. "Bureaucratic Politics in Comparative Perspective." *Journal of Comparative Administration* 1 (May 1969): 5-38.

Riker, William H. "The Two-party System and Duverger's Law: An Essay on the History of Political Science." *American Political Science Review* 76 (December 1982): 753-766.

Robinson, Richard. *Contemporary Portugal: A History*. London: George Allen and Unwin, 1979.

Rodrigues, Avelino, et al. *O Movimento dos Capitães e o 25 de Abril*. Lisbon: Moraes, 1974.

Rose, Richard. *Electoral Behavior: A Comparative Handbook*. New York: The Free Press, 1974.

Rose, Richard, and Derek W. Urwin. "Social Cohesion, Political Parties and Strains in Regimes." *Comparative Political Studies* 2 (April 1969): 7-67.

Safran, William. *The French Polity*. New York: David McKay, 1977.

Sartori, Giovanni. *Parties and Party Systems: A Framework for Analysis*. Cambridge: Cambridge University Press, 1976.

Schmitter, Philippe C. *Corporatism and Public Policy in Authoritarian Portugal*. London and Beverly Hills, Calif.: Sage Publications, 1975.

_____. "Liberation by *Golpe*: Retrospective Thoughts on the Demise of Authoritarian Rule in Portugal." *Armed Forces and Society* 2 (1974): 5-33.

_____. "Le Parti Communiste Portugais entre 'Pouvoir Social' et le 'Pouvois Politique,'" *Études Internationales*, September 1975, pp. 375-388.

Schmitter, Philippe C., and G. Lehmbruch, eds. *Trends toward Corporatist Intermediation*. London and Beverly Hills, Calif.: Sage Publications, 1979.

Schwab, George, ed. *Eurocommunism: The Ideological and Political-Theoretical Foundations*. Westport, Conn.: Greenwood Press, 1981.

Secretariat for Administrative Reform. *Principles and Directives of the Administrative Reform in Portugal*. Lisbon, 1968.

Seers, Dudley, et al., eds. Underdeveloped Europe: Studies in Center-Periphery Relations. Atlantic Highlands, N.J.: Humanities Press, 1979.

Shively, W. Philips. "The Elusive 'Psychological Factor': A Test for the Impact of Electoral Systems on Voters' Behavior." Comparative Politics 3 (October 1970): 115-125.

_____. "Party Identification, Party Choice, and Voting Stability: The Weimar Case." American Political Science Review 56 (December 1972): 1203-1225.

Silva, Fernando Diogo da. "Uma Administracão Envelhecida." Revista da Administração Pública 2 (October-December 1979): 621-650.

Smith, Gordon. Politics in Western Europe. New York: Holmes and Meir, 1973.

Soares, Mário. Portugal's Struggle for Liberty. London: Allen and Unwin, 1975.

Solomon, Richard H. Mao's Revolution and the Chinese Political Culture. Berkeley and Los Angeles, Calif.: University of California Press, 1971.

Spínola, António de. Portugal e o Futuro. Lisbon: Arcádia, 1974.

Spiro, Herbert J. Government by Constitution. New York: Random House, 1959.

Waldo, Dwight. The Administrative State. New York: Ronald Press, 1948.

Weiner, Myron, and Ergun Ozbundun, eds. Competitive Elections in Developing Countries. Forthcoming.

Wheeler, Douglas L. The First Portuguese Republic. Madison, Wis.: University of Wisconsin Press, 1978.

_____. "Portuguese Elections and History." Paper presented at the Conference on Modern Portugal, Yale University, 1975.

Wiarda, Howard J. Corporatism and Development: The Portuguese Experience. Amherst, Mass.: University of Massachusetts Press, 1977.

_____. Does Europe Stop at the Pyrenees? Or Does Latin America Begin There? Iberia, Latin America and the Second Enlargement of the European Community. Washington, D.C.: American Enterprise Institute Occasional Paper Series No. 2, n.d.

_____. From Corporatism to Neo-Syndicalism: The State, Organized Labor, and the Changing Industrial Relations Systems of Southern Europe. Cambridge, Mass.: The Center for European Studies, Harvard University, 1981.

_____. "Portuguese Corporatism Revisited." Iberian Studies 3 (1974), 78-79.

_____. "The Portuguese Revolution: Towards Explaining the Political Behavior of the Armed Forces Movement." Iberian Studies 4 (Autumn 1975): 54-61.

Wiarda, Howard J. "Toward a Framework for the Study of Political Change in the Iberic-Latin Tradition: The Corporate Model." World Politics 25 (January 1973): 206-235.

_____. Transcending Corporatism? The Portuguese Corporative System and the Revolution of 1974. Columbia, S.C.: Institute of International Studies, The University of South Carolina, 1976.

_____, ed. Politics and Social Change in Latin America: The Distinctive Tradition. Amherst, Mass.: University of Massachusetts Press, 1974.

Wilson, Frank L. "Alternative Models of Interest Intermediation: The Case of France." British Journal of Political Science 12 (1982): 173-200.

_____. "French Interest Group Politics: Pluralist or Neocorporatist?" American Political Science Review 77 (December 1983): 895-910.

Zuckerman, Alan, and Mark I. Lichbach. "Stability and Change in European Electorates." World Politics 29 (July 1977): 523-551.

Index

Abrilada, 37
Absolutists, 24, 34, 36-38, 85, 145
Academic Center of Christian Democracy (Centro Académico de Democracia Cristã: CADC), 89-90
Actos Adicionais (Additional Acts), 39, 85
Afonso Henriques, king of Portugal, 15, 16, 18-19, 24-26
Afonso II, king of Portugal, 19, 28-30
Afonso III, king of Portugal, 19, 21, 30
Afonso IV, king of Portugal, 21, 31
Afonso V, king of Portugal, 31, 35
Agrarian reform, 79
Al-Andalus, 18-19
Alcácer-Quiver, battle of, 22, 68
Alcaide, 29, 31, 33
Alcântara, battle of, 23
Alegre, Manuel, 198
Alentejo
  medieval administration in, 29
  socio-economic characteristics of, 124
  mentioned, 19, 79, 104, 119
Alexander III, pope, 25
Alfonso VI, king of León, 17, 25

Alfonso VII, king of León, 18, 24-25
Aljubarrota, battle of, 22
Almeida, António José, 88
Almohad Empire. See Almohads
Almohads, 18-19
Almond, Gabriel A., 175-176
Almoxarifado (alms-shire), 33
Almoxarife (alms-sheriff), 33
Alves, Lima, 92
Amaro, Adelino da Costa, 102
Anarchists, 92, 103
Anarchosyndicalists, 103
Angola, 1, 60
António, prior of Crato, 22-23
  as king of Portugal, 37
Antunes, Major Melo, 71, 73-74
Antunistas, 71
Armada, Portuguese-Spanish, 23
Armed Forces Movement (Movimento das Forças Armadas: MFA)
  as self-defined liberation movement, 71
  background of members, 68
  beginnings of, 66-67
  factions within, 71-73
  interference of in constitution-making process, 148

223

Armed Forces Movement
  (cont'd)
  protocols with political
    parties, 72
  mentioned, 66, 69, 70-71,
    74-75, 77, 80, 94, 96
Arriaga, General Kaulza de,
  104
Assembleia de freguesia
  (parish assembly), 177
Assembly of the Armed Forces
  (Assembleia das Forças
  Armadas), 71-72
Assembly of the Republic
  (Assembleia da República:
  AR), 95-97, 102,
  152, 154
  organization and powers
    of, 149-150, 155-156
Association of Socialist
  Culture--Worker's
  Brotherhood (Associação
  de Cultura Socialista-
  Fraternidade Operária)
  106. See also Union of
  the Left for Social
  Democracy
Asturia. See León
Atestados, 176, 179
Authoritarian regimes
  definition of, 49-50
  presumed strength of, 51
  typology of, 50
  weakness of, 51-52
Authoritarianism, 1, 2.
  See also Authoritarian
  regimes
Avis, House of, 22-23
Azores, 100, 153, 176

Bairros (neighborhoods), 76-77
Balsemão, Francisco, 100-102
Barbosa, Luís, 103
Barcelos, Count of. See
  Duke of Bragança
Barracas (shantytowns), 77
Barreto, António, 98
Beatriz, daughter of Fernando and wife of Juan I
  of Castile, 21
Behavioralism, 5-6
Belgium, comparisons
  with, 43

Beresford, William, 27
Berger, Suzanne, 84, 109,
  161
Board of National Salvation (Junta da Salvação Nacional: JSN),
  69-72
Board of Patriotic Action
  (Junta da Acção
  Patriótica: JAP), 96
Braga, bishopric of, 21,
  30
Bragança family, 31
Bragança, house of, 24
Bragança and Guimarães,
  duke of, 31-32
Branco, Aresta, 88
Bureaucratic-military
  regimes, 50, 54, 60
  definition of, 50
Bureaucrats, types of, 163

Caciquismo, 87, 91, 108,
  119, 125
Cadiz, constitution of, 27
Caetano, Marcello, 58, 60,
  66-69, 75-76, 79, 91-92, 94, 100, 162, 198-199
Calatrava, religious military order of, 19, 22
Camacho, Brito, 88
Câmara de Deputados (House
  of Deputies), 37-39,
  145
Câmara de Pares (upper
  House), 37-38, 145
Câmara de Senadores (House
  of Senators), 38
Câmara Municipal (Municipal Chamber), 176-178,
  191
Campinos, Jorge, 98
Carbonária, 27
Cardoso, Lopes, 98, 106
Cargos vitalícios, 162
Carmo, Isabel do, 94
Carmona, General Óscar de
  Fragosa, 53, 92
Carneiro, Francisco Sá,
  98, 100-101, 151
Carvalho, Alfredo, 98
Carvalho, Brigadier Otelo
  Saraiva de, 68, 70,
  73-74

Casas do Povo (People's
    Houses), 54
Casas dos Pescadores
    (fishermen's houses),
    54
Castile, 15-16, 19, 21-22,
    35
Castilianization, 22, 36
"Catch-all" parties, 127,
    140
Catholic Church, the
    conflict with crown over
    royal patrimony, 29-31
    disestablishment of, 28
    resistence to corporatism
    from, 57
    role in creation of Portu-
    guese national iden-
    tity, 20
    support for absolutism by,
    85
Centrist Party (Partido
    Centrista), 88
Chancelor-mor (Great
    Chancellor), 33
Chartists, 85. See also
    Regenerators
Chief of the General Staff
    of the Armed Forces
    (Chefe do Estado-Maior
    General das Forças
    Armadas: CEMGFA), 74
Christian Democrats, 83,
    See also Party of the
    Social Democratic Center
Christian Social Democratic
    Party (Partido Cristão
    Social Democrático:
    PCSP), 104
Cistercians, 32
Civil service, 57
Civil war, 37
Código Administrativo (Ad-
    ministrative Code), 179
Comarcas, 33
Combate Socialista, 107
Communists, 73, 75-76, 80,
    83, 93, 96-97, 99. See
    also Portuguese Commun-
    ist Party
Concordat of 1940, 57
Congresso da República (Con-
    gress of the Republic),
    39, 119, 146

Conselho de Minístros
    (Council of Ministers),
    162
Constancio, Vítor, 98
Constant, Benjamin, 144-145
Constitutional Charter
    (Carta Constitucional),
    27, 36, 38-39, 85, 145
Constitutionalism, theories
    of, 143-147
Constitutional Tribunal,
    153-154
Constitution
    of 1822, 36, 38, 85, 144-
    145
    of 1838, 38, 85, 145
    of 1911, 39, 146
    of 1933, 55, 146
    of 1976, 8, 143, 147, 151,
    153-157
Constituent Assembly, 49,
    97, 72, 121
Continental Operations
    Command (Comando Opera-
    cional do Continente:
    COPCON), 68, 70, 73
Coordinating Committee of
    the MFA, 71-72
Corporações (Corporations),
    55. See also corpora-
    tism; corporative
    chamber
Corporatism
    as analytical framework,
    4-5, 6
    as ideology of Salazar, 54
    attempted revival of, 58
    failure to institutional-
    ize, 57-59
    organization of corporate
    structure, 54-55
Corporative Chamber (Câmara
    Corporativa), 55-58, 69,
    91, 146, 149
Corregador de Corte, 31, 33
Cortes, 22, 23, 35-38, 41,
    45, 59, 86, 144-145
Cortesão, Jaime, 95
Costa, Afonso, 88
Costa, Alfredo Nobre de, 151
Costa, General Gomes de, 68
Council of Portugal, 23

Council of the Revolution
(Conselho da Revolução:
CR), 72-74, 148, 151-
153, 156
Council of State, 33, 153-
156
Council of the Republic,
153
Council of Twenty. See
Superior Council of
the MFA
Council of Two-Hundred.
See Assembly of the
Armed Forces
Coutinho family, 31
Crespo, Vítor, 102
Crises and Sequences model
of the SSRC
comparisons, 43-44
outlined, 13-15
patterns for Portugal,
41-43
theoretical light shed,
44-45
Critics (críticos), 101
Cunhal, Álvaro, 103
Curto, Marcelo, 98

Delgado, General Humberto,
68, 93, 105
Democratic Alliance
(Aliança Democrática:
AD), 98-99, 101-103,
129-138 passim, 152-
154, 203
Democratic and Socialist
Left (Esquerda Socia-
lista e Democrática),
98, 106. See also
Union of the Left for
Social Democracy
Democratic Electoral Com-
mittee (Comissão Demo-
crática Eleitoral:
CDE), 92, 96, 119. See
also Portuguese Demo-
cratic Movement
Democratic Party (Partido
Democrático). See
Portuguese Republican
Party
Democratic Student Left
(Esquerda Democrática
Estudantil: EDE), 107.

Democratic Student Left
(cont'd)
See also Reorganizing
Movement of the Party
of the Proletariat
Developmental crises
analysis of, 22-24
definition of, 22
d'Hondt proportional sys-
tem, 89, 149
dinaminazação (mobiliza-
tion), 77
Dinis I, king of Portugal,
20, 28, 30-31
Directores-Gerais (Directors-
General: DGs), 162
compared with counterparts
in Western Europe,
170-171
political attitudes of,
169-171
social origins of, 165-
169
Distribution crisis
application to Portugal, 40-41
definition of, 13
District governor, 179
Distritos (districts), 176
Domingos, Emídio da Veiga
Duarte, Duke of Bragança,
23-24
Duverger, Maurice, 147,
156, 200

Eanes, General Ramalho,
as chief of staff after
1974, 74
as president, 97, 101-
102, 150-151, 153-154
École Nationale d'Administration, 162
Electoral Committee for
Democratic Unity
(Comissão Eleitoral
para a Unidade Demo-
crática: CEUD), 93,
95-96, 119
Electoral laws
after 1974, 94-95
during First Republic,
89-90
during liberal era, 86
during New State, 91

Escrivão da puridade (private scribe), 33
Estado Novo. See New State
European Christian Democratic Union, 102
Expresso, 100

Fabião, Otelo, 74
Fátima, affect on voting behavior, 125
Federações (federations), 54
Ferdinand II, king of León, 19
Ferdinand VII, king of Spain, 27
Fernando, grandson of Pedro I, 21
Finland, comparison with, 156
First Republic
  parties within, 87-88
  political life during, 39-40
  voting behavior during, 119, 125, 127
  mentioned, 7, 28, 52-53, 59, 65, 88-89, 90, 118, 139, 147, 149, 167, 200-201
Fourth French Republic, comparisons with, 7
Forais (town charters), 32
France, comparisons with, 1-2, 8, 23, 27, 43, 45, 54, 109, 118, 144, 147, 149, 156, 161, 197-198, 200-203
Franchise, the
  after 1974, 94-95
  during Liberal era and First Republic, 86
  during New State, 119, 120 (table)
Franco, António Sousa, 100-101
Freemasonary, 26
Freitas, do Amaral, Diogo, 102-103
Friedrich, Carl J., 147
Front of Popular Action (Frente de Acção Popular: FAP), 103

Galicia, 17-19
Gama, Jaime, 98
General Confederation of Portuguese Workers (Confederação Geral de Trabalhadores Portugueses: CGTP), 104
General Directorate of Security (Direcção Geral de Segurança: DGS), 69. See also International Police for the Defense of the State
Geraldo Geraldes, 19
Germany, Imperial, 43, 84
Glória, Maria da, 36
Gomes, General Costa, 70-74
Gomes, Sousa, 98
Gonçalves, Colonel Vasco, 70-71, 73-74, 76
Gonçalvistas, 71, 73, 74-75
Gonelha, Maldonado, 98
Graham, Lawrence S., 69
Great Britain, comparisons with, 1, 43, 84, 140, 170
Greece, 1, 90
Grêmios (guilds), 54-55
Grew, Raymond, 43-44
Group of Nine (Grupo dos Nove), 74-148
Gueterres, António, 98
Guinea (Bissau), 1, 60, 69

Hammond, John, 124
Hardliners (duros), 101
Harvesters (seareiros), 95
Henri, count of Portugal, 17-18, 28-29
Henry, son of Manuel I, 22
Herculano, Alexandre, 16
Hispanophiles, 16
Históricos
  as faction of Socialist Party, 98
  during Liberal era, 39, 86
Holy Alliance, 36
Holy See, 24-25, 29-30
Hospitlers, religious military order of, 19

"Hot Summer" of 1975, 73
Identity crisis
  application to Portugal, 15-24
  definition of, 13
Independent Movement of National Reconstruction (Movimento da Reconstrução Nacional: MIRN), 104-105. See also Party of the Portuguese Right
Independent Social Democratic Association (Associação Social Democrata Independente: ASDI), 99, 101
Independent Social Democratic Party (Partido Social Democrático Independente: PSDI), 104
Inquiries (inquerições), 30
Institutionalism, 5-6
Institutions, definition of, 23
Interest intermediation, 5
International Communist League (Liga Comunista Internacionalista: LCI), 107
International Monetary Fund (IMF), 97
International Police for the Defense of the State (Polícia Internacional e Defesa do Estado: PIDE), 92-93, 103
Intersindical, 75-76. See also General Confederation of Portuguese Workers
"Italianization" of the party system, 129
Italy, comparisons with, 1, 2, 27, 43-45, 54, 90, 147, 165, 170

Jacobinism. See Jacobins
Jacobins, 24, 34, 36-38, 145
João I, king of Portugal, 35

João II, king of Portugal, 28, 31-32, 35
João IV, king of Portugal, 24
João VI, king of Portugal, 36, 144-145
João VII, king of Portugal, 26
João, master of Avis, 22
Juízes de fora (outside judges), 31
Junta de Freguesia (parish board), 77, 176, 178-181

Kingdom of León. See León

Latifundia, 124
Left Union for Social Democracy (União de Esquerda para a Democracia Social: UEDS), 98-99, 106. See also Democratic and Socialist Left.
Legião Portuguesa (Portuguese Legion), 56
Legitimacy crisis
  application to Portugal, 24-28
  definition of, 13
Legitimist Party (Partido Legitimista), 89
León, 16-17, 24, 27-28
Liberal era. See Liberalism.
Liberalism, 26, 34-35, 39, 50, 54, 85-86, 92, 118
Liberal Party (Partido Liberal: PL), 89
Liberals. See Liberalism
Linz, Juan J., 49-50, 52, 65
Lisbon
  rise of as national capital, 21
  mentioned, 18, 23-24, 26, 36, 67, 70, 74, 87, 88, 89, 96, 104, 118, 119, 124, 125, 167, 169, 171
Lourenço, Brigadier Vasco, 73-74
Loures, by election in, 99
Lowenstein, Karl, 157

Luís, brother of Manuel I, 22

Madeiros, Ferreira, 98
Manuel I, king of Portugal, 22, 28, 32-33
Maoists, 83, 105, 109, 129
Marxist-Leninist Communist Party of Portugal (Partido Comunista de Portugal, Marxista-Leninista: PCP, M-L), 103, 106
Marxist-Leninist Revolutionary Communist Committees (Comités Comunistas Revolucionários, Marxistas-Leninistas: CCR, M-L), 107
Marxist-Leninist Revolutionary Union (União Revolucionária Marxista-Leninista: UR, M-L), 107
Marxist Revolutionary Groups (Grupos Marxistas Revolucionários: GMR), 107
Masons, 27. See also Freemasonary
Mattos, General Morton de, 93
Meireles, Admiral Quintão, 92
Meirinhos-mores (bailiffs), 31, 33
Melo, Eurico de, 101
Melo family, 31
Menenses family, 31
Miguel, king of Portugal, 36-39, 145
Milícianos (conscript officers), 66-67
Minifundia, 124
Ministry of Agriculture, 79
Ministry of Finance, 90
Ministry of Internal Administration, 179
Mobil Local Support Service (Serviço Ambulatório de Apoio Local), 77-78
Mocidade Portuguesa (Portuguese Youth), 56
Monarchist Cause (Causa Monárquia), 89-90, 105

Monarchists, 83, 92-93, 145. See also Monarchist Cause, Monarchy Electoral Committee, and Popular Monarchist Party
Monarchy Electoral Committee (Comissão Eleitoral Monarquica: CEM), 93, 105
Moniz, Egas, 89
Morais, Tito de, 98
Moslems, 16-22, 25, 29, 30
Mota Magalhães, 100
Mota Pinto, Carlos, 101-102, 151
Movement of Antifascist National Unity (Movimento de Unidade Nacional Antifascista: MUNAF), 93
Movement of Democratic Unity (Movimento de Unidade Democrático: MUD), 92, 95
Movement of the Socialist Left (Movimento de Esquerda Socialista: MES), 105
Mozambique, 1, 60
Municipal Assembly (Assembleia Municipal), 177-181
Municipalities (municípios), 177-178

National Assembly (Assembleia Nacional), 56, 69, 71, 100, 119, 146, 149
National Democratic Movement (Movimento Nacional Democrático: MND), 92, 95
National Foundation for Joy in Work (Fundação Nacional para a Alegria no Trabalho), 56
National Institute of Administration (Instituto Nacional de Administracão: INA), 161-162
Nationalist Party (Partido Nacionalista: PN), 89

Nationalizations, 72
National Popular Action (Acção Nacional Popular: ANP), 91
National Republican Party (Partido Nacional Republicano: PNR), 88
National Union (União Nacional: UN), 56-57, 59, 90-91, 94, 102, 107-108, 119, 177
Naval Brigade (Brigada Naval), 69
Neo-fascists, 83
New Harvest (Seara Nova), 95
New Socialists, faction of the Socialist Party, 98
New State (Estado Novo)
  breakdown of, 59-61
  clandestine resistance to, 93-94
  emergence of, 52-56
  liberalization of, 94
  partisan activity during, 91-93
  policymaking process during, 58-59, 178-180
  mentioned, 7, 8, 15, 49, 60-61, 65-66, 69, 75, 80, 83, 95-96, 103, 105, 108, 118, 121, 124, 147-149, 161, 165, 169, 191, 198, 200-201
Novistas, 74

Officer corps, social composition of, 66-67
Olivares, Count-Duke of, 23
Ordinações Manuelinas (Manuelian Ordinances), 32
Order of Christ. See Templers
Organic-Statist regimes, definition of, 50, 54, 60, 162, 198
Overinstitutionalization, concept of, 59

Pais, General Sidónio, 68, 88
Panelinhas, 68

Parish (freguesia), 176-181
Participation crisis
  application to Portugal, 34-40
  definition of, 13
Party of Christian Democracy (Partido da Democracia Cristã: PDC), 102, 104, 121. See also Party of the Social Democratic Center.
Party of Popular Unity (Partido de Unidade Popular: PUP), 106
Party of the Portuguese Right (Partido da Direita Portuguesa: PDP), 104, 129
Party of the Social Democratic Center (Partido do Centro Democrático Social: CDS)
  as AD partner, 97, 101-102
  electoral behavior of, 129-138, passim
  founding of, 102
  ideology of, 102
  support base of, 125-127
  mentioned, 107, 109, 151, 197
Patriotic Front for the Liberation of Portugal (Frente Patriótico para a Libertação de Portugal: FPLP), 93
Peasants and Worker's Alliance (Aliança Operária Camponesa: AOC), 106
Peculiar, John, bishop of Braga, 21
Pedro I, king of Portugal, 21
Pedro II, king of Portugal, 35-36
Pedro IV, king of Portugal, 37-38
Penetration crisis
  application to Portugal, 28-34
  definition of, 13
Pereira, Carmelinda, 106

Pereira, Eduardo, 98
Pereira, Nun'Alvares, 22
Peres, Fernando, consort of Teresa, 18
Permanent Commission of the Assembly of the Republic, 155
Philip II, king of Spain, 22-23
Philip III, king of Spain and Portugal, 23
Philip IV, king of Spain and Portugal, 23-24
Pimlott, Ben, 68
Pires, Lucas, 103
Polarized pluralism, concept of, 129
Policymaking process, 9
 after 1974, 161-162
 during New State, 58-60, 162-163
Political archaeology, concept of, 84
Political actors, citizens' perception of themselves as, 187-190
Political brokers, lack of, 191
Political culture
 analysis of, 183-190
 culture vs. structure debate, 175-176
 definition of, 182
 subject political culture, 190-191
Pombal, Marquis de, 33-34
Popular Action Front (Frente de Acção Popular: FAP), 103
Popular Democratic Party (Partido Popular Democrático: PPD), 100. See also Social Democratic Party
Popular Democratic Union (União Democrática Popular: UDP), 107
Popular Monarchist Party (Partido Popular Monárquico: PPM), 101-102, 105, 109, 129
Popular Socialist Front (Frente Socialista Popular: FSP), 98, 105

Popular Socialist Movement (Movimento Socialista Popular: MSP), 98, 105
Populism, how manifested in Portugal, 66, 68-69
Porto, 27, 38, 39, 87, 89, 96, 118, 125
Portugal e o Futuro (Portugal and the Future), 69
Portuguese Communist Party (Partido Comunista Português: PCP)
 electoral behavior of, 129-138 passim
 founding of, 103
 ideology and political strategy since 1974, 103-104
 membership and support base, 103-104, 125-127
 schisms within, 103
 mentioned, 92, 107, 121, 124, 204
Portuguese Democratic Movement (Movimento Democrático Português: MDP), 92. See also Democratic Electoral Committee
Portuguese Integralist Movement (Integralismo Lusitano), 90
Portuguese Legion (Legião Portuguesa), 69
Portuguese Marxist-Leninist Committee (Comité Marxista-Leninista Portuguesa: CM, L-P), 106
Portuguese Maximalist Federation, 89, 103. See also Portuguese Communist Party
Portuguese Republican Party (Partido Republicano Português: PRP), 87-88
Portuguese Socialist Action (Acção Socialista Portuguesa: ASP), 96
Portuguese Worker's Communist Party (Partido Comunista de Trabalhadores Portugueses: PCTP), 107. See also Reorganizing Movement of the Party of the Proletariat

Presidente da Câmara (mayor),
role since 1974, 178-182
under New State, 176-177
Progressives (Progresistas),
39, 86-87
Provisional governments
the First, 70
the Second, 70
the Fourth, 73
the Fifth, 73
the Sixth, 74
Purges. See Saneamentos.

Quadruple Alliance, 38
Quental, Antero de, 95

Radical communists, 106, 129
Radical socialists, 105-106, 129
Rebelo, António de Sousa, 101
Recensaemento (registration of voters), 176
Reconquest (Reconquista), 25, 32
Reformers (Reformadores), 98, 101
Reformist Party (Partido Reformista: PR), 89
Reformists, 86
Regador, 176-177
Regenerators (Regeneradores), 39, 85-87
Regimento dos Contadores das Comarcas, 32
Regimentos e Ordenações da Fazenda, 32
Reorganizing Movement of the Party of the Proletariat (Movimento Reorganizativo do Partido do Proletariado: MRPP), 107
Republican and Socialist Alliance (Aliança Socialista), 95
Republican and Socialist Front (Frente Republicana e Socialista: FRS), 98-99
Republican centers (Centros Republicanos), 88

Republican Evolutionist Party (Partido Republicano Evolutionista: PRE), 88
Republicanism, advent and spread of, 27, 34, 39, 87-88. See also Portuguese Republican Party
Republican National Union (União Nacional Republicana: UNR), 88
Republican Revolutionary Boards (Juntas Revolucionários Republicanos), 88
Republicans, 92, 93, 95, 118. See also Republicanism and Portuguese Republican Party.
Republican Union (União Republicana: UR), 88
Resposta PS, 99
Revolution
elite revolutions, 80
misuse of the concept of, 65-66
negative revolutions, 147
Revolutionary Brigades (Brigadas Revolucionárias: BR), 94
Revolutionary Party of the Proletariat (Partido Revolucionário do Proletariado: PRP), 105
Revolutionary Party of the Workers (Partido Revolucionário dos Trabalhadores: PRT), 106-107
Revolutionary Socialist Party (Partido Socialista Revolucionário: PSR), 107
Rodrigues, Aires, 106
Rodrigues, Martins, 106
Rotativism (Rotativismo), 39, 86
Rousseau, Jean-Jacques, 144-145

Salazar, António de Oliveira
appointed prime minister, 55

Salazar, António de
  Oliveira (cont'd)
  as minister of finance,
    53
  establishes New State,
    53-54
  implements corporatism,
    55-56
  mentioned, 7, 40, 49, 52-
    53, 56-60, 75, 79, 83,
    90-93, 108, 146-147,
    162, 198-199.
  See also New State,
    National Union, Corpora-
    tism
Saldanha, Duke of, 68
Salqueiro, João, 101
Sancho I, king of Portugal,
  19
Sancho II, king of
  Portugal, 19
Saneamentos (purges), 162
Santiago, religious mili-
  tary order of, 19, 32
Santo, Teófilo Carvalho, 92
Santos, Machado, 89
Sartori, Giovanni, 129
Scandinavia, comparisons
  with, 43, 84
Schmitter, Philippe C.,
  51, 56, 119
Seara Nova (New Harvest), 89
Sebastianism, 198
Sebastião, king of Portugal,
  22, 68
Secretário d'el Rei (public
  secretary), 33
Secretary of State for Cor-
  porations and Social
  Welfare, 56
Semi-presidentialism, 147-
  148, 154-156
Senado (Senate), 39
Septemberists, 38, 85, 119
Sequeira, Vítor Hugo, 98
Serra, Manuel, 98, 105
Sesmarias, decree of, 40
Silva, Cavaco, 101
Sindicatos (syndicates), 54
Sinédrio, 26
"Situation" the, 66, 68,
  70-76, 80
Smith, Gordon, 83, 143

Soares, Mário
  as founder of Socialist
    Party, 96
  as prime minister of
    first constitutional
    government, 97
  conflict with President
    Eanes, 153-154
  quarrels with socialist
    leaders, 99
  mentioned, 98, 100, 106
Social Contract, the, 144
Social Democratic Action
  (Acção Social Democrata:
  ASD), 101. See also
  Independent Social
  Democratic Association
Social Democratic Movement
  (Movimento Social
  Democrata: MSD), 100.
  See also Social Demo-
  cratic Party
Social Democratic Party
  (Partido Social Demo-
  crata: PSD)
  electoral behavior, 129-
    138 passim
  ideology of, 100
  leadership quarrels with-
    in, 100-102
  support base, 125-128
  mentioned, 107, 109,
    121, 151, 203
Social Democratic Union
  (União Social Democrá-
  tico: USD), 104
Social democrats, 73-74,
  83, 93, 96. See also
  Social Democratic Party
Socialism, 54
  utopian, 87, 100
  See also Socialist Party
Socialist Front. See
  Socialist Party
Socialist Intervention
  Group (Grupo de Inter-
  venção Socialista: GIS),
  106
Socialist Party (Partido
  Socialista: PS)
  activities during period
    of exception, 97
  alliance with communists
    and social democrats, 96

Socialist Party (cont'd)
  coalition with social democrats, 100
  constitutional revision, 153
  first constitutional government, 99
  founding of, 96
  leadership quarrels within, 97-99
  support base of, 125-128, 129-138 passim
  mentioned, 102- 105-106, 109, 121, 154, 203
Socialists, 73-74, 83, 92, 93. See also Socialist Party, Socialism
Socialist Union (União Socialista), 95
Socialist Youth Alliance (Aliança Socialista de Juventude: ASJ), 107
Social Science Research Council (SSRC)
  crises and sequences framework of, 13-15
  mentioned, 7, 198
Society for Economic and Social Development (Sociadade para o Desenvolvimento Económica e Social: SEDES), 94, 100, 102
Society for the Defense of the Family (Sociadade para a Defensa da Família), 56
Soldiers United Will Win (Soldados Unidos Vencerão: SUV), 73
Spain, 1, 4, 16, 18, 19-20, 27, 36, 54, 90
Spanish Union, the, 16, 25
Spínola, General António de, 69-71
Spinolistas, 69-71, 75
Spiro, Herbert J., 156
Superior Council of National Defense, 153, 155
Superior Council of the MFA (Conselho Superior do MFA), 71
Superior Council of the National Economy, 55

Support Committee for the Reconstruction of the Marxist-Leninist Party (Comité de Apoio da Reconstrução do Partido Marxista-Leninista: CARP, M-L), 107. See also Popular Democratic Union
Suspensitive veto, 144
Sweden, comparisons with, 170

Templers, religious military order of, 19, 32
Teresa, wife of Henri, Count of Portugal, 17-18
Terras, 29-30, 33
Third Republic, France, comparisons with, 7
Tomás, Admiral Américo, 69
Trotskyists, 83, 106-107, 129
Tutela administrativa (administrative tutelage), 174

Ultimatum of 1890, 27
Unified Socialist Worker's Party (Partido Operário Unificado Socialista: POUS), 98, 106
Uniões (unions), 54
Unionists, 88
Union of the Christian Democratic Center (União do Centro Democrático Cristão: UCDC), 104
Union of the Left for Social Democracy (União de Esquerda para a Democracia Social: UEDS), 98
United Organization of Workers (Organização Unida de Trabalhadores: OUT), 105
United People's Action (Acção Povo Unido: APU), 104
United Revolutionary Front (Frente Unida Revolucionária: FUR), 73

Urban Resident's Commissions (Comissões de Moradores), 76-77
Urraca, wife of Alfonso VI, 17

Vereadores, 31, 178, 181
Vila Francada, 36
Vilar, Rui, 98
Vila Viçosa, Marquis of. See Duke of Bragança
Vintistas (Twentiethists), 38, 85
Viseu, Duke of, 32
Visigothic Empire, 25

Vogais, 176

Weimar Republic, 7, 156, 202-203
West Germany, 1-2, 70, 147
Wheeler, Douglas L., 52
Workers' Commissions (Comissões de Trabalhadores), 77
Work of the Mothers for National Education (Obra das Maēs para a Educação Nacional), 56
World War I, 66
World War II, 143, 147